2500 Keywords to Get You Hired

JAY A. BLOCK, CPRW
MICHAEL BETRUS, CPRW

McGraw-Hill

New York   Chicago   San Francisco
Lisbon   London   Madrid   Mexico City   Milan
New Delhi   San Juan   Seoul   Singapore
Sydney   Toronto

The McGraw·Hill Companies

Library of Congress Cataloging-in-Publication Data

Block, Jay A.
    2500 keywords to get you hired / by Jay A. Block and Michael Betrus.
        p.   cm.
Includes index.
    ISBN 0-07-140673-5 (alk. paper)
1. Résumés (Employment)   2. Applications for positions.   3.   Job
hunting.   4. Keyword searching.   I. Title: Twenty-five hundred keywords
to get you hired.   II. Title: Keywords to get you hired.   III. Betrus,
Michael.   IV. Title.
    HF5383 .B5355   2003
    650.14'2—dc21

                                                           2002151839

2 3 4 5 6 7 8 9 0   PBT/PBT   0 9 8 7 6 5 4 3

ISBN 0-07-140673-5

McGraw-Hill books are available at special quantity discounts to use
as premiums and sales promotions, or for use in corporate training
sessions. For more information, please write to the Director of
Special Sales, Professional Publishing, McGraw-Hill, Two Penn
Plaza, New York, NY 10121-2298. Or contact your local bookstore.

 This book is printed on recycled, acid-free paper containing a
minimum of 50% recycled, de-inked fiber.

Contents

Contents

Contents

Contributors

Rolande L. LaPointe, CPC, CIPC, CPRW, IJCTC, CCM   30, 136, 139, 146, 152
RO-LAN Associates, Inc.
725 Sabattus Street
Lewiston, Maine 04240
207) 784-010
Rlapointe@aol.com

Anne Follis   79, 89, 94, 97, 106, 149, 153
CareerPro Resume Service
6738 N. Frostwood Parkway
Peoria, Illinois 61615
(309) 691-2445
AAAProfessionalResumes@yahoo.com or AAAProResumes@aol.com
www.AAAProfessionalResumes.com

Jean Cummings   54, 58, 123, 138, 145, 173
A Resume For Today
123 Minot Road
Concord, MA 01742
Phone: 978-371-9266   Email: jc@AResumeForToday.com
Web site www.AResumeForToday.com

Barb Poole   33, 37, 56, 103, 126, 160, 172
Hire Imaging
1812 Red Fox Road
St. Cloud, MN 56301
(320) 253-0975
eink@astound.net

Peter Hill, CPRW   64, 87, 99, 107, 133, 157, 165
Distinctive Resumes
Honolulu, Hawaii
(808) 306-3920
distinctiveresumes@yahoo.com
www.peterhill.biz

Camille Carboneau, CPRW, CEIP   32, 50, 53, 72, 125, 154, 158
CC Computer Services & Training
PO Box 50655
Idaho Falls, Idaho 83405
208.522.4455
Camille@ccComputer.com
http://www.SuperiorResumes.com

Roleta Fowler   100, 119, 127, 134, 140, 144, 162, 164
Wordbusters Resume and Writing Services
433 Quail Court
Fillmore, California 93015-1137
(805) 524-3493
resumes@wbresumes.com
http://www.wbresumes.com

Debbie Ellis   34, 40, 67, 81, 93, 108, 121, 161
Phoenix Career Group
Danville, KY 40422
(800) 876-5506
info@phoenixcareergroup.com
www.phoenixcareergroup.com

Kathy Renzulli   29, 51, 78, 85, 117, 159
Connecticut Department of Labor
555 Main Street
Ansonia, Connecticut 06401
(203) 736-1059
Kathy.Renzulli@po.state.ct.us
www.ctdol.state.ct.us

Susan Guarneri   36, 44, 46, 96, 124, 167, 171
Guarneri Associates / Resumagic
1101 Lawrence Road
Lawrenceville, NJ 08648
(609) 771-1669
Resumagic@aol.com
www.resume-magic.com

Freddie Cheek   63, 65, 71, 86, 128, 143, 169, 170
Cheek & Cristantello Career Connections
4511 Harlem Road, Suite 3
Amherst, New York 14226
(716) 839-3635
fscheek@adelphia.net
CheekandCristantello.com

M. J. FELD, MS, CPRW   62, 66, 68, 75, 98, 102, 109
Careers by Choice, Inc.
205 East Main Street, Suite 2-4
Huntington, NY 11743
(631) 673-5432
mjfeld@bestweb.net

Wendy J. Terwelp   41, 61, 70, 112, 116, 156
Opportunity Knocks of Wisconsin, LLC
11431 N. Port Washington Road, Ste. 101-C
Mequon, WI 53092
262.241.4655
consultant@knocks.com
www.knocks.com

Ann Baehr   80, 82, 92, 105, 118, 122, 148, 155
Best Resumes
122 Sheridan Street
Brentwood, NY 11717
(631) 435-1879
resumesbest@earthlink.net
www.e-bestresumes.com

Tracy M. Parish, CPRW   28, 45, 76, 77, 95, 113, 120, 142
CareerPlan, Inc.
PO Box 325
Kewanee, IL 61443
(888) 449-2200
Resume@CareerPlan.org
www.CareerPlan.org

Introduction

Welcome to the seventh installment in our series of reference guides designed to help you in your career. Our previous guides have been focused on the structure and development of resumes and cover letters. They include:

- *101 Best Resumes*
- *101 More Best Resumes*
- *101 Best Cover Letters*
- *101 Best .Com Resumes*
- *101 Best Resumes for Grads*
- *101 Best Tech Resumes*

Keywords represent a subset of this matter. Keywords are nouns and adjectives that serve to describe you professionally.

This guide offers a variety of tools for you. For the top professions we identified, you will find a list of at least 20 keywords, an example of their use in a sample resume, and their use in a sample interview question. Not every keyword is illustrated in every respective resume or sample interview. Inserting every keyword would have made them too wordy and in many cases unrealistic. These samples will give you some ideas, but your use really depends on your own experiences and objectives. Each profession showcases the work of both the authors and the members of the Professional Association of Resume Writers.

Really look over "Tips to Get You Hired" starting on Chapter 3. They will provide you with savvy tips you won't find anywhere else. The tips are divided into six categories and are very tactical in nature. We always try to stay away from theory and instead emphasize hands-on tactics.

Part I

1

What Is a Keyword?

Keywords are those descriptive words, usually nouns, that are associated with specific disciplines or industries. Keywords are important because they are considered standardized for specific industries. For example, if you were an accountant, keywords would include: cost accounting, budget analysis, auditing, tax, etc. Keywords can be critical in the world of software management and job searching. Employers and recruiters may take your resume and cover letter (especially if sent electronically) and do a computerized search for keywords or descriptors that match the profile they are seeking. Think of it as a prescreening process. For example, a finance director for Microsoft hiring a staff accountant might have a scan or search of resumes and cover letters completed for the words listed above, and if they aren't on your materials, you could miss the first cut.

Keywords play an integral role in two areas of the resume screening process. One is the human element, when hiring and nonhiring managers are screening resumes for words and phrases that match the criteria they are seeking. The second is the computer search, where computers search the data on many different resumes to select those that match the words and phrases. That is how posted resumes on Web sites like Monster.com work.

Prescreening by Personnel

Keywords can be very important outside the computer search arena. In many cases, the initial scan of resumes is completed by either a human resources person or an assistant to the hiring manager. Even the most competent people doing this function can only do a high-level job of resume scanning if they are not intimately aware of the position or are not hiring for themselves. That is why it is important to keep a certain amount of "boilerplate" in your resume.

A client of ours named David Robinson comes to mind. He worked for Verizon Wireless and was curious about an advertisement he saw for a position with Ericcson. We updated his resume in the style that looks like that on pages 56–57 from our first book, *101 Best Resumes*. The key to that resume style was the use of the left column for a listing of accounts—that really becomes the core of the resume if you work in an account-driven environment like sales. The hiring manager called David for an interview and told him: "We've had so many resumes that I told my assistant not to bring me any more unless they look like a perfect fit. The way that you listed your accounts on the first page of the resume was a great way to show us who your contacts are." So, the initial screening was conducted by his assistant, who was only scanning resumes for key items (words, even things like industry-specific terms, product names, etc.), and his resume effectively illustrated his sales accounts.

Don't make the readers work to learn what you're all about. Even in a four percent unemployment environment, the competition for good jobs is too stiff.

The Online Environment

Today, the Internet environment brings a new way of distributing your resume. As part of the "boilerplate" activities that people do when beginning to market themselves to potential employers, using the Internet is now a standard resource tool. One of the first things many people do is post their resumes on Web sites like Monster.com or Headhunter.net. Corporate recruiters and independent recruiters do review resumes posted on these sites. It works best when the search field is very narrow. If you were to do a keyword search of all the resumes posted on Monster.com for *telecommunications*, for example, the return would be in the thousands. However, if you narrowed the search to *MMDS narrowband spectrum management*, the return would be significantly lower. So, you need to whittle your skills down as much as possible to help the right people find you through these keyword searches. Keywords make your traditional resume electronically retrievable in resume databases like Monster.com or Headhunter.net.

After your resume is entered electronically into a resume database like that on Monster.com, it is ready to be searched and ranked. A hiring manager or recruiter then decides which keywords best identify the skills needed in a candidate, and based upon those keywords, has the system search the resume database. Typically, the reviewer will have several keywords that are required and others that are optional.

When the search engine recognizes a keyword in your resume, it is called a "hit." Your resume is ranked according to the number of keyword hits. Only resumes that have the required keywords are found. Of those, resumes that have more of the desired keywords rank higher, and will be selected first to be read by a human reviewer. Other factors that can affect search rankings include proximity to other keywords and how close to the top of the page keyword hits occur. Therefore, in addition to placing keywords relevant to your field throughout your resume and cover letter, an extra "keyword summary" should be created near the top of your resume specifically for a resume search engine. Our resume guides provide many examples of how to do this in constructing the opening part of your resume.

A good "Summary of Qualifications" provides an opportunity to include listings of keywords that may not fit in the rest of the written part of the resume. The more keywords you have, the greater the likelihood of ranking high in the search.

Keywords

Below is a plain-formatted resume that is representative of something that might be pasted in the application area on Monster.com. Highlighted in gray are the keywords. Granted, this resume is an exaggerated version of the use of keywords. Still, it will give you a good perspective. Also, it's no secret that the more specialized a position is, the greater the role that keywords will play. However, even if you're in sales or general management, key industry terms can be very helpful.

Dan Schmitz
1234 Hereford Highway
Kansas City, MO 12345
H: (913) 555-1111 W: (913) 555-1111; E-mail: danschmitz@technology.net

Keyword Summary

Systems Engineer. Client Server System Architect. Systems Analysis. Systems Integration. Network Administration. Database Administration. Systems Administration. Software Engineering. Troubleshooting Computing Systems.
DOS. Windows NT. TCP/IP. OSI. Microsoft LAN Manager. Novell Netware. Project Management. Trade Studies. Consulting. BETA Tester. Technical Presentations. Sales Presentations. Instructor. BS Degree. Mathematics and Computer Science. UCLA. Air Force Institute of Technology. Computer Engineering.

Summary of Qualifications

Seven years of experience in designing, installing, and troubleshooting computing systems.

Programming: C, C++, Visual BASIC, FORTRAN, Pascal, SQL, OSF/Motif, UNIX Shell Script (sh, ksh, csh), BASIC, Clipper, Algol 68, and 80X86 Assembler.

Operating Systems: UNIX (bsd & SVr3/r4), MS Windows, MS DOS, MS Windows NT, Solaris, HP-UX, Ultrix, AIX, VAX/VMS, and Macintosh System 7.

Networking: TCP/IP, OSI, Microsoft LAN Manager, Novell Netware, DDN, Internet, Ethernet, Token Ring, SNA, X.25, LAN-WAN interconnection.

Applications: Microsoft Office, Microsoft Access, Microsoft Visual C++, Microsoft Project, Microsoft Publisher, Lotus 123, Lotus Freelance, System Architect, and others.

Professional Experience

Network Engineer

Netcom, Dallas, Texas 1996–Present

* Provide systems engineering, software engineering, technical consulting, and marketing services as a member of the Systems Integration Division of a software engineering consulting company.

* Designed and managed the development of an enterprise-level client/server automated auditing application for a major financial management company migrating from mainframe computers, db2, and   to a workgroup-oriented, client/server architecture involving Windows for Workgroups, Windows NT Advanced Server, Microsoft SQL Server, Oracle7, and UNIX.

* Designed an enterprise-level, high-performance, mission-critical, client/server database system incorporating symmetric multiprocessing computers (SMP), Oracle7's Parallel Server, Tuxedo's on-line transaction processing (OLTP) monitor, and redundant array of inexpensive disks (RAID) technology.

* Conducted extensive trade studies of a large number of vendors that offer leading-edge technologies; these studies identified proven (low-risk) implementations of SMP and RDBMS systems that met stringent performance and availability criteria.

Education

University of Kansas, B.S. Software Engineering and Computer Communications

GPA: 3.43

Specialized Training

Database Administration, Performance Tuning, and Benchmarking with Oracle7; Oracle Corporation.

Interactive UNIX System V r4 (POSIX) System Administration; ETC, Inc.

Effective Briefing Techniques and Technical Presentations; William French and Associates, Inc.

Transmission Control Protocol/Internet Protocol (TCP/IP); Technology Systems Institute.

LAN Interconnection Using Bridges, Routers, and Gateways; Information Systems Institute.

OSI X.400/X.500 Messaging and Directory Service Protocols; Communication Technologies, Inc.

2
Skills Lead to Keywords

Have you ever known a highly successful sales professional who didn't have a firm grasp and knowledge of his or her product? An award-winning professor that did not know his or her material? Ask experienced salespeople what the secret to success is, and they'll say that it's knowing the product, knowing the customer, and matching the benefits of the product to the needs of the customer. This is a powerful success formula.

The job search is a sales and marketing endeavor. There is simply no way around this: You are the product, you are the salesperson, and you must define your customers and promote yourself to them. So, like the highly successful salesperson, the key to your success is to know your product (you) inside and out, and match the benefits of the product to the needs of your potential customers (prospective employers). In sales, we call this selling features and benefits. You must know the features of the product, known as "marketable skills," and determine what specific benefits result from those features that would interest a prospective employer. In other words, the only reason for someone to hire you is for the benefit that you offer that person or company. If interviewers were to ask you what your strengths are, what skills you bring to the table, or what contributions you feel you could make to the company, they are actually asking you to identify your features and the benefit that the company would realize by hiring you.

In order to communicate effectively the features and benefits of the product, namely you, you must first take an inventory of your skills. In the simplest of terms, there are three categories of skills:

- Job-related (or academic) skills
- Transferable skills
- Self-management skills

JOB-RELATED/TECHNICAL SKILLS

There are four categories of job-related skills: 1) working with people, 2) working with data and information, 3) working with things, and 4) working with ideas. Though most of us work with all four categories at one time or another, we tend to be attracted to one or two areas in particular. Successful teachers, customer service representatives, and salespeople must be particularly skilled at working with people. Financial controllers, weathermen, and statistical forecasters possess outstanding skills in working with data and information. Engineers, mechanics, and computer technicians enjoy using their skills to work with things, and inventors, writers, and advertising professionals must have solid creativity and idea skills.

For the keyword exercise, place most emphasis on working with data and information; uncover skills that are objective and as specific as possible.

TRANSFERABLE SKILLS

Transferable skills are just that—transferable from one environment to another. If you enjoy working with people, your specific transferable skills might include leadership, training, entertainment, mentoring, mediation, persuasion, public speaking, conflict resolution, or problem-solving skills. If you enjoy working with data and information, your specific transferable skills might include research, analysis, proofreading, editing, arranging, budgeting, assessing, measuring, evaluating, surveying, or pricing. If you enjoy working with things, your specific transferable skills might include knowledge of equipment, repair, maintenance, installation, setup, troubleshooting, or building. And finally, if you enjoy working with ideas, your specific transferable skills might include creating, developing, reengineering, restructuring, painting, writing, problem solving, planning, or brainstorming.

So take 15 minutes, sit down with a pen, and paper and write down all the skills and abilities you possess that have value to a company. Transferable skills are marketable and tangible qualifications that will have value to many organizations. An accountant, human resources manager, or logistics manager at General Motors has tangible transferable skills that are of value to many companies both in and out of the automotive industry.

SELF-MANAGEMENT SKILLS

Self-management skills are skills that are personality and value oriented. Self-management skills are those that describe your attitude and work ethic. They include creativity, energy, enthusiasm, logic, resourcefulness, productive competence, persistence, adaptability, and self-confidence. One cautionary note, however: *Try not to be too general in describing your self-management skills*. When you identify a specific skill, always be prepared to explain how that skill will benefit a prospective employer. For example, if you're analytical, how does that make you better prepared for a position you have designed for yourself?

When you identify and recognize your skills, you begin to know your product. If you know your product inside and out, you will never be caught off guard in an interview. In fact, you will be able to reinforce your value by emphasizing specific accomplishments you've achieved in the past, using those specific skills.

In summary, writing a resume with good keyword descriptors requires that you identify your marketable skills because they represent the heart of the resume. Your ability to sell yourself confidently in an interview despite stiff competition depends on knowing your skills and communicating the benefits of those skills to the interviewer. Strategic resume preparation begins with identifying what you have to offer based on where you plan to market yourself. It is the foundation for developing a powerful resume, and will be the foundation of successful interviewing as well.

3
Tips and Techniques

25 TIPS FOR USING THE INTERNET IN YOUR JOB SEARCH

1. When typing your resume out with the intent of emailing, make sure it is in an ASCII format.
2. Use keywords heavily in the introduction of the resume, not at the end.
3. Keywords are almost always nouns, related to skills, such as financial analysis, marketing, accounting, or Web design.
4. When sending your resume via email in an ASCII format, attach (if you can) a nicely formatted one in case it does go through and the reader would like to see your creativity and preferred layout. If you do attach it, use a common program like MS Word.
5. Don't focus on an objective in the introduction of the resume, but rather accomplishments, using keywords to describe them.
6. Don't post your resume to your own Web site unless it is a very slick page. A poorly executed Web page is more damaging than none at all.
7. Before you email your resume, experiment sending it to yourself and to a friend as a test drive.
8. Look up the Web site of the company you are targeting to get recent news information about new products, etc., and look for their job posting for new information.
9. Before your interview or verbal contact, research the company's Web site.
10. Use a font size between 10 and 14 point, make it all the same for an ASCII format resume, and don't create your resume for emailing with lines exceeding 65 characters.
11. In case your resume may be scanned, use white paper with no borders and no creative fonts.
12. Include your email address on your resume and cover letter.
13. Don't email from your current employer's IP network.
14. Don't circulate your work email address for job search purposes.
15. In the "subject" of your email (just below the "address to" part), put something more creative than "Resume Enclosed." Try "Resume showing 8 years in telecommunications industry" (if that is your chosen industry), for example.
16. For additional sources of online job searching, do a "search" on the Web for job searching, your company, and your specific discipline for additional information.
17. Be careful of your spelling on the Internet. You will notice more spelling errors on email exchanges than you will ever see in mailed letter exchanges.
18. Try to make sure your resume is scannable. This means it has a simple font, no borders, no creative lining, no bold face, no underlining, no italics, and limited if any columning. Though the practice of scanning is overestimated, it should still be a consideration.
19. Purchase or check out of a library an Internet directory listing the many links to job opportunities out there. There are thousands.
20. If you are using the email as your cover letter, keep it brief. If the reader is reading on screen, their tolerance for reading long information is reduced dramatically.
21. Always back up what you can on a disk.
22. If you post your resume to a newsgroup, first make sure that this is acceptable to avoid any problems with other participants.
23. Remember that tabs and spaces are the only formatting you can do in ASCII.
24. Make sure you check your email every day. If you are communicating via the Internet, people may expect a prompt return.
25. Don't send multiple emails to ensure that one gets through. Try to send it with a confirmation of receipt, or keep a look out for a notice from you ISP that the message didn't go through.

25 NETWORKING TIPS

1. Two-thirds of all jobs are secured via the networking process. Networking is a systematic approach to cultivating formal and informal contacts for the purpose of gaining information, enhancing visibility in the market, and obtaining referrals.
2. Effective networking requires self-confidence, poise, and personal conviction.
3. You must first know the companies and organizations you wish to work for. That will determine the type of network you will develop and nurture.
4. Focus on meeting the "right people." This takes planning and preparation.
5. Target close friends, family members, neighbors, social acquaintances, social and religious group members, business contacts, teachers, and community leaders.
6. Include employment professionals as an important part of your network. This includes headhunters and personnel agency executives. They have a wealth of knowledge about job and market conditions.
7. Remember, networking is a numbers game. Once you have a network of people in place, prioritize the listing so you have separated top-priority contacts from lower-priority ones.
8. Sometimes you may have to pay for advice and information. Paying consultants or professionals or investing in Internet services is part of the job search process today, as long as it's legal and ethical.
9. Know what you want from your contacts. If you don't know what you want, neither will your network of people. Specific questions will get specific answers.
10. Ask for advice, not for a job. You should not contact someone asking if they know of any job openings. The answer will invariably be no, especially at higher levels. You need to ask for things like industry advice, advice on geographic areas, etc. The job insights will follow but will be almost incidental. This positioning will build value for you and make the contact person more comfortable about helping you.
11. Watch your attitude and demeanor at all times. Everyone you come in contact with is a potential member of your network. Demonstrate enthusiasm and professionalism at all times.
12. Keep a file on each member of your network and maintain good records at all times. A well-organized network filing system or database will yield superior results.
13. Get comfortable on the telephone. Good telephone communication skills are critical.
14. Travel the "information highway." Networking is more effective if you have email, fax, and computer capabilities.
15. Be well prepared for your conversation, whether in person or over the phone. You should have a script in your mind of how to answer questions, what to ask, and what you're trying to accomplish.
16. Do not fear rejection. If a contact cannot help you, move on to the next contact. Do not take rejection personally—it's just part of the process.
17. Flatter the people in your network. It's been said that the only two types of people who can be flattered are men and women. Use tact, courtesy, and flattery.
18. If a person in your network cannot personally help, advise, or direct you, ask for referrals.
19. Keep in touch with the major contacts in your network on a monthly basis. Remember, out of sight, out of mind.
20. Don't abuse the process. Networking is a two-way street. Be honest and brief and offer your contacts something in return for their time, advice, and information. This can be as simple as a lunch, or offering your professional services in return for their cooperation.

21. Show an interest in your contacts. Cavette Robert, one of the founders of the National Speakers Association, said, "People don't care how much you know, until they know how much you care." Show how much you care. It will get you anywhere.
22. Send thank-you notes following each networking contact.
23. Seek out key networking contacts in professional and trade associations.
24. Carry calling cards with you at all times to hand out to anyone and everyone you come in contact with. Include your name, address, phone number, areas of expertise, and/or specific skill areas.
25. Socialize and get out more than ever before. Networking requires dedication and massive amounts of energy. Consistently work on expanding your network.

25 "WHAT DO I DO NOW THAT I HAVE MY RESUME?" TIPS

1. Develop a team of people who will be your board of directors, advisors, and mentors. The quality of the people you surround yourself with will determine the quality of your results.

2. Plan a marketing strategy. Determine how many hours a week you will work, how you'll divide your time, and how you'll measure your progress. Job searching is a business in itself—and a marketing strategy is your business plan.

3. Identify 25 (50 would be better) companies or organizations that you would like to work for.

4. Contact the companies, or do some research, to identify hiring authorities.

5. Define your network (see "Networking Tips"). Make a list of everyone you know including relatives, friends, acquaintances, family doctors, attorneys, and CPAs, the cleaning person, and the mail carrier. Virtually everyone is a possible networking contact.

6. Prioritize your list of contacts into three categories: 1) Strong, approachable contacts, 2) good contacts or those who must be approached more formally, and 3) those who you'd like to contact but can't without an introduction by another party.

7. Set up a filing system or database to organize and manage your contacts.

8. Develop a script or letter for the purpose of contacting the key people in your network, asking for advice, information, and assistance. Then start contacting them.

9. Attempt to find a person, or persons, in your network who can make an introduction into one of the 25 or 50 companies you've noted in number 3.

10. Spend 65 to 70 percent of your time, energy, and resources networking because 65 to 70 percent of all jobs are secured by this method.

11. Consider contacting executive recruiters or employment agencies to assist in your job search.

12. If you are a recent college graduate, seek out assistance from the campus career center.

13. Scout the classified advertisements every Sunday. Respond to ads that interest you, and look at other ads as well. A company may be advertising for a position that does not fit your background, but say in the ad they are "expanding in the area," etc. You have just identified a growing company.

14. Seek out advertisements and job opportunities in specific trade journals and magazines.

15. Attend as many social and professional functions as you can. The more people you meet, the better your chances are of securing a position quickly.

16. Send out resumes with customized cover letters to targeted companies or organizations. Address the cover letter to a specific person. Then follow up.

17. Target small to medium-sized companies. Most of the opportunities are coming from these organizations, not large corporations.

18. Consider contacting temporary agencies. Almost 40 percent of all temporary personnel are offered permanent positions. Today, a greater percentage of middle and upper management, as well as professionals, are working in temporary positions.

19. Use online services. America Online, Prodigy, and CompuServe have career services, employment databases, bulletin boards, and online discussion and support groups, as well as access to the Internet. This is the wave of the future.

20. If you are working from home, be sure the room you are working from is inspiring, organized, and private. This is your space and it must motivate you!

21. If your plan is not working, meet with members of your support team and change the plan. You must remain flexible and adaptable to change.

22. Read and observe. Read magazines and newspapers and listen to CNBC, CNN, and so on. Notice which companies and organizations are on the move and contact them.

23. Set small, attainable, weekly goals. Keep a weekly progress report on all your activities. Try to do a little more each week than the week before.

24. Stay active. Exercise and practice good nutrition. A job search requires energy. You must remain in superior physical and mental condition.

25. Volunteer. Help those less fortunate than you. What goes around comes around.

25 INTERVIEWING TIPS

1. Relax. The employment interview is just a meeting. And although you should not treat this meeting lightly, don't forget that the organization interviewing you is in need of your services as much as, or perhaps more than, you are of theirs.

2. The key to successful interviewing is rapport building. Most people spend their time preparing for interviews by memorizing canned responses to anticipated questions. Successful interviewers spend most of their time practicing the art of rapport building through the use of powerfully effective communicating techniques.

3. Prepare a manila folder that you will bring to the interview. Include in the folder:
   * company information (annual reports, sales material, etc.)
   * extra resumes (6–12) and your letters of reference
   * 15 questions you've prepared based on your research and analysis of the company
   * a blank legal pad, pen, and anything else you consider helpful (e.g., college transcripts)

4. Dress appropriately. Determine the dress code and meet it. If their dress is business casual, you still need to be dressed in business professional. Practice proper grooming and hygiene.

5. Shoes, of course, must be polished.

6. Wear limited jewelry.

7. Call the day before and confirm the appointment—it will set you apart.

8. Be certain that you know exactly where you're going. Arrive in plenty of time. You should be at the receptionist's desk 10–12 minutes before the scheduled interview.

9. Prior to meeting the receptionist, check your appearance. Check your hair, clothing, and general image. Test your smile.

10. Secretaries, administrative assistants, and receptionists often have a say in the hiring process. Make a strong first impression with them.

11. Look around the office and search for artifacts that disclose the personality and culture of the company—and possibly the interviewer. This information will be helpful in initially breaking the ice, when you first begin discussions.

12. Be aware of your body language. Sit erect, with confidence. When standing and walking, move with confidence!

13. Your handshake should be firm, made with a wide-open hand, fingers stretched wide apart. Women should feel comfortable offering their hands and firm and friendly handshakes. A power handshake and great smile will get you off to a great start.

14. Eye contact is one of the most powerful forms of communicating. It demonstrates confidence, trust, and power.

15. During the interview, lean forward toward the interviewer. Show enthusiasm and sincere interest.

16. Take notes during the interview. You may want to refer to them later in the interview. If you are uncomfortable with this, ask permission first.

17. Be prepared for all questions, especially uncomfortable ones. Before the interview, script out a one-page response for each question that poses a problem for you, and practice repeating it until you're comfortable with it.

18. Communicate your skills, qualifications, and credentials to the hiring manager. Describe your market value and the benefits you offer. *Demonstrate how you will contribute to the bottom line.* Show how you can 1) improve sales, 2) reduce costs, 3) improve productivity, or 4) solve organizational problems.

19. Key in on *specific accomplishments*. Accomplishments determine hireability. They separate the winners from the runners-up.

20. Listening skills are priceless! Job offers are made to those who listen well, find hidden meanings, and answer questions in a brief but effective manner.
21. Let the interviewer bring up salary first. The purpose of an interview is to determine whether there is a match. Once that is determined, salary should then be negotiated.
22. There is no substitute for planning and preparation, practice and rehearsing—*absolutely none*.
23. Practice interviewing techniques using video technology. A minimum of five hours of video practice, preferably more, guarantees a stellar performance.
24. Close the sale. If you find that you want the position, ask for it. Ask directly, "Is there anything that would prevent you from offering me this position now?" or "Do you have any reservations or concerns?" (if you sense that). At the very least, this should flush out any objections and give you the opportunity to turn them into positives.
25. Always send a thank-you note within 24 hours of every employment meeting.

25 SALARY NEGOTIATING TIPS

1. From the moment you make initial contact with any company or organization you wish to work with, you are in negotiation. You may not be discussing money openly, but you are making a permanent imprint on the minds of the hiring authorities.
2. Delay all discussions of salary until there is an offer on the table.
3. You are in the strongest negotiating position as soon as the offer is made.
4. Know your value. You must know how you can contribute to the organization. Establish this in the mind of the hiring manager.
5. Get employers enthusiastic about your candidacy, and they will become more generous.
6. There is no substitute for preparation. If you are well prepared, you'll be confident, self-assured, and poised for success.
7. Prior to going into employment negotiations, you must know the average salary paid for similar positions with other organizations in your geographical area.
8. Prior to going into employment negotiations you must know, as best you can, the salary range that the company you're interviewing with will pay, or what former employees were earning.
9. Prior to going into employment negotiations, you must know your personal needs and requirements, and how they relate to numbers 7 and 8 above.
10. Remember, fringes and perks, such as vacation time, flex time, health benefits, pension plans, and so on, have value. Consider the "total" salary package.
11. Salary negotiations must be win-win negotiations. If they're not, everybody loses in the end.
12. Be flexible; don't get hung up on trivial issues, and always seek compromise when possible.
13. Listen carefully and pay close attention. Your goals will most likely be different from the goals of the employer. For instance, the firm's main focus might be "base salary." Yours might be "total earning potential." So a win-win solution might be to negotiate a lower base salary but a higher commission or bonus structure.
14. Anticipate objections and prepare effective answers to these objections.
15. Try to understand the employer's point of view. Then plan a strategy to meet both the employer's concerns and your needs.
16. Don't be afraid to negotiate out of fear of losing the offer. Most employers expect you to negotiate as long as you negotiate in a fair and reasonable manner.
17. Always negotiate in a way that reflects your personality, character, and work ethic. Remain within your comfort zone.
18. Never lose control. Remain enthusiastic and upbeat even if the negotiations get a little hot. This might be your first test under fire.
19. Play hardball only if you're willing to walk away from, or lose, the deal.
20. What you lose in the negotiations will most likely never be recouped. Don't be careless in preparing for or conducting the negotiation.
21. Be sure to get the offer and final agreement in writing.
22. You should feel comfortable asking the employer for 24 to 48 hours to think about the deal if you need time to think it over.
23. Never link salary to personal needs or problems. Compensation should always be linked to your value.
24. Understand your leverage. Know if you are in a position of strength or weakness and negotiate intelligently based on your personal situation.
25. End salary negotiations on a friendly and cheerful note.

25 UNCONVENTIONAL TECHNIQUES FOR UNCOVERING AND SECURING NEW OPPORTUNITIES

1. If you see a classified ad that sounds really good for you but only lists a fax number and no company name, try to figure out the company by trying similar numbers. For example, if the fax number is 555-4589, try 555-4500 or 555-4000, and get the company name and contact person so you can send a more personalized letter and resume.

2. Send your resume in a Priority Mail envelope for the serious prospects. It only costs $3, but will stand out and get you noticed.

3. Check the targeted company's Web site; they may have postings there that others without computer access haven't seen.

4. If you see a classified ad for a good prospective company but for a different position, contact them anyway. If they are new in town (or even if they're not), they may have other nonadvertised openings.

5. Always have a personalized card with you in the event that you meet a good networking or employment prospect.

6. Always have a quick personal briefing rehearsed to speak to someone.

7. Network in nonwork environments, such as a happy-hour bar (a great opportunity to network) or an airport.

8. Network with your college alumni office. Many college graduates list their current employers with that office, and they may be a good source of leads, even out of state.

9. Most newspapers list all the new companies that have applied for business licenses. Check that section and contact the ones that appear appealing to you.

10. Call your attorney or accountant and ask them if they can refer you to any companies or business contacts; perhaps they have a good business relationship that may be good for you to leverage.

11. Contact the Chamber of Commerce for information on new companies moving into the local area.

12. Don't give up if you've had just one rejection from a company you are targeting. You shouldn't feel that you have truly contacted that company until you have contacted at least three different people there.

13. Join networking clubs and associations that will expose you to new business contacts.

14. Ask stockbrokers for tips on which companies they identify as fast growing and good companies to grow with.

15. Make a list of everyone you know and use them as a network source.

16. Put an endorsement portfolio together and mail out with targeted resumes.

17. Employ the hiring proposal strategy. (See *101 Best Cover Letters*.)

18. Post your resume on the Internet, selecting news groups and bulletin boards that will readily accept it and match your industry and discipline.

19. Don't forget to demonstrate passion and enthusiasm when you are meeting with people, interviewing with them, and networking through them.

20. Look in your industry's trade journals. Nearly all industries and disciplines have several, and most have advertising sections in the back that list potential openings with companies and recruiters. This is a great resource in today's low-unemployment environment.

21. Visit a job fair. For most professionals, there won't be managerial positions recruited for, but there will be many companies present, and you may discover a hot lead. If they are recruiting in general, you should contact them directly for a possible fit.

22. Don't overlook employment agencies. They may seem like a weak possibility, but that may uncover a hidden opportunity or serve as a source to network through.

23. Look for companies that are promoting their products using a lot of advertising. Sales are probably going well, and they may be good hiring targets for you.

24. Call a prospective company and simply ask them who their recruiting firm is. If they have one, they'll tell you, and then you can contact that firm to get in the door.

25. Contact every recruiter in town. Befriend them, and use them as networking sources if possible. Always thank them, to the point of sending them a small gift for helping you out. This will pay off in dividends in the future. Recruiters are always good contacts.

Part II

4

Keywords by Profession

ACCOUNT EXECUTIVE (ADVERTISING/MARKETING/PR)

Keywords

Market Penetration/
Expansion

Negotiations

Presentations

Relationship
Building

Incentive
Development

Territory
Penetration

Competitive Market
Analysis

Prospecting

Solution-Based
Selling

Consultative Selling

Client Needs
Analysis

Trade Show
Management

Lead Generation

Sales & Marketing

Sales Promotions

Product Introduction

Market Research &
Analysis

Staff Training &
Development

New-Business
Planning/
Development

Goal
Setting/Personal
Development

Resume

Anita Cooley
234 Shoshue Blvd.
Cincinnati, Ohio 45237
(513) 555-1122 / anita666@hotmail.com

Account Executive
Growing and sustaining revenues in highly competitive markets.

New-Business Planning/Development • Market Research & Analysis
Competitive Market Analysis • Market Penetration/Expansion

Core Strengths

Presentations / Negotiations
Relationship Building
Incentive Development
Territory Penetration

Problem Resolution
Consultative / Solution-Based Selling
Client Needs Analysis
Lead Generation

Professional Experience

ROCCO MARKETING AGENCY, Detroit, Michigan   1999 to Current

Account Executive

Exercise full sales and marketing accountability for major local account list with territory extending from Detroit to Philadelphia and reaching to Toms River, NJ. Coordinate annual trade shows, develop and execute sales promotions, and create power methods to introduce new products. Challenged with ensuring peak performance of team through effective staff training and development as well as ambitious goal setting while emphasizing personal development.

- Received Stellar Seller Award (2000) for generating first-quarter new business.
- Increased local sales by 16% in 2000 over 1999 by employing consultative sales approach.
- Aggressively negotiated contract with major client, netting over $1 million 2000.
- Lead team in turning around distress territory of underperforming executive.

Education

University of Cincinnati, Cincinnati, Ohio
Bachelor of Arts: Business & Communications, 1990

- Interned with One2all Communications, New York
- GPA 3.75

References Furnished Immediately upon Request

Interview Q&A Using Keywords

Why should we hire you, what are your strengths, and how do you see yourself contributing to our company?

Consistently, I have demonstrated my ability to meet or exceed sales goals. Planning and developing ways to attract new business have always distinguished me from my colleagues. Based on my ability to conduct thorough market research and analysis, I have repeatedly been successful in implementing creative sales, marketing and promotional strategies that have produced desired results. Your company has a product/service that will assist clients in getting ahead of their competition; I offer expertise in market expansion and solution selling to attract new clients and thus maximize your revenue.

ACCOUNTING MANAGER

Resume

Heather Shuster
1234 North Colorado Boulevard
Burbank, California 91304
(818) 555-1234 / email@email.com

> **ACCOUNTING MANAGER**
> **Experienced in All Aspects of General Accounting and Financial Reporting**
>
> **Team Building and Leadership / Hiring, Training, & Supervision**
> **Strong Analytical, Mathematical, and Problem Solving Skills**
> **Experienced in Integrated Accounting Software**

Accounting manager with bachelor's degree in Finance and five years' related supervision and accounting systems experience. Proven ability to plan and supervise work of others to achieve department and organizational goals. Expertise in QuickBooks Pro, Great Plains, Peachtree, Word, Excel, and Access.

Core Strengths

General Accounting
Financial Systems & Reporting
Oral & Written Communications
Accounts Receivable/Payable

Budget Management
Hiring, Training & Supervising
Payroll/Employment Taxes
Expense Tracking & Analysis

Professional Experience

WC SPECIALTY PRODUCTS, INC., Los Angeles, CA   1997–Present

Accounting Manager

Direct activities of accounting department for manufacturer of specialty gift items. Supervise, train, and evaluate team of twelve involved with general accounting, accounts receivable/payable, payroll processing, data collection and analysis, banking activities, and employment tax reporting. Ensure month-end closings and timely financial statement preparation. Prepare and manage annual budget process. Report to VP Finance.

- Consolidated benefits accounting system for divisions located in four states throughout United States.
- Directed implementation of state-of-the art accounting software; trained staff on use.
- Improved accuracy of financial reporting systems and asset accounting procedures.
- Coordinated audit process with outside CPA. Collaborated in due diligence process on anticipated acquisition.

Education

CALIFORNIA STATE UNIVERSITY, Los Angeles, CA
B.A. in Accounting; 1996

Keywords

Account Reconciliations

Accounting Software

Accounts Receivable/Payable

Banking

Budgets

Computer Skills

Data Collection & Analysis

Data Processing

Expense Tracking

Financial Reporting

Mergers and Acquisitions

General Accounting

Information Systems

Month-End Closing

Payroll

Revenue Accounting

Employment Tax Reporting

Problem Solving

Project Management

Uniform Capitalization

Interview Q&A Using Keywords

Why should we hire you, what are your strengths, and how do you see yourself contributing to our company?

I have more than five years' experience in all aspects of general accounting and financial reporting. I am strong with all required software programs, including Word, Excel, and accounting software such as QuickBooks Pro, Great Plains, and Peachtree. From a management perspective, I practice team building and leadership skills and have experience in hiring, training, and coaching. My financial strengths include budgeting, reporting, auditing, and GL work.

ACCOUNTS RECEIVABLE SUPERVISOR

Keywords

Accounts Receivable

Cash Management

Cost Reduction

Key Accounts

Financial Audits

Internal Controls

Credit & Collections

Strategic Planning

Financial Reporting

Negotiate

Collections

Profit/Loss (P&L)

Corporate Mergers

Profit Gains

Regulatory
   Compliance
   Auditing

Audit Controls

Risk Management

Revenue Gain

Work Paper

Financial Controls

Resume

Mark Williams
123 S. Fourth Street
Kewanee, Illinois 61443
(309) 555-1234 / email@email.com

> **Accounts Receivable Supervisor**
> **Proven Background in Cost Reduction, Credit, and Collections**
>
> **Financial Reporting / Strategic Planning Skills**
> **Full Range of P&L / Key Account Financial Management Experience**

Results-oriented, dedicated, and highly accomplished Accounts Receivable Supervisor with a proven track record of reducing costs and improving collection results. Experienced in working with corporate mergers.

Core Strengths

Accounts Receivable	Strategic Planning
Collections	Key Accounts
Profit/Loss (P&L)	Credit & Collections
Financial Reporting	*Audit* Controls
Financial Controls	Risk Management

Professional Experience

JT ENTERPRISES—Lawson, IL   1989 to Current

Accounts Receivable Manager

Direct, train, and mentor a staff of four full-time accounting clerks in managing domestic and international accounts receivable operations, financial reporting, strategic planning, and credit/collection activities. Implement policies, procedures, and programs to streamline operations, reduce costs, and increase efficiency. Negotiate payment terms and serve as the main point of contact in resolving issues at all levels.

- Negotiated key account terms, resulting in $7,000 in annual savings.
- Spearheaded collection methods, clearing $45,000 in past-due accounts.
- Trained staff members on new collection techniques to improve profit gains.
- Oversaw accounts receivables during two corporate mergers.

Education

UNIVERSITY OF ILLINOIS STATE—Knox, Illinois
Bachelor of Science: Accounting 1988
Certifications: **Certified Public Accountant (CPA) 1989**

Interview Q&A Using Keywords

Why Should Our Company Hire You?

I have extensive experience as an Accounts Receivable Manager and have been involved in many corporate-level teams in implementing audit controls, ensuring regulatory compliance, managing corporate mergers, and ensuring profit gains. I have also worked with many high-level and international clients in effectively directing collections activities.

ACTUARY

Resume

Laura Longevity
999 Concourse Boulevard
Meriden, Connecticut 06456
(860) 555-1122 / email@email.com

> **Actuary**
> **Society of Actuaries Fellow**
>
> **Life and Health Insurance/Employee Benefits/Pensions**
> **American Society of Pension Actuaries**

Pensions specialist with a background in insurance plans. Proficient in mortality and disability table construction. Skilled in *statistical* analysis software. Trained in latest valuation techniques.

Core Strengths

Pension valuations	Calculating employee contributions
Earnings distribution	Risk management
Annuity and Pension design	Computer programs and applications
Solid communication skills	Data analysis

Professional Experience

Milk M Enterprises, Chicago, Illinois   1987–2000

Actuary

Managed rate and product development functions of benefits department. Calculated rates for insurance plans. Projected and reported on yields. Recommended equitable earnings distributions. Designed pension and annuity products. Reviewed legislation for product compliance and design. Researched demographic and social issues for impact on group and individual plans. Certified pension plans for federal and state agencies.

- Acted as Consultant to Health and Human Services Administration
- Introduced a complex lattice model for higher accuracy in valuations
- Provided technical assistance to a legislative team working on health-care reforms
- Created a multitiered pension plan for a company with 8,000 employees

Education

University of Pennsylvania
Bachelor of Science, Mathematics   1982
- Pi Mu Epsilon, Math Honors Society

University of Pennsylvania, Wharton School of Business
Asset Liability Management   2002

References Furnished Immediately upon Request

Keywords

Statistical Data
Probability Tables
Mortality
Yield
Insurance Plans
Pensions
Annuities
Premiums
Demographics
Social Issues
Legislative Review
Data Analysis
Earnings Distribution
Rate Calculation
Disability
Liability
Benefits
Group Contracts
Risk
Valuation

Interview Q&A Using Keywords

Why should we hire you, what are your strengths, and how do you see yourself contributing to our company?

I bring an understanding of contemporary political, social, and health issues. My expertise includes extensive research and training in current mortality and disability trends in light of those issues as well as cutting-edge interest rate theory and valuation constructs. Having consulted with both HHS and state legislatures, I have knowledge of upcoming legislation and regulatory changes. I have excellent presentation skills and can translate complex formulas into the vernacular.

ADMINISTRATIVE ASSISTANT

Keywords

Assistant to
  Administrator

Computer Skills

Word Processing

Dictation

Transcription

Spreadsheets

Appointment
  Management

Travel
  Arrangements

Letter Composition

Newsletter Creation

Itinerary
  Management

Message Taking

Call Screening

Office Management

Petty Cash

Presentation
  Preparation

Professional
  Appearance

Commissioned
  Notary Public

Staff Supervision

Project Management

Resume

Linda B. Boisvert
123 James Street
Auburn, Maine 04210
(207) 555-1111 / email@email.com

Credentialed *Administrative Assistant*
Certified Professional Secretary

Commissioned Notary Public
Office Management Capabilities

Unique paraprofessional with outstanding skills resulting in becoming recently certified in advanced secretarial skills. Ability to totally run and manage a small office or work as a team member in a larger environment.

Core Strengths

Executive Assistant	Accurate Message Taking
Varied Computer Skills	Dictation/Transcription
Letter Composition	Newsletter Creation
Appointment Management	Petty Cash Account

Professional Experience

Bates Manufacturing Co., Lewiston, Maine   1995 to Present

Administrative Assistant

Provide secretarial and administrative support to the vice president of manufacturing. Notarize documents when needed for entire organization. Coordinate all incoming business news and create monthly newsletter distributed to all employees and clients. Utilize the Internet extensively to research products, competitive businesses, and current trends. Compile information for weekly presentations for department heads.

- Serve as corporate librarian for all Internet research compiled.
- Completely prepare newsletter from scratch to "camera-ready."
- Saved the company $10,000 in printing costs in one year.
- Introduced software and applications to upgrade and network office.

Education

Mid-State College, Auburn, Maine   Completed 2 Years
Associate Degree Computer Science
Associate Degree Secretarial Science

Interview Q&A Using Keywords

Why should we hire you, what are your strengths, and how do you see yourself contributing to our company?

Having recently earned my CPS (Certified Professional Secretary) status, I feel confident that my additional five (5) years of experience as an executive secretary would qualify me for your position. The strengths I would bring to your position would be in all areas of secretarial support with an emphasis on administrative-level assisting. In particular, I have worked successfully in the areas of special project management, presentation preparation, itinerary management, and all levels of travel scheduling and tracking. I am also very proficient with all Microsoft programs and using a Palm Pilot.

ANESTHESIOLOGIST

Resume

Roberto Sanchez, M.D.
123 Alvarado Lane
Dallas, Texas 75243
(972) 555-5432 / email@email.com

> **BOARD CERTIFIED ANESTHESIOLOGIST**
> with 20 years of experience
>
> **Cardiovascular and Emergency/**
> **Research and Clinical Studies**

Perioperative, preoperative, intraoperative, and postoperative practical experience in administering anesthetics, pain control, and moderate sedation, and an active participant in ongoing research.

Core Strengths

Provide excellent medical care
Prescribe pain-relieving medication
Cardiovascular and respiratory
Board certified—ASAHQ

Focused consultations with patients
Monitor and control all situations
Infection control techniques
Licensed by the State of Texas

Professional Experience

NORTH TEXAS MEDICAL ASSOCIATES, Dallas, Texas   1982 to present

Senior Anesthesiologist

Provide Perioperative, Preoperative, Intraoperative, and Postoperative Medicare Care for anesthesia care, pain management, respiratory and cardiovascular disease, and emergency situations. Perform medical assessments, *diagnose* situations, monitor and control anesthetics, and prescribe pain-relieving medication. Actively participate in research and clinical studies.

- Treated over 20,000 patients in hospitals and clinics since 1982.
- Patient satisfaction rated very high in interpersonal interactions.
- Conducted more than 25 clinical studies since 1995.
- Recognized by the ASAHQ as a "Top 25" Anesthesiologist in 2001.
- Selected as a member of the ASAHQ Board of Directors in 2002.

Education

Johns Hopkins University School of Medicine, Baltimore, Maryland
Doctor of Medicine in Anesthesiology; 1981
University of Houston, Texas
Bachelor of Science Degree; Major: Medicine

Keywords

Anesthesiology
Pain
Board Certified
Moderate Sedation
Medical Care
Consultations
Perioperative
Preoperative
Intraoperative
Postoperative
Anesthetics
Medical Assessment
Monitor and Control
Pain-Relieving
  Interventions
Diagnosis
Respiratory
Cardiovascular
Infection Control
Emergency
  Situations
Research and
  Clinical Studies

Interview Q&A Using Keywords

Why should we hire you, what are your strengths, and how do you see yourself contributing to our company?

I have 20 years of experience as a Board Certified Anesthesiologist providing perioperative, preoperative, Intraoperative, and postoperative medicare care. After performing medical assessments on each patient, I diagnose their situation, monitor and control anesthetics, and prescribe pain-relieving interventions. I have practical experience in anesthesia, moderate sedation, respiratory and cardiovascular disease, infection control, and emergency situations. I believe my research and clinical studies will help the practice greatly.

Keywords

Visual Basic/
  VBScript

Java

Active Server Pages

JavaScript

XTML

XML

DHTML

ActiveX

Com/COM+

.Net

IIS

SQL Server

MTS

ADO

Windows 2000

Linux

Design Development

Infrastructure

Code Testing

Programming

Resume

Jonas Gorauskas
11027 Southeast 21 Boulevard
Anywhere, Idaho 00000
(208) 555-0000 / email@email.com

Application Developer

Expert Web Application Developer
Proven ability to transform concepts into working, stable applications.

Outstanding analytical, problem-solving and decision-making skills. Able to solve complex problems with efficient solutions. Proficient in managing multiple projects. Multilingual—fluent in Portuguese and English.

Core Strengths

Programming Ability	Deliver Solutions
Business Management Skills	Read German and Spanish
Infrastructure Planning	Customer Service Oriented
Code Testing	Integrate Web sites

Professional Experience

AKTIVTEK.com, Sierra, Nevada   2001 to Present

Web Application Developer/Owner

Develop applications, analyze data, plan infrastructure and deployment for Web sites. Define and analyze requirements, design, code, and implement core elements in the company's product line. Perform object-oriented Web application development, integrate Web sites with database servers, and code new programs and new server components. Address and resolve numerous technical issues.

- Reader's Choice Award, WebOnline, 2000.
- Published "Using the FileSystemObject," Pinnacle Publishing, Inc. 2001.
- Published "User Authentication and Management Without a Database," ActiveWeb Developer, 1999.

Education

Lewis-Clark State College, Lewiston, Idaho
Bachelor of Science Degree in Computer Science   **1999**

- Selected to lead the development of the WinBridge game client product.
- Key player selected to implement compiled server-side components to improve robustness and efficiency of client solutions.

Interview Q&A Using Keywords

Why should we hire you, what are your strengths, and how do you see yourself contributing to our company?

My hands-on technical expertise makes me a great candidate for the job. I meet all qualifications outlined in the advertisement. I earned a Bachelor of Science degree in Computer Science. I have designed, developed, and programmed a number of successful Web projects, always being cost-conscious. Completing the Pet.com e-commerce site required dedication to the project from conception to completion. I have excellent communications skills and understand that providing superior customer service is the key to success.

ARCHITECT

Resume

Christopher Aron
8705 Cleveland Avenue
St. Paul, Minnesota 55104
(651) 555-2599 / email@email.com

Licensed Architect
Registered in Minnesota, Wisconsin, Iowa, and Michigan

Fluent in English, Spanish, and French
Proficient with AutoCAD, FormZ, 3D Studio, MS Office, Pagemaker

---

Demonstrated success in exploring the relationship between architecture and the environment, preservation, and accessibility through the discourse of design. Able to enhance the understanding, knowledge, and philosophy brought forth in quality architecture.

Core Strengths

Public architecture	Preservation consultant
Program definition	Drawings and models
Presentation graphics	Historic log structures
Americans with Disabilities Act	Trade/crossover skills

Professional Experience

STATE OF MINNESOTA, St. Paul, Minnesota 1995 to Current

Architect: Bureau of Engineering

Midwest region's recognized authority in the analysis, documentation, and restoration of historic log structures, completing 54 projects to date. Scope of project management encompasses manpower allocation, feasibility studies, site and cost analysis, estimating, and management budgets. Served on the Technology Planning Committee, reviewing and implementing tools and systems for the Architectural Unit. Design, develop, and manage public park, rural, and city projects, from proposal development through new and restorative construction phases.

- "The Bremerton Estate" featured in *The Log Home Tradition* magazine
- "Volunteer of the Year" award recognition, The St. Paul Area Historical Society
- Design Finalist, Elderly Housing (Exhibited at National Institute of Health)
- "Architecture Responds to Americans with Disabilities," featured in the *St. Paul Chronicle*

Education

University of Minnesota, Minneapolis, Minnesota
Master of Architecture, 1999
Bachelor of Architecture, 1989

- Design Finalist, Contemporary Healthcare Facility (Exhibited in New York, New York)
  References Furnished Immediately upon Request

Keywords

Multistate Architect Licensure

Program Definition

Americans with Disabilities Act Compliance

Documents

Construction Estimating and Management

Site and Cost Analysis

Presentation Graphics

Feasibility Studies

Program Definition

Drawings and Models

Public Architecture

Design Finalist

Zoning and Codes

Historic Log Structures

Commercial and Residential Architecture

Manpower Allocation

Preservation Consultant

Exhibits

Multilingual Fluency

Trade/Crossover Skills

Interview Q&A Using Keywords

Why should we hire you, what are your strengths, and how do you see yourself contributing to our company?

I am able to handle all phases of design: from program definition through design, models, and drawings. My works have received design finalist and exhibit recognition in academic and professional environments, including the Design of the Year award in Minneapolis in 1999. Because of multilingual fluency, as well as historic and public architecture expertise, my range of influence is broad. Multistate licensure and broad experience encompass commercial and residential, codes, zoning, and ADA compliance. I have led manpower allocation, feasibility studies, site and cost analysis, estimating and management of projects. Trade/Crossover skills in plumbing, electrical, build-out, and renovation projects have been valuable assets to my work.

ART DIRECTOR

Keywords

Layout & Design

UI/Site Architecture

Typography

Pre-Press/Print
Production

Visual Media

Concept
Development

Paste-Up

Point-of-Sale
Materials

Trade Promotions

Dealer Sell Sheets

Event Graphics

Branding &
Advertising

Print, Logo, &
Identity

Bounce-Back

Trade Show Exhibits

Branding Identity

Brand Building

Interface Design

Product Design

Global Brand
Strategy

Resume

Chris Smith
178 Green Street
Albuquerque, New Mexico 87104
(505) 555-1122 / email@email.com

Art Direction / Design
Specializing in branding, identity development, and team leadership

Resource Allocation / Load Balancing
Extensive knowledge of interface design and Internet technologies

---

Dynamic, experienced professional with an eye on the bottom line. Special ability to motivate teams and develop creative brand identity and advertising campaigns that consistently improve market position.

Core Strengths

Strong Visual Skills	Creative Problem Solving
Resource Management	Budget Development / Management
UI/Site Architecture	New Product Launch
On-Site Promos	Formal Graphic Design Training

Professional Experience

SICOLA MARTIN, Austin, TX   1995 to Present

Art Director

Art Direct ad campaigns in all divisions including Web site design, catalogs, dealer sell sheets, product graphics, packaging, point-of-sale materials, trade show promotions, and event graphics. Oversee all licensee groups as International Creative Director. Manage art department. Assisted in the development and presentation of global brand strategies for key client accounts.

- Designed and rendered accompanying point-of-sale materials.
- Utilizing illustrative talents, selected to complete product illustrations for bounce-back coupons and ad slicks.
- Directed paste-up and type-setting activities for direct mail pieces.

Education

Syracuse University, Syracuse, New York
Bachelor of Fine Arts / Advertising Design, 1986

- Design of gallery graphics
- Gallery scheduling

Interview Q&A Using Keywords

Why should we hire you, what are your strengths, and how do you see yourself contributing to our company?

I understand that you are looking for a professional with a minimum of 5 years of senior art direction experience. I have more than 10 years of hands-on direction experience. What makes me unique is that I have frequently done lettering as part of the product design projects on which I'm working. I specialize in typography, brand building, and identity design, which add collateral value to my candidacy. With a long track record of success in advertising and multimedia design, I will immediately add value to your team!

ARTIST

Resume

Maria Lane
5555 Ridgeway Lane
Sherman Oaks, California 91340
(818) 555-2222 / email@email.com

> **ILLUSTRATOR / ARTIST / DESIGNER**
> **Creative Artist/Designer Experienced in Diverse Mediums.**
>
> **Strong Sense of Color, Detail, Balance, and Proportion.**
> **Talented in Interpreting Needs of Clients.**

Creative artist/designer who consistently exceeds client expectations. Developed business images and design graphics, logos, illustration, murals, and textiles for wide range of corporate and private clients. B.A. in art with strong computer skills including CAD, Adobe Illustrator, PageMaker, Photoshop, Quark, etc. Works well independently as well as collaboratively in a team environment. Skilled in monitoring trends and styles.

Core Strengths

Illustrations	Textile Design
Sketch Artist	Packaging
Logos	Murals
Business Images	Graphic Design
Creative Direction	Design Elements

Professional Experience

HEARTFELT GRAPHICS, Encino, CA   1995–Present
Textile Artist / Designer
Design product line for multimillion manufacturer of textiles. Monitor fashion trends and styles to conceive new designs that "win" accounts and meet consumer demand. Created seasonal and proprietary branded designs for retail mass market. Create business images including logos, packaging, illustrations, and murals for office decor.

- Conceived innovative designs that generated widespread industry recognition for company and increased sales fourfold.
- Created designs that have become classics and broke all sales records.
- Consistently met critical deadlines in a fast-paced environment.
- Developed specialty packaging for soft-drink product launch.

Education

UNIVERSITY OF CALIFORNIA, Los Angeles, CA
B.A. in Art and Art History
Excellent Recommendations Available upon Request

Keywords

Artistic
Balance
Branding
Business Images
Color
Creative Direction
Designer
Graphic Design
Illustrator
Logos
Murals
Packaging
Painting
Product Development
Promotional Material
Proportion
Sketch Artist
Talent
Textile Design
Trends

Interview Q&A Using Keywords

Why should we hire you, what are your strengths, and how do you see yourself contributing to our company?

I am a creative designer with talent and experience across diverse mediums. I possess a strong sense of color and have an innate sense of design. I have worked with several design software programs and graphic designers, and like to interpret client needs and preferences and produce a magical end result that seems always to impress them. I have conceived innovative designs that generated industry recognition and increased sales.

ASSOCIATION MANAGER

Resume

Robert S. Dawson, CAE
977 Marlboro Court
Lawrenceville, New Jersey 08648
(609) 555-1234 / email@email.com

Association Manager / Executive Director
Proven track record of advocacy and chapter development

Program Administration / Development Coordination
Member-driven organization management

Certified Association Executive (CAE) and Executive Director of not-for-profit association. Noted for leadership in member recruitment and retention, budget allocation, revenue generation, and program expansion.

Core Strengths

Financial/Budget Management	Member Development
Legislative Advocacy	Educational Programming
Public/Media Relations	Fund-Raising/Grant Writing
Staff Development/Training	Special Events Management

Professional Experience

HUNTERDON TEACHERS ASSOCIATION, Ewing, New Jersey   1998 to Current

Executive Director

Recruited to revitalize 2500-member professional association of teachers in Hunterdon County. Guide policy for Board of Directors, provide educational programming, legislative advocacy, and member communications. Manage $800,000 annual budget along with $500,000 in strategic funds and investments. Lead conference planning, community outreach, and fund-raising. Represent HTA at local, state, regional, and national events.

- Spearheaded goal-based strategic visioning and planning committee, which has implemented benchmarked objectives for member services.
- Increased membership by over 50% within two years, with record-breaking recruitment and renewal rates and targeted program expansion.
- Controlled costs and saved $55,000 through in-depth insurance review.

Education

Rider University, Lawrenceville, New Jersey
Bachelor of Arts, Sociology and Business Administration—1992

- Certified Association Executive, Society of Association Executives
- Management Certificate, Zenger-Miller Leadership Program

Keywords

- Advocacy
- Chapter Development
- Program Administration
- Development
- Member-Driven Organization
- Certified Association Executive (CAE)
- Not-for-Profit
- Leadership
- Member Recruitment
- Member Retention
- Member Services
- Budget Allocation
- Revenue Generation
- Member Development
- Educational Programming
- Fund-Raising
- Grant-Writing
- Special Events Management
- Public Relations
- Member Communications

Interview Q&A Using Keywords

Why should we hire you, what are your strengths, and how do you see yourself contributing to our company?

As an experienced Association Executive, my proactive organization leadership has included key elements in the long-term success of a member-driven organization: viable organization mission and policy development coupled with tangible, high-benefit member services and revenue development activities. This combination drives member recruitment and retention, promotes positive public relations, and stimulates productive board relations. I would like to do the same for you.

Resume

Hunt Wesley, CPA
3459 Summit Avenue
St. Paul, Minnesota 55102
(651) 555-9713 / email@email.com

Auditing Specialist
15-Year Career Ensuring Tight Financial Controls
Internal Revenue Service / Public Accounting / Corporate Accounting
Operational Audit and Corporate Development Expertise

Broad career path has enhanced auditing expertise from the perspectives of government regulatory and compliance auditor, public accounting auditor, and corporate controller. Stay proactive with audit techniques, accounting methods, and codes and regulations.

Core Strengths

Cost avoidance & reduction	**Financial audits**
Tax audits	Audit controls
Asset & liability management	Financial models
Profit/loss (P&L) analysis	Audit management

Professional Experience

INTERNAL REVENUE SERVICE, St. Paul, Minnesota   1995 to Current

Auditor

Planned and managed tax and financial audits for businesses throughout Minnesota, designing and implementing a comprehensive program of financial controls and accountability. Enforced internal controls governing finance, accounting, capital assets, and technology acquisitions. Introduced proactive management techniques to strengthen focus on cost avoidance and reduction. Led a team of 10 responsible for corporate tax filings in more than 600 local, state, and federal jurisdictions.

- Integrated audit controls that reversed the previous external audit review findings.
- Helped client reduce debt by 28% through improved credit and collection processes.
- Implemented financial controls reversing several companies' previous year's losses.
- Led operational audits of Salvation Army, ensuring federal/organization compliance.

Education

University of Minnesota, Minneapolis, Minnesota
Bachelor of Business Administration: Accounting, 1985

- C.P.A., State of Minnesota, since 1986
- Accounting Club Treasurer, 2 years

Keywords

Audit Management

Audit Controls

Asset & Liability Management

Tax Audits

Corporate Development

Public & Corporate Accounting

Cost Avoidance

Cost Reduction

Cost/Benefit Analysis

Due Diligence

Financial Audits

Financial Controls

Financial Models

Internal/External Controls

Internal/External Audit Reviews

Operational Audits

Internal Revenue Service

Profit/Loss (P&L) Analysis

Regulatory Compliance Auditing

Computer Savvy

Interview Q&A Using Keywords

Why should we hire you, what are your strengths, and how do you see yourself contributing to our company?

I offer exemplary performance within Internal Revenue Service, "Big 8" accounting firms, and corporate settings. I have a track record of directing financial and operational audit management programs of businesses worldwide. In doing so, I have established a structured process to expedite regulatory compliance auditing, reporting, and defense. One of my strengths is in implementing stringent audit controls to accommodate internal and external audit reviews. I can create sound financial status through internal and external controls focused on due diligence. Strong computer systems expertise also ensures my ability to distinguish between problems caused by systems errors or flawed input.

AUTOMOBILE PARTS MANAGER

Resume

Greg Fantin
66220 Magnolia Boulevard
Encino, California 91316
(818) 555-1111/ email@email.com

AUTOMOBILE PARTS MANAGER
Five Years' Automotive Industry Experience; Three Years as Manager

Strong Customer Service Orientation
Track Record of Sales Growth and Increased Staff Productivity

---

In-depth automotive and auto parts knowledge. Strong entrepreneurial drive with excellent communication, organizational, and problem-solving abilities. Proven ability to increase sales, reduce costs, and motivate teams to achieve high levels of productivity.

Core Strengths

OEM & After-Market Parts	Inventory Management
Client Relations	P&L Responsibility
Expense Control	Warehouse Operations
Shipping/Receiving	Staff Development
Team Building & Leadership	Organizational Skills

Professional Experience

AUTO UNIVERSE, Los Angeles, CA   Encino, CA   1997–Present

Auto Parts Manager

Direct day-to-day operations of leading auto parts retailer with full P&L responsibility. Ensure high level of customer service/support.

- Increased sales by average of 15% annually through combination of excellent staff training and mentoring, improved merchandising efforts, and continued focus on customer service.
- Implemented inventory controls that streamlined product delivery while concurrently reducing theft and loss.
- Recruited, trained, and developed #1 team out of 25 stores in Western Region.
- Initiated mentoring program with local schools, culminating in recognition by local government officials for community support, and generating positive publicity for company.

Education

CALIFORNIA STATE UNIVERSITY, Los Angeles, CA
B.A. in Business Administration

Interview Q&A Using Keywords

Why should we hire you, what are your strengths, and how do you see yourself contributing to our company?

I am familiar with all aspects of automotive parts operations, with five years direct experience including three years management level experience. You need strong customer service skills since this position deals with customers constantly, and I am very comfortable working with the public. I am also experienced at managing tight inventory controls that ensured timely delivery of products while reducing losses and theft. Finally, at Auto Universe, sales increase by about 15% annually through combination of excellent staff training and improved merchandising.

BANK BRANCH MANAGER

Resume

Jeff Kilpatrick
192-35 32nd Avenue
Flushing, NY 11358
(718) 555-1122 / email@email.com

Banking Branch Manager
Five Years' Profitable Branch Operations Experience

Deep Knowledge of Bank Products, Practices, and Procedures
Committed to Customer Service and Community Relations

High-energy professional with fast-track hands-on banking experience. Skilled in the strategic planning, sales building, and local brand building needed for a branch's visibility and viability in this competitive industry.

Core Strengths

Business Development	Cash Management
Action Plans/Sales Goals	Budgets/Staffing
Consumer Banking Programs	Relationship Management
Bank Compliance	Staff Coaching/Monitoring

Professional Experience

Astoria Federal Savings, Bayside, NY   1997 to Current

Branch Manager, Bayside and Flushing

Manage all banking activities and 20-member staff for two neighborhood branches of this leading New York Metro retail banking institution. Direct and train staff in deposit and loan production, merchant services, consumer credit and mortgage administration, Internet and ATM banking, and customer service strategies. Actively develop relationships with local businesses and community leaders.

- Generated 22% revenue increase by increasing customer retention.
- Managed turnkey opening and staffing of new Flushing branch.
- Initiated profitable "Neighborhood Days" branch promotions.
- Partnered with merchants to raise visibility through community events.

Education

Queens College, The City University of New York, Flushing, NY
Bachelor of Arts: Business Administration, 1997

- GPA 3.75
- Graduated with Honors

References Furnished Immediately upon Request

Keywords

Branch Operations

Bank Compliance

Cash Management

Business Development

Relationship Management

Customer Relations/ Service

Branch Sales Action Plans

Sales Goals

Staff Coaching/ Monitoring

Deposit/Loan Production

Alternative Systems

Internet Banking

ATM Banking

Merchant Services

Community Relations

Budgets

Staff Scheduling/ Management

Consumer Credit/Mortgage Administration

Customer Service Strategies

Consumer Banking Programs

Interview Q&A Using Keywords

Why should we hire you, what are your strengths, and how do you see yourself contributing to our company?

As an experienced branch manager who has fast-tracked from teller, to assistant manager, to branch manager within a few short years, I have a hands-on understanding of all facets of banking at the branch level. I've used that knowledge to develop innovative customer-driven programs that have delivered a 22% revenue increase this year, despite a lagging economy. Customer retention rates have grown by over 20% as well. Our customers and staff are happy, our operations are lean, and our margins reflect that.

BANK TELLER

Keywords

Banking

Safe Deposit

ATM Processing

Vault Operations

Bank Teller

Foreign Currency
Exchange

Audit Examination

Transaction
Approval

Processed Data
Retrieval

Accountability of
Transactions

Daily Settlement
Sheet

Lockbox Processing

Funds Transfer
Operations

Transaction
Banking

Reconciliation
Projects

Ancillary Sales
Referrals

Reconnet Software

Loan Documentation

Back Operations
Accounting

Branch Automation
Banking

Resume

Patricia A. Evans
1234 Olde Post Road
Lovington, New Mexico 88260
(506) 555-1122 / email@email.com

BANK TELLER
Accuracy / Dependability / Efficiency

Bonded to handle large sums
Reconciliation Project Specialist / Back Operations Accounting

---

Highly qualified **Bank Teller** with extensive experience as a cash handler and customer service representative. Customer focused, goal oriented, with excellent verbal communication and interpersonal skills.

Core Strengths

Funds Transfer Operations — Reconciliation & Audits
Foreign Exchange Conversions — Reconnet Software Proficiency
Processed Data Retrieval — Ancillary Sales Referrals

Professional Experience

WELLS FARGO, Lovington, New Mexico — 1996 to Current

Teller

Process customer transactions within established guidelines. Identify and make ancillary sales referrals, recommend alternate channels, cross-sell bank services and products for Wells Fargo partners, and render consistently superior customer service. Provide access to processed data retrieval for banking customers. Additional responsibilities include safe deposit, merchant, and vault operations, ATM processing, bond and coupon sale, foreign currency exchange, night shift lockbox processing, and funds transfer operations.

- Noticed for maintaining full accountability of transactions.
- Recognized for computing figures with speed and accuracy.
- Able to satisfy consistently stringent audit examinations.
- Awarded "Teller of the Year" for providing continuously superior customer service.

Education

City University of New York, New York, New York
Bachelor of Science / Accounting, 1993

- NSF Scholarship recipient
- Past President, City University Alumni Association

References Furnished Immediately upon Request

Interview Q&A Using Keywords

Why should we hire you, what are your strengths, and how do you see yourself contributing to our company?

With over five years of experience in transaction and branch automation banking, a degree in accounting, and a superior record for accuracy, I offer immediate value to your team. My biggest strengths are my mathematical ability, my enthusiasm, and my total dedication to quality and personal and professional growth. I will always do my best to provide your customers, my colleagues, and my supervisors with the level of performance they expect and deserve.

BENEFITS COORDINATOR

Resume

Wilma F. Sandstone
1972 North 82nd Street
Milwaukee, WI 53223
(414) 555-1122 / email@email.com

Benefits Coordinator
Expertise in health, dental, life, AD&D, LTD, STD, and pension plans

Certified Employee Benefits Specialist/Employee Education
Cost-effective approach to benefits administration

A cost-effective professional with expertise in administering health, dental, life, AD&D, LTD, STD, and pension plans. Skilled analyzing existing plans and examining new insurance plans that meet employee and corporate goals.

Core Strengths

Employee education and training	Benefits analysis and administration
Cost-effective plan selection	New plan rollout and integration
Insurance billing reconciliation	Knowledge of employment law
Employee satisfaction survey	Compliance with standards

Professional Experience

FRIENDSHIP VILLAGE, Milwaukee, Wisconsin   1990 to Present

Benefits Coordinator

Research, select, and administer insurance plans and employee benefit packages for approximately 400 employees, including health, dental, life, AD&D, LTD, STD, and pension plans. Coordinate employee surveys to assess satisfaction levels and needs. Conduct biweekly employee benefit orientations. Process family and medical leave paperwork. Reconcile insurance billings. Keep abreast of current employment laws.

- As a result of an employee survey, adopted new dental plan that improved employee satisfaction and increased enrollment.
- Analyzed/coordinated integration of benefits for pending acquisition and its 73 employees.
- Developed and administered successful on-site education program.

Education

WHARTON SCHOOL OF THE UNIVERSITY OF PENNSYLVANIA
(International Foundation of Benefits), Philadelphia, Pennsylvania
Certified Employee Benefits Specialist (CEBS), 1990

- Benefits Discussion Group, MRA Student Chapter

References Furnished Immediately upon Request

Keywords

- Certified Employee Benefits Specialist
- Health, Dental, Life, AD&D, LTD, STD Administration
- 401K and Pension Plan Administration
- Family Medical Leave Act
- Employee Education and Training
- Benefits Integration
- Insurance Plan Research and Selection
- Benefits Assessment/ Analysis
- Employee Satisfaction Survey
- Compliance
- Employee Relations
- Increased Enrollment
- On-site Educational Programs
- Resolve Benefit Issues
- Liaison
- Insurance Billing Reconciliation
- New Plan Rollout
- Knowledge of Employment Laws
- Benefits Orientation
- Documentation

Interview Q&A Using Keywords

Why should we hire you, what are your strengths, and how do you see yourself contributing to our company?

As a Certified Employee Benefits Specialist with more than a decade of experience researching, selecting, and administering cost-effective health, dental, life, AD&D, LTD, STD, 401K, and pension plans, I am confident I can select and administer plans benefiting both employee and company goals. As a successful liaison and resource, I educate new and existing personnel in plan benefits, while ensuring satisfaction.

BOOKKEEPER

Resume

Trisha Thompson
5151 Valjean Avenue
Encino, California 91316
(818) 555-1122 / email@email.com

> **Full Charge Bookkeeper**
> **15 Years' Experience in All Aspects of Bookkeeping through Trial Balance**
>
> **Proactive in Streamlining Procedures / Adept at Multitasking**
> **Excellent Computer Skills Including QuickBooks, ADP, and Peachtree**

Detail-oriented professional committed to efficiency and thoroughness. Works well independently as well as collaboratively in a team environment. Proven ability to process high volume of work accurately and meet critical deadlines with attention to detail.

Core Strengths

Accounts Payable/Receivable	Journal Entries & General Ledger
Trial Balance	Account & Bank Reconciliations
Payroll	Expense Tracking & Reports
Collections	Client Relations

Professional Experience

STUDIO CITY BMW, Studio City, CA   1995 to Current

Full Charge Bookkeeper

Handle all bookkeeping functions for busy BMW dealership, including Accounts Receivable/Payable, Payroll Processing, and Invoicing. Accurately processed high volume of records in a fast-paced environment. Generate monthly trial balance. Reconcile bank statements and key accounts identifying, researching, and analyzing all variances. Process expense accounts and generate reimbursements. Tactfully follow up on and resolve overdue receivables and collections. Consistently meet critical deadlines. Provide additional general office support.

- Upon hire, organized six-month backlog of bookkeeping and accounting documentation.
- Collected on accounts that were seriously delinquent.
- Created standardized forms to process more expense accounts on timely basis.
- Transitioned bookkeeping and payroll processes to QuickBooks and ADP respectively in response to increasing work volume.

Education

Los Angeles Valley College, Valley Glen, CA
A.A. in General Education; 1994

References Furnished Immediately upon Request

Interview Q&A Using Keywords

Why should we hire you, what are your strengths, and how do you see yourself contributing to our company?

I have a thorough knowledge of all aspects of bookkeeping through trial balance. I am experienced in accounts receivable, accounts payable, and payroll processing. You mentioned you have a fast-paced environment, and our current operation processes a high volume of records. I consistently meet critical deadlines. Technically, I reconcile monthly accounts and bank statements, accounting for all variances, manage the GL, and oversee all invoicing. I work well independently as well as collaboratively in a team environment.

Resume

Grace Matherly
927 The Maples
Pennington, NJ, 08534
(609) 555-1122 / email@email.com

Senior Brand Manager
Vice President of Pepperidge Farm Division, Campbell Soup Company

Fifteen Years' Experience in Product Development, Launch, and Marketing
Cradle-to-Grave Product Line Oversight

Inspire teams to achieve, create, and bring products to market, develop strategies to increase sales, develop systems to grow productivity, reengineer processes to reduce costs, and lead business to profitability.

Core Strengths

Cradle-to-Grave Product Life Cycle	Cross-Functional Team Management
Profit & Loss (P&L) Management	Multigeneration Product Plans
Product/Market Positioning	Competitive Intelligence
Product/Market Launch	Trend Identification/Analysis

Professional Experience

Campbell Soup Company, Camden, NJ   1992 to Current

VP Marketing, Pepperidge Farm / Senior Brand Manager

Spearheaded revitalization and new product development for one of Campbell's leading divisions, delivering five successful new products, creative pricing and service strategies, and innovative purchasing and cost-reduction initiatives. Manage full product life cycle, C-level relationship building, strategic distribution partnerships, and continuous market research for competitive advantage. Initiatives have produced over $50 million in new sales in five years. Manage a multimillion-dollar P&L and a staff of 10 directs.

- Led Cookie/Cracker division to $100 million in annual sales (+30%).
- Delivered top profit contribution of company's three divisions (+25%).
- Saved plant from closure by developing successful new snack product.
- New product has generated $30 million in sales in first two years.

Education

The Wharton School, University of Pennsylvania, Philadelphia, PA
M.B.A.: Marketing, 1990

Temple University, Philadelphia, PA
Bachelor of Arts: Economics, 1985

References Furnished Immediately upon Request

Keywords

Brand Management

Advertising

Campaign Management

Multigeneration Product Plan

Marketing Communications

Cross-Functional Product Team

Trend Identification/ Analysis

Competitive Advantage

Pricing Strategies

Service Strategies

Purchasing/Cost-Reduction Initiatives

Market Share

Relationship Building

Product/Market Launch

Product/Market Positioning

Competitive Intelligence

Market Research

Product Lifecycle Management

Cradle-to-Grave Product Life Cycle

Profit & Loss (P&L) Management

Interview Q&A Using Keywords

Why should we hire you, what are your strengths, and how do you see yourself contributing to our company?

With over 15 years' participation in the development, growth, or turnaround of leading brands, I offer you a proven history of innovative marketing initiatives. The skills and passion that I bring to brand management, business development, and campaign management translate directly to the bottom line. My leadership of cross-functional product teams has led major divisions in Kraft, Mars, and Campbell Soup to new highs in productivity, market share, and brand success. Your market domination is my goal.

BUILDING INSPECTOR

Keywords

General Building
Inspector

International
Conference of
Building Officials
(ICBO)

Certified Inspector

Field Inspections

Automated
Permitting

Residential and
Commercial
Construction

Building Trade
Construction

Building Inspections

Materials Standards

Inspection
Ordinances

Code Compliance

Customer Service

Building Code
Requirements

Material Assembly
Practices

Code Enforcement

Team Building

Customer
Relationship
Management

Building Plans

Blueprints

Construction Laws

Resume

Theresa Mascagni
17 Mercer Street
Mt. Laurel, New Jersey 08054
(856) 555-4586 / email@email.com

General Building Inspector
International Conference of Building Officials (ICBO) Certified

Skilled Field Inspections / Automated Permitting
Residential and Commercial Construction

Certified Inspector (ICBO) experienced in building trade construction and building inspections, materials standards, inspection ordinances, and code compliance. Team player with exemplary customer service commitment.

Core Strengths

Building Code Requirements	Automated Permitting/Inspections
Building Materials Standards	Code and Ordinance Enforcement
Material Assembly Practices	State and Local Construction Laws
Team Building and Motivation	Customer Relationship Management

Professional Experience

TRENTON PUBLIC WORKS, Trenton, New Jersey 1985 to Current

General Building Inspector III

Perform skilled field inspections of residential and commercial buildings under construction or renovation. Review building plans and blueprints to determine compliance with codes, ordinances, and regulations. Committed to providing quality customer service, and ensuring structurally sound and safe buildings. Train, evaluate, and supervise team of six junior inspectors.

- Lead inspection team in producing up to 300 field inspections monthly, overseeing project coordination with other city and county departments.
- Captured high level of customer satisfaction (88% approval rating) by providing timely inspection work and responsive code enforcement.
- Introduced and maintain automated permitting and inspection software, increasing department efficiency by 147% and reducing labor costs.

Education

Burlington Community College, Pemberton, New Jersey
Associate of Science Degree, General Engineering—1984

- International Conference of Building Officials Certification—1985
- Member, Construction Technology Association of New Jersey

References Furnished Immediately upon Request

Interview Q&A Using Keywords

Why should we hire you, what are your strengths, and how do you see yourself contributing to our company?

With training in general engineering and 17 years' experience in skilled inspectional work, I have gained extensive knowledge in building inspections, as well as state and local code compliance issues. Moreover, I have been able to build cohesive inspection teams (with little employee turnover), generate cost-saving automated processes, and win the trust and approval of builders, contractors, and homeowners alike. I am ready for a new challenge—when can I begin?

Resume

Patti Coury
123 S. Fourth Street
Kewanee, Illinois 61443
(309) 555-1234 / email@email.com

> **Call Center Director**
> **Highly Accomplished and Globally Experienced**
>
> **Network Administration / Operational Leadership**
> **Expertise in Quality Improvement and Business Development**

Goal-oriented, technically adept, and highly motivated call center manager with a proven track record in building, mentoring, and motivating highly effective teams and exceeding corporate sales goals.

Core Strengths

Contract Negotiations	Multisite Operation
Strategic Planning	Outsourcing
Cost Reduction	Vendor Negotiations
Supplier Management	Cost Analysis
Network Administration	Total Quality Management (TQM)

Professional Experience

TELECOM COMPANY   1987 to Current

Call Center Director

Recruited to turn around operations, reduce turnover, drive profits, and boost morale. Developed and implemented continuous process improvement approaches, integrated technology solutions, reengineered internal systems, and played a key role in business development. Led benchmarking project to achieve productivity improvement and increase customer retention on inbound calls; significantly improved customer relations and communications.

- Played a key role in supporting a key client's global market expansion.
- Championed Total Quality Management (TQM) programs.
- Spearheaded employee recognition programs, reducing turnover by 20%.
- Oversaw network administration and achieved cost reductions in hardware by assigning a technical equipment manager to manage accessories.

Education

ILLINOIS STATE COLLEGE, MORGAN, Illinois
Bachelor of Arts: Business Communications 1983

Keywords

Telecommunications

Customer Relations

Multisite Operations Management

Quality Improvement

Network Administration

Call Center

Technology Solutions

Business Development

Total Quality Management (TQM)

Advanced Technology

Reengineering

Continuous Process Improvement

Customer Service

Productivity Improvement

Global Market Expansion

Cost Reduction

Performance Improvement

Low Employee Turnover

Customer Retention

Efficiency Improvement

Interview Q&A Using Keywords

Why Should Our Company Hire You?

I have a successful track record of managing call centers, both from a technology standpoint and personnel. I have improved failing call centers on two occasions in different industries, while increasing profits, boosting morale, and reducing employee turnover. The key factors in achieving these results have been my ability to analyze operations quickly and spearhead numerous programs, policies, and procedures to reengineer systems and achieve the corporate mission.

CAREER COUNSELOR/COACH

Resume

Cathy Quigley
1040 Shaker Drive
Columbia, Maryland 21046
(410) 555-1245 / email@email.com

Career Counselor / Career Coach
Career Development and Job Search Coaching

Career Assessment Instruments / Career Decision Making
Individual and Group Facilitation

Confident, compassionate, licensed professional counselor and National Certified Career Counselor with 18 years of demonstrated career services effectiveness facilitating adult career transitions and job search skills.

Core Strengths

Career Development and Planning	Program/Workshop Design
Career Assessments and Interpretations	Group Facilitation/Training
Business Networking/Job Development	Multimedia Presentations
Vocational Counseling and Guidance	Portfolio Preparation

Professional Experience

KENT COMMUNITY COLLEGE, Columbia, Maryland, 1995 to Current

Senior Career Counselor

Provide career, job search, academic and transfer counseling to diverse student population. One of three career counselors for 1800-student campus. Administer career assessments, individual and group facilitation sessions, and career information workshops. Deliver intake counseling, needs assessment, career research and planning, employment preparation, resume writing, and mentoring programs. Supervise two career technicians.

- Expanded career services program to include Internet-based delivery, including on-line student support group and interactive career research.
- Achieved highest student satisfaction rating (96%) for department (as compared to other campus departments) for the last four years.
- Teamed cross-departmentally to deliver highly successful career fairs.

Education

The Johns Hopkins University, Baltimore, Maryland
Master of Science, Guidance and Counseling—1985

- National Certified Career Counselor (NCCC)
- Certified Career Management Coach (CCMC)

Interview Q&A Using Keywords

Why should we hire you, what are your strengths, and how do you see yourself contributing to our company?

As a Myers-Briggs Type ENFJ, I bring a "big picture" perspective to the career development issues of students, as well as to department constraints. With that perspective, I have developed up-to-date delivery of career services utilizing Web-based tools that ensure quality, interactive information at low cost. As an "NF" I genuinely care about meeting each student's career counseling needs. Finally, as a "J," I get things done! Do *you* need an innovative, proactive career counselor?

CERTIFIED PUBLIC ACCOUNTANT

Resume

Emma Thompson, CPA
55 Amanda Avenue
Encino, California 91316
(818) 555-9875 / email@email.com

**CPA—"Big 5" Experience
Expertise in Taxation / Forensic Accounting / Auditing / Financial Analysis
Cutting-Edge Technology Solutions / Hiring, Training, & Supervising**

Senior-Level Accounting Professional with excellent qualifications in accounting, client relationships management, and financial/tax reporting. In-depth knowledge of generally accepted accounting principles as well as federal and state tax guidelines. Proven ability to work well under pressure with attention to detail and meeting critical deadlines. Highly developed skills in analyzing/interpreting/summarizing data, problem solving, building client rapport, and organizational management.

Core Strengths

Research & Analysis	Tax Planning
State & Federal Income Taxes	P&L Evaluation
Financial Reporting & Projections	Budget Development/Management
Compilation & Reviews	Business Development
Client Relations	Hiring, Training & Supervision

Professional Experience

JONES, STEIN & WILLIMS, CPAS, Beverly Hills, CA   1995–Present

CPA / Senior Accountant

Provide full range of accounting and tax services including audits, projections, compilations and review, and tax return preparation for corporations, partnerships, and individuals. Develop and manage client relationships across diverse industries including entertainment, real estate, construction, and nonprofits, as well as high net worth individuals. Research complex tax issues. Train and supervise junior staff members.

- Introduced technology solutions that standardized in-house tasks including audit working papers, financial reports, and tax returns. Reduced time required to complete audits and tax returns by 30%.
- Advised real estate holding company through various complex due diligence and financing procedures.
- Directed preacquisition audit of manufacturing operation considered for purchase by major client. Findings resulting in recommendation that purchase not be completed.
- Successfully negotiated IRS tax settlements on behalf of clients.

Education

UNIVERSITY OF CALIFORNIA, Los Angeles, CA; B.A. in Economics

Keywords

Auditing

Banking & Lines of Credit

Budgeting

Client Relationships

Compilation & Reviews

CPA

Financial Analysis

Financial Reporting

Financial Projections

Forensic Accounting

Generally Accepted Accounting Principles/GAAP

Hiring, Training, & Supervising

P&L Evaluation

Problem Solving

Research & Analysis

State & Federal Income Taxes

Tax Guidelines

Tax Planning

GAAP

Training & Supervision

Interview Q&A Using Keywords

Why should we hire you, what are your strengths, and how do you see yourself contributing to our company?

I am a senior-level accounting professional with "Big 6" experience. Above all else, I have an impeccable record of managing accounting practices consistent with GAAP and have never been involved with any improper practices. My references will echo that trait. I have an in-depth knowledge of federal and state tax codes and regulations and am skilled in all aspects of tax and financial planning and budgeting.

CFO

Keywords

Financial Strategies/
Analysis

Asset/Liability
Management

Strategic Planning

Profitability Modeling/
Forecasting

Profit & Loss (P&L)
Management/
Analysis

Financial Statement
Preparation

Regulatory Compliance

Capital/Operating
Budgets

Cross-Functional Team
Leadership

Financial Restructuring

Margin Improvement

M&A Due Diligence/
Management

Audit Management

Policy Development

Financial
Planning/Controls

Return-on-Assets (ROA)

Return-on-Equity (ROE)

Return-on-Investment
(ROI)

Corporate Tax
Planning/Oversight

Regulatory Affairs
Oversight/Compliance

Resume

Frank Thompson
62 Rancho Rio Boulevard
Northridge, CA 91326
(818) 555-1122 / email@email.com

> **Diversified Senior-Level Finance Specialist**
> **Special Expertise in MIS**
>
> **Extensive Mergers and Acquisitions Experience**
> **Skilled in Financial Integration of IT and Business Process**

Ten-year, cross-functional corporate and entrepreneurial finance experience. Core contributions to successful start-ups and established leaders. Expert in M&A due diligence and systems/culture integration.

Core Strengths

Financial Strategies/Analysis
Capital/Operating Budgets
Profit & Loss (P&L) Management
M&A Due Diligence/Management

Corporate Tax Planning/Oversight
Profitability Modeling and Forecasting
Financial Restructuring
Regulatory Affairs Oversight

Professional Experience

R&D Technology Associates, Los Angeles, CA   1999 to Current

Chief Finance Officer

Report directly to the CEO, maintaining full business operations authority and P&L responsibility for all financial strategic planning, asset/liability management, financial statement preparation, audit management, finance policy development, financial planning/control, and regulatory compliance. Cross-functional team leadership as member of core management team. Solid contributions in return-on-assets (ROA), return-on-equity (ROE), and return-on-investment (ROI). Structured accounting, administration, and MIS areas.

- Participated in five major corporate acquisitions and related integrations.
- Received *LA Biz Award* for creating employee-owned subsidiary.
- Negotiated joint venture with Malaysian firm to test/correct software.
- Took $16 million contract to $50 million, five-contract revenue stream.

Education

Boston College, Carroll Graduate School of Management, Chestnut Hill, MA
Master of Science: Finance, Highest Honors, 1997

Massachusetts Institute of Technology, Sloan School of Management, Cambridge, MA
Bachelor of Science: Management Science, concentration in Finance, 1995

References Furnished Immediately upon Request

Interview Q&A Using Keywords

Why should we hire you, what are your strengths, and how do you see yourself contributing to our company?

As a skilled and accessible manager, I can run large organizations yet do a spreadsheet when needed, I can see "the big picture" yet reduce a complex problem to a simpler explanation, and I can manage the details of multimillion-dollar organization. My financial background is very sound, with an emphasis on audit management, policy controls, and when necessary, financial restructuring. Under my direction my current corporation manages the best ratio of SG&A expenses to revenues in our industry.

CHANGE/REENGINEERING CONSULTANT

Resume

Henry L. Crawford
27 Elm Circle
Miamisburg, Ohio 45347
(937) 555-1573 / email@email.com

> **Change/Reengineering Consultant**
> **Experience Building Start-Up, Turnaround, & High-Growth Companies**
>
> **Facilitate Corporate Cultural Change & Build Strategic Partnerships Skilled**
> **Relationship Manager / Customer-Driven Management Style**

Entrepreneurial spirit and multiindustry experience. Facilitate business development and profit growth through emphasizing continuous process improvement and cost containment.

Core Strengths

Business Consulting	Contract Negotiations
Corporate Image	Sales Management
Problem Solving	Teaming & Leadership
Product & Service Pricing	Training & Development

Professional Experience

CRAWFORD & SEALS, INC., Miamisburg, Ohio   1985 to Current

Business Consultant

Successful leading start-up and underperforming organizations to industry leadership positions and profitability through analyzing operations, identifying problems, and restructuring processes. Expert in competitive market positioning and key customer relationship management. Deliver strong and sustainable financial gains in challenging markets through decisive leadership.

- Directed start-up of multimillion-dollar real estate investment firm.
- Managed chain of 400 health clubs from loss to $5M annual profit.
- Streamlined manufacturing plant to cut costs $500K per month.
- Negotiated merger between two major medical facilities.

Education

Wright State University, Dayton, Ohio
M.B.A., 1995

- B.S., Finance & Accounting, 1984
- Graduate GPA: 4.0

References Furnished Immediately upon Request

Keywords

Reengineering Consultant

Strategic Partnership

Competitive Market Positioning

Cost Containment

Profit Growth

Relationship Management

Cross-Cultural Communication

Business Development

Multiindustry Experience

Customer-Driven Management

Start-Up

Turnaround

Continuous Process Improvement

Corporate Cultural Change

Contract Negotiations

Corporate Image

Sales Management

Business Reengineering

Efficiency Improvement

Problem Solving

Interview Q&A Using Keywords

Why should we hire you, what are your strengths, and how do you see yourself contributing to our company?

I have cross-industry experience and significant achievements working with start-up, turnaround, and high-growth businesses. I have comprehensive management experience, and have been successful in restructuring sales, marketing, strategic and business planning, and information technology. I am a tough but fair negotiator who can create win/win outcomes. I am a skilled public speaker who is comfortable communicating cross-culturally and across management and functional lines.

CHEMIST

Keywords

Science

Organic

Research

Development

Composition

Structure

Elements

Synthetics/Polymer

Modeling

Simulation

Measure

Independent

Chemistry

Meticulous

Mathematics

Analytical

Corrosion

Reaction

Kinetics

Spectrographic

Resume

Mary Beth Brissette
2345 Spyglass Circle
Waterford, Michigan 00000
(208) 555-0000 / email@email.com

Chemist

Expertise in Chemical Corrosion Research

Strong science, inorganic, and organic chemistry background. Exceptional knowledge of chemistry specializing in research and development of polymer compounds and the effects of chemical corrosion on super alloy metals.

Core Strengths

Organic Chemistry	Reaction Kinetics
Proficient Computer Skills	Gibbs Energy of Formation
Data Analyzation	Spectrographic Analysis
Quality Control	Chemical Corrosion Research

Professional Experience

CHEMICAL MANUFACTURER, Cascade, Michigan   1997 to Current

Chemist

Prepare instructions for plant workers that specify ingredients, mixing times, and temperatures for each stage in the process. Monitor automated processes to ensure proper product yield, and test samples of raw materials or finished products to ensure that they meet industry and government standards. Report and document test results and analyze those results to improve existing theories or develop new test methods.

- Developed a new process to reduce costs in mixing chemical compounds resulting in a $250,000 cost savings per year.
- Chairperson of a Regional Conference of Chemists and Material Scientists on Corrosion Research.

Education

Michigan State University, East Lansing, Michigan
Master of Science Degree in Chemistry   1997

- Contributor to the JANAF Thermochemical Tables
- Dean's List, Four Years

Interview Q&A Using Keywords

Why should we hire you, what are your strengths, and how do you see yourself contributing to our company?

I am accurate, pay attention to detail, and have the ability to focus. I am curious and thrive on research and experiments. I rely on collaboration with other professionals and work well with or without supervision. I enjoy working with my hands building scientific apparatus, performing laboratory experiments, and computer modeling. I value the integrity of my work. I am a meticulous and organized record keeper. I have a well-established network of professional chemists with whom I collaborate regularly.

CITY MANAGER

Resume

Dana Urban
5555 72nd street
Omaha, Nebraska 68102
(402) 555-1122 / email@email.com

> **City Manager**
>
> **Economic Development/Business Liaison**
> **Member International City/County Management Association**

Goal-oriented administrator with vision and skills to bring municipalities into the twenty-first century. Skilled in cost-saving strategies and planning that bring initiatives to life while maintaining the integrity of existing communities.

Core Strengths

Economic Development	Project Management
Regional Collaboration	Community Relations
Zoning Regulations	Contract Negotiations
Budget Administration	Strategic Planning

Professional Experience

City of Des Moines, Des Moines, Iowa   1995–present

City Manager

Prepared and administered $120MM annual municipal budget. Attended Council meetings and implemented policy of elected officials. Managed Human Resources with final decision on hiring and firing key personnel. Developed positive relationships with local media, businesses and community. Negotiated contracts and reviewed proposals for development projects. Reported progress of City departments in reaching goals.

- Leveraged services through regional collaboration saving $6.2MM annually
- Designed Youth Leadership Project under Iowa state renewable grant
- Coordinated five-year neighborhood revitalization project
- Des Moines named in 100 best places to live in America 1999

Education

Creighton University, Omaha, Nebraska
Bachelor of Arts/Political Science 1987
Master of Arts/ Urban/Suburban Administration 1992

Keywords

Planning

Zoning Regulations

Local Ordinances

Public Services

Economic Development

Annual Budget

Community Relations

Policy

Municipal Operations

Contracts

City Council

Media Relations

Human Resources

Project Management

Budget Administration

Infrastructure

Business Liaison

Neighborhood Revitalization

Statutes and Legislation

Regional Collaboration

Interview Q&A Using Keywords

Why should we hire you, what are your strengths, and how do you see yourself contributing to our company?

With my background in economic development, I am able to attract businesses appropriate to communities and consistent with their future plans. Coordinating infrastructure projects by leading a team of civil engineers and public works specialists has yielded positive results, meeting deadlines and exceeding expectations. I am able to design and implement program initiatives. I have extensive experience in regional collaborations that increase services while trimming the cost of delivery and maintaining quality.

CIVIL ENGINEER

Keywords

Industry Knowledge

Conceptual
  Knowledge

Hands-on
  Experience

Project Oriented

Scientific
  Instrumentation

AutoCad

GenericCad

GPS/GIS

VISIO

Excel

Licensed
  Professional Civil
  Engineer

Self-Insured

Building
  Construction

Results Oriented

Transit

Technical
  Mathematics

Eaglepoint

SoftDesk

Design

Logic

Resume

Kendall Koplin
11027 Southeast 21 Boulevard
Anywhere, Idaho 00000
(208) 555-0000 / email@email.com

Civil Engineer

Accomplished Multilingual Engineer
Successful Project Management and Supervisory Experience

Competent in building construction, local transit, pipelines, electric, gas, and sanitary services. Effective problem-solving and decision-making skills. Proficient in managing multiple projects. Fluent in English, Spanish, and Portuguese.

Core Strengths

Solid Management Capabilities	Excellent Technology Skills
Team Player	Project Oriented
Schematics	Results Oriented
Design	Quality Conscious

Professional Experience

L&A ENGINEERING, Idaho Falls, Idaho   1988 to Present

Civil Engineer

Oversee and conduct daily operations of a $3.6M sewer renovation project. Plan and oversee a variety of field projects, including making recommendations for design of parking and maintenance facilities.

- Successfully completed a $1.2M City Greenbelt renovation project, on time and within budget.
- Successfully completed a $5.6M street and landscape redesign project saving the company $51,000.
- Improved record-keeping database by redesigning input logic.

Education

Idaho State University, Pocatello, Idaho
Bachelor of Science Degree in Civil Engineering; 1988

- Dean's List, 4 Years.
- Junior and Senior Internship, L&A Engineering; only offered to top two students.

Interview Q&A Using Keywords

Why should we hire you, what are your strengths, and how do you see yourself contributing to our company?

I meet all qualifications outlined in the job posting including a Bachelor's degree. I have designed and managed several multimillion-dollar projects in the Boise area. I have the dedication it takes to visualize the project, start the project, and see it to completion. My proficient use of computer software makes me most productive, reducing any training time, and I can assist in training other coworkers. I have successfully coordinated a number of project professionals. I am available immediately and have directly related experience.

CIVIL SERVICE (POLICE OFFICER)

Resume

Michael Lendl
113 Bartlett Street
Lewiston, Maine 04240
(207) 555-7777 / email@email.com

**Police Officer
Crime Scene Investigator**

**Crime Scene Lab Fingerprinting Specialist
Certified in the Use of Varied Surveillance Equipment**

Law enforcement professional with active involvement in all areas of police work including numerous court appearances as a witness, volunteer participation in self-defense programs, and monitoring, reviewing, and making recommendations for lock-up and jail security procedures.

Core Strengths

Fingerprint Analysis	Undercover Operations
Crime Investigations	Surveillance
Interrogations	Witness Questioning

Professional Experience

Lewiston Police Department, Lewiston, Maine   1997–Present

Police Officer

Monitor a specified geographic area for unlawful or suspicious activities, and in some cases providing and dispatching assistance to those requiring medical assistance. Perform duties on a rotation basis while either walking a beat with a fellow officer, driving a cruiser, or operating a motorcycle. Specialized work involving crime scene investigations and undercover work is scheduled as needed.

- Recognized as the department's fingerprinting expert.
- Proficient at operating an intoxilyzer; train other officers.
- Volunteer, labor relations liaison assisting union steward.
- Member, Jail Security Committee.

Education

University of Maine (L/A Center), Lewiston, Maine
Bachelors Degree: Criminal Justice, 1996

- Attended, Waterville Police Academy, Waterville, Maine
- Graduated, Police Training Program, 1997

Keywords

Law Enforcement

Surveillance

Criminal Law

Investigations

Doppler Traffic Radar

Intoxilyzer Operation

Dispatching

Self-Defense

Traffic Control

Court System

Labor Relations

Jail Security

Management

Undercover

Witness

Suspect

Victim

Lineup

Finger Printing

Firearms

Interview Q&A Using Keywords

Why should we hire you, what are your strengths, and how do you see yourself contributing to our company?

I am a police academy graduate with specialized training in fingerprinting and analysis and crime scene investigations. With five years of experience as a police officer, I have had many opportunities to put to use much of my training and expertise on the job. Duties have also included walking a beat, driving a cruiser, and operating a motorcycle. Prior formal education in criminal justice has prepared me for management and/or supervisory roles, as I become eligible.

COLLEGE GRADUATE—ACCOUNTING

Keywords

Accounts Payable

Accounts Receivable

General Ledger

Account Reconciliations

Expense Reports

Collections

Finance

GPA

Accounting Major/Degree

Auditing

Cost Accounting

GAAP

Oral and Written Communication Skills

Payroll

Benefits

Financial functions

Microsoft Excel and Word

Quicken, QuickBooks, Peachtree

Bookkeeping

Bachelor of Science in Accounting

Resume

Susan Quinn
35 Memorial Boulevard
Newark, NJ 07104
(973) 555-1212 / email@email.com

Entry-Level Accountant
Record of cost reduction and collections improvement

Self-starter / Streamlining accounting processes
Leveraging technology to increase efficiency and accuracy

Motivated college graduate with a Bachelor of Science degree in Accounting. Strong academic performance. Four years of part-time experience performing basic bookkeeping/accounting functions.

Core Strengths

Organizational skills	Computer proficient
Multitasking	Talented in basic accounting
Detail oriented	Strong work ethic
Numerically accurate	Integrity

Education

University of Syracuse, Syracuse, NY
Bachelor of Science: Accounting, 2001
Minor: Computer Science

- 3.7 GPA in Major

Professional Experience

REED ANIMAL HOSPITAL, Newark, NJ Part-time 1999–Present

Administrative Assistant, Reception, Bookkeeping

Handle all front-desk duties at a busy small-animal practice. Schedule appointments, take orders for medicines, field questions, and solve problems. Bookkeeping/accounting activities include maintaining computerized records using Quicken, and reconciling accounts.

- Created an Excel spreadsheet to track past-due invoices
- Decreased aging reports and increased monies collected by over 40%
- Saved $2000 annually by negotiating a bulk-buying agreement
- Helped automate AP and AR
- Streamlined staff payroll operations by creating an electronic form

Interview Q&A Using Keywords

Why should we hire you, what are your strengths, and how do you see yourself contributing to our company?

As a new Accounting graduate, I stand out in two ways. First, I offer a record of improving accounting processes in a small office. Second, I know how to use software applications to improve the speed and accuracy of accounting operations. My organizational, communication, and problem-solving skills are equally strong. I am able to benefit a company significantly by accurately performing basic accounting functions as well as introducing efficiencies that reduce costs.

COLLEGE GRADUATE—COMMUNICATIONS

Resume

Glenna Hazen
1167 Frederick Valley Pike
Huber Heights, Ohio 45428
(937) 555-7377 / email@email.com

College Graduate—Communications
Seeking Entry-Level Position in Communications

**Multimedia Training: Advertising Communications, Broadcast & Electronic Media,
Trade Show Presentations, & Public Relations**

Strong combination of classroom training and hands-on experience. Enthusiastic and energetic top performer graduating in top five percent of class. Internships completed with major advertising agencies and corporations.

Core Strengths

Planning & Organization   Self-Motivated
Creative Problem Solving   Attention to Detail
Multitasking   Computer Proficiency
Team Leadership   Concept Development

Professional Experience

FLYNN-BRODERICK, INC., Cincinnati, Ohio   1995 to Current

Intern

Assisted with campaign planning and management. Conducted market research, wrote direct mail letters and press releases, and designed electronic media (home page). Produced corporate identity through creating letterhead and logo. Contracted for creative services. Helped develop publications, i.e., newsletters and training manuals. Planned and managed conferences and special events; coordinated complex logistics.

- Expanded AIDS Awareness effort to community outreach programs.
- Secured corporate sponsorship for Communications College scholarship.
- Spearheaded fund raising campaign that produced $10K for food pantry.
- Led grassroots campaign that defeated proposed teen center closing.

Education

Wright State University, Dayton, Ohio
Bachelor of Science, Organizational Communication, 2002

- GPA: 3.65
- President of Spanish Club; Member of Campus Actors Guild

References Furnished Immediately upon Request

Keywords

Advertising Communications

Broadcast Media

Campaign Management

Conference Planning

Event Management

Logistics

Corporate Identity

Direct mail Campaign

Market Research

Multimedia Advertising

Press Release

Public Relations

Publications

Grassroots Campaign

Fund-Raising

Community Outreach

Corporate Sponsorship

Trade Shows

Electronic Media

Creative Services

Interview Q&A Using Keywords

Why should we hire you, what are your strengths, and how do you see yourself contributing to our company?

While attending college, I held part-time and summer jobs for companies that ranged from Web-based businesses to the performing arts, advertising communications, and radio. This, together with internships my junior and senior years, gave me hands-on experience in multimedia, public relations, and creative services. This combination of broad-based experience and formal education will help me quickly come up to speed in your company, and enable me to make valuable contributions from day one.

COLLEGE GRADUATE—CONSTRUCTION

Resume

Jason Pertowski
8215 Harriet Avenue South
Minneapolis, Minnesota 55406
(651) 555-3409 / email@email.com

Construction Manager

B.S., Construction Management / 10 Years' Experience

Talented Builder of Physical Facilities Beneficial to Society
Eclectic Talents Blend Technology, Techniques, and Communications

---

Experience in the planning, development, and management of construction operations, with a record of consistent achievement in improving quality, accountability, and efficiency. Proficient at managing simultaneous projects to meet costs/deadlines successfully.

Core Strengths

Supervision and labor productivity	Planned Use Development (PUD)
Land development and surveying	Mechanics and materials
Competitive estimating and bidding	Building construction and codes
Specifications and contracts	Safety and quality control

Professional Experience

JP BARTLETT COMPANIES, Minneapolis, Minnesota   1995 to Current

Construction Manager

Supervise and coordinate construction management contract services for Rivertown, a 450,000-square-foot facility. Direct monthly safety meetings. Coordinate layout and design, communicate with engineers and key personnel. Perform on-site inspection during all phases of construction projects, including commercial, single and multifamily, water towers, plants and wastewater treatment facilities, barracks, fire stations, and other facilities. Interpret specifications, review bids, and prepare concise activity reports. Manage budget process and financial expenditures.

- Implemented program for in-house precast concrete that reduced materials costs by 24%
- Member of senior management team leading Minneapolis's first PUD projects
- Directed construction affairs for the mall renovation, a five-year, $2.8 billion project
- Coordinated $25 million in mixed-use property development project, as part of revitalization

Education

North Dakota State University, Fargo, North Dakota
Bachelor of Science: Construction Management, May 2002

- Peer Assistant, Construction Management Mentoring Program, 2001–2002
- Home Builders Care Foundation Scholarship Recipient, 2002

References Furnished Immediately upon Request

Interview Q&A Using Keywords

Why should we hire you, what are your strengths, and how do you see yourself contributing to our company?

Success in construction management prompted me to enhance my real-world experience with a related B.S. degree. I have supervised 2 to 100-person crews—staff and subcontractors, with high productivity, through all phases of projects. Both professors and supervisors have commended my ability to come in or ahead of time with deadlines, within or below costs. "Ground-up" work with a major contractor and developer has exposed me to commercial and residential construction. My concentrated studies in land development and soils/foundations help me balance environmental and economic issues. I have significant cost estimating and competitive bidding experience on concrete and steel design structures. My scope of abilities ranges from technical specifications and contracts, to articulate communications at all levels.

Resume

Hanna Thomas
212-37 Corporal Kennedy Street
Bayside, NY 11360
(718) 555-1122 / email@email.com

> **Experienced Finance and Marketing Professional**
> **Recent M.B.A. Recipient—Columbia University**
>
> **Three Years' Background with Ernst & Young**
> **Committed to Achieving and Supporting Corporate Objectives**

Contribute to cross-functional success by facilitating communication across individual account teams; supporting the sales process; interfacing with partners, clients, and support staff; and crafting value propositions.

Core Strengths

Marketing/Positioning Strategies   Niche Marketing
Marketing Communications   Strategic Analysis
Speed-to-Market Support   Event Planning
Relationship Management   Presentation Abilities

Professional Experience

Ernst & Young, LLP, New York, NY   1997 to Current

MarCom Specialist, Marketing Support

Work closely with sales and marketing executives in support of E&Y partners in the Metro New York Tax Practice. Using experience and education in finance and marketing, provide a wide array of marketing communications including pursuit packs, collateral pieces, and newsletters. Using technology abilities, produce multimedia presentations/communications. Handle public relations initiatives and seminar creation.

- Produced unplanned, speed-to-market seminar for managing partner.
- Created Practice's first standardized, area-specific collateral pieces.
- Suggested and supported development of Practice's first intranet site.
- Contributed ideas and content for Tax Practice's yearly marketing plan.

Education

Columbia University, New York, NY
M.B.A.: Finance, 2002
Fordham University, New York, NY
Bachelor of Arts: Business, 1999

References Furnished Immediately upon Request

Keywords

M.B.A.

High GPA

Presentation Abilities

Positioning Strategies

Finance

Strategic Analysis

Marketing Communications

Public Relations

Event Planning

Sales Support

Partner Support

Marketing Strategy

Technology Abilities

Multimedia Communications

Sales and Marketing

Speed-to-Market Support

Seminar Creation

Relationship Management

Cross-Functional Teaming

Collateral Material Production

Interview Q&A Using Keywords

Why should we hire you, what are your strengths, and how do you see yourself contributing to our company?

As a recent MBA recipient with three years' background in finance, marketing, and sales support with Ernst & Young, I offer hands-on experience in an array of business functions in several industries, including health care, retail, and hospitality. E&Y is a great training ground and I have learned much in my time there, fast tracking from entry-level support positions to managing team leader. It has been my practice to learn everything possible in every department, and I have done so while completing a rigorous MBA program at Columbia.

COLLEGE GRADUATE—MECHANICAL ENGINEER

Keywords

BSME

Analytical

Detail-Oriented

AutoCAD

Numerical aptitude

Engineering

Mechanical
Engineering

Design

Mathematics

Internship

Documentation

Team Player

Parts Design/Repair/
Replacement

Project Development
Life Cycle

Spreadsheets—
Excel, Lotus 1-2-3

Project Costing

Project Planning

Quality Assurance

Mechanically Adept

Detailed Drawings

Resume

Louise B. Brown
22 Acton Road
Acton, MA 02478
(978) 555-1212 / email@email.com

> **Mechanical Engineer—College Graduate**
> **Combining sound academic training with hands-on experience**
>
> **Mechanically Adept / Making Solid Project Contributions**
> **Team Player / AutoCAD Proficient**

Technically-skilled, highly motivated BSME with hands-on mechanical engineering experience. Intensive co-op experience assisting with the development of an alternative energy project.

Core Strengths

Math and technical skills	Organizational skills
Design and documentation skills	Detail-oriented
Communication skills	Parts repair/replacement
Working knowledge of welding	AutoCAD layouts

Education

Northeastern University, Boston, Massachusetts
Bachelor of Science: Mechanical Engineering 2001

- 3.4 GPA
- Proficient in AutoCAD, Excel, and Lotus 1-2-3

Professional Experience

MILLDAM HYDRO, Gardner, MA   Part-time 2001–2002

Co-op Position

Performed duties in support of day-to-day operations at a low-head hydropower generating station. Developed Excel spreadsheets and entered line-items to assist with project costing. Evaluated engineering problems and made recommendations. Developed AutoCAD layouts. Responded to FERC (Federal Energy Regulatory Commission) correspondence. Specified materials. Performed cost estimating and price comparisons.

- Performed preventative maintenance on parts of hydraulic turbines
- Helped design an eel-way to maintain the Fish and Wildlife license
- Saved $2000 by negotiating more advantageous sheet metal contracts
- Contributed to executing endangered mussels recovery program

Interview Q&A Using Keywords

Why should we hire you, what are your strengths, and how do you see yourself contributing to our company?

My co-op placement gave me an opportunity to participate in the design, development, and implementation of several engineering projects. On the job, I supported the Mechanical Engineer at various stages of the project life cycle. I identified opportunities to reduce costs, recommended engineering solutions, and solved project problems. My AutoCAD skills are excellent. In the role of entry-level mechanical engineer, I am ready to "hit the ground running" and make valuable project contributions to a company.

Resume

John Justin
10231 Linden Lane
Los Angeles, California 90049
(310) 555-1111/ email@email.com

> **RECENT COLLEGE GRADUATE WITH B.A. IN ENGLISH**
> **Track Record of Professional Accomplishments in Retail Sales**
>
> **Excels in Customer Service**
> **Tenacious / Motivated / High Energy**

Hard working and highly motivated with a strong work ethic. Consistently goes beyond the requirements of the job to achieve company goals. Learns quickly, enjoys challenges and works well independently as well as collaboratively in a team setting. Track record of accomplishments in retail sales positions.

Core Strengths

Organizational Abilities	Team Building & Leadership
Client Relations	Oral & Written Communications
Time Management	Presentations
Problem Solving	Sales Experience
Relationship Building	Presentation Delivery
Computer Skills	Report Preparation

Education

University of California at Los Angeles; 2002
B.A. in English

Professional Experience

FASHION WORLD, Los Angeles, CA   1997–Present

Part-Time and Seasonal Positions
Assistant Manager (2000–Present)
Sales Associate (1997–2000)
Promoted to Assistant Manager of $2.5 million location of national retailer. Oversee smooth functioning of day-to-day operations, consistently meeting or exceeding sales goals while maintaining stable payroll expense. Ensure high level of customer satisfaction. Hire, train, schedule, and motivate team of 15–20 sales associates.

- Increased sales in men's department by more than 50%.
- Developed reputation for skilled merchandising.
- Implemented weekly coaching meetings that enhanced staff morale, fostered team building, and reduced absenteeism.

Keywords

College Graduate

GPA

Computer Skills

Major: Marketing

Prospecting

Account Relationship

Leadership

Motivation

Organizational Skills

Presentations

Problem Solving

Professional Image

Relationship Building

Report Preparation

Sales Experience

Team Building

Time Management

Well Organized

Work Ethic

Work Experience

Interview Q&A Using Keywords

Why should we hire you, what are your strengths, and how do you see yourself contributing to our company?

I am a recent college graduate with previous part-time and seasonal experience in a retail sales environment. My achievements in school represent a strong work ethic and sense of responsibility, having graduated with a 3.4 GPA while working all four years at UCLA. I achieved top store sales on several occasions and was promoted to Assistant Manager.

COMMERCIAL OR CORPORATE PILOT

Keywords

Aircrew Training

Pilot

Charter Flight

Aviation

Air Traffic Control

Altitude

Airport

Commercial Flight

Corporate Travel

Close Coordination
with Maintenance
and Operations

Cost Control

Crew Coordination

Customer Focus

Flexible Training

Managing Complex
In-Flight
Emergencies

Mentoring Crew
Members

Safety-First
Orientation

Simulator
Instruction

Upgrading Skills

Resume

Charles R. Miller
1400 West Street
Montgomery, Alabama 36100
(334) 555-1212 / email@email.com

Corporate or Commercial Pilot
7500 PIC, accident- and incident-free flying hours

Crew Coordination & Mission Planning Skills
Expert Ambassador

A team-oriented, safety-driven pilot who can balance operational needs with reliable, quality flight operations. Regularly tested on my ability to upgrade across types quickly and capably.

Core Strengths

Flexible mission planning	Natural instructor skills
Solid FAR knowledge	Confidence-inspiring appearance
Crew coordination skills	Managing multiple emergencies

Professional Experience and Qualifications

Commercial Pilot, Multi Engine, Land, Instrument
FAA Class I Medical Certification, No restrictions, July 2003
Total time: 10,500 PIC 7500 Instrument 8600 Multi-engine 7500 IP 4000

Blue Sky Airlines   2000 to Current

First Officer promoted to Captain

Responsible for safe flight operations of B727-200 series passenger service. Insure full compliance with corporate and flying safety regulations. Project a positive image to our passengers. Subject to no-notice, in-flight evaluations.

- Selected as simulator instructor over three more experienced captains
- Met or exceeded Federal on-time departure standards every quarter for the last eight quarters

Education

Auburn University, Auburn, Alabama
Bachelor of Business Administration, 1985

References Furnished Immediately Upon Request

Interview Q&A Using Keywords

Why should we hire you, what are your strengths, and how do you see yourself contributing to our company?

I bring a combination of flying skills and business acumen that can serve all your customers—internal and external—very well. I know that our company will be judged by how smoothly, efficiently, and safely a flight proceeds under my command. I can bring that same dedication to every crewmember because I enjoy mentoring aviation professionals. Finally, you might consider the cost savings I can offer you as a simulator instructor.

CONSTRUCTION FOREMAN

Resume

Joseph A. Smith
121 Carpenter Way
Mequon, Wisconsin 53092
(262) 555-1186 / email@email.com

> **Construction Foreman**
> **Proven track record of meeting time, labor, and project goals**
>
> **Project/Job site management**
> **Estimating time, labor, materials/Cost containment**

Results-oriented, quality-focused Construction Foreman with a consistent track record of meeting project timelines and budgetary constraints. Skilled managing general contractor/subcontractor crews and other trades.

Core Strengths

Project management	Team leadership
Rough/finish carpentry	Plumbing, HVAC, electrical
Vendor sourcing	Time, labor, materials estimating
Code compliance	Quality commitment

Professional Experience

RITZY BUILDERS, Pewaukee, Wisconsin   1995 to Present

Construction Foreman

Interact with general and subcontractors, architects, crews, and other trades to coordinate projects on site from blueprints to completion, while meeting time, labor, material estimates, and project specifications. Source and negotiate terms with suppliers, ensuring materials meet quality specifications and delivery timelines.

- Built eight 320,000-square-foot, $10 million supermalls.
- Restored $1.2 million Victorian mansion to its original specifications.
- Instituted use of proprietary construction management system to produce estimates, takeoffs, and bids.

Education

Milwaukee Area Technical College
Carpentry Diploma, 1992

- Member of the National Vocational Honor Society
- Recipient of Scholastic Achievement Award

References Furnished Immediately upon Request

Keywords

Project Management

Job Site

Crew/Skilled Trades

Cost Estimating

Time, Labor, Materials

Residential/Commercial

Rough/Finish Carpentry

Plumbing, HVAC, Electrical

Interior/Exterior Painting

Architect

General Contractor

Subcontractors

Takeoffs, Bids

Building Codes

Compliance

Team Leadership

Remodeling/Build-Outs

Restoration

Renovation

New Construction

Interview Q&A Using Keywords

Why should we hire you, what are your strengths, and how do you see yourself contributing to our company?

As a results-oriented Construction Foreman, I am consistently on time and under budget with my projects, whether our company is serving as the general contractor or the subcontractor. I have experience with commercial and residential properties including new construction, remodeling, and renovation. Projects range from $100,000 to more than $10 million. My team leadership skills also enable me to coordinate the efforts of multiple trades including plumbing, HVAC, electrical, painting, and rough/finish carpentry.

CONTRACTS SPECIALIST

Resume

David Robinson
3 Bradford Drive
Bristol, CT 06010
(860) 555-1212 / email@email.com

Contracts Specialist

Four years of progressive responsibilities facilitating contractual sales

---

Full accountability negotiating and overseeing the contracts process with our customers. Excellent skills in expediting the entire purchasing process from inquiry to delivery.

Areas of Expertise

Contract Language	Reimbursements
Letters of Intent	Credit Authority
Purchase Agreements	Promissory Notes
Documentation	Export Regulations

Professional Experience

RAYTHEON COMPANY, El Segundo, CA   1997 to Present
Contracts Specialist (1999–Present)
Contracts Associate (1997–1999)

Submit proposals and negotiate sales terms with purchasers of Raytheon goods. Validate the creditworthiness of international companies by verifying commercial credit authorizations. Monitor the progress of contracts tracking purchase orders, deliverables, and milestones. Hold signature authority up to $3M.

- Successfully negotiated lease agreements with favorable finance terms.
- Resolved technical and logistical matters in advance of contractual deadlines, avoiding a potential breech of contract on the company's largest sale in history.
- Considered the company expert on export regulations.

Education

University of California, Sacramento
Bachelor of Science, Business Administration, 1997

- Summa Cum Laude graduate
- Honors Program

References Furnished Immediately upon Request

Keywords

Signature Authority

Documentation

Purchase Agreements

Letters of Intent

Promissory Notes

Finance Terms

Reimbursements

Inquiries

Negotiation of Terms

Deliverables

Breech of Contract

Milestones

Lease Agreements

Contractual Deadlines

Export Regulations

Proposal Submissions

Contract Language

Creditworthiness

Credit Authorizations

Purchase Orders

Interview Q&A Using Keywords

Why should we hire you, what are your strengths, and how do you see yourself contributing to our company?

I believe that what I do has a substantial impact on the bottom line of my organization, and I take that responsibility very seriously. You mentioned you are looking for a self-starter, and I am pleased to be able to say that since I became a contracts specialist, my management has commented on my ability to handle the job more effectively than my predecessors. In particular, my ability to evaluate creditworthiness, knowledge of contract language, and commitment to making sure contractual deadlines are met, are what sets me apart.

CONTROLLER

Resume

Michael A. Schenker
722 Woodbridge Road
Williamsville, New York 14221
(716) 555-1029 / email@email.com

> **Controller**
> **Private Sector and Public Accounting**
>
> **Profit Oriented / Cost Conscious with Successful**
> **Record as Change Agent, Introducing New**
> **Technologies and Progressive Business Models**

Senior executive with complete financial management of all accounting and finance activities. Researched and designed comprehensible road map for lucrative acquisitions and mergers.

Core Strengths

Profit Forecasting	Cash Flow Analysis
Contingency Planning	Feasibility Study
Debt Consolidation	Systems Integration

Professional Experience

OPEN ROAD, INC., Lackawanna, New York   1993 to Present

Controller / Director of Finance

Provide fiscal leadership for manufacturer of automotive aftermarket products with $26.7 million in annual sales. Protect business and financial assets through internal controls, independent audits, and aggressive insurance management. Prepare annual budgets and strategic plans.

- Negotiated insurance settlement that realized $220,000 in incremental loss recovery.
- Facilitated acquisition of four small companies, consolidating production lines and warehouse space with significant expense reduction.
- Reduced audited adjustments from 40 to 4 by standardizing accounting practices.
- Saved over $600,000 in property and sales tax reduction and discovered $98,000 in double-paid charges on utility taxes.

Education

Canisius College, Buffalo, New York
Master of Business Administration, 1987
Certified Public Accountant—New York

References Furnished Immediately upon Request

Keywords

Financial Leadership/ Management

Audit Adjustments and Internal Controls

Asset Protection

Report Creation

Tax Reduction

Budgeting and Strategic Planning

Loss Recovery

Cost Containment/ Expense Reduction

Change Agent

Systems Integration

Profit Forecasting

Business Acquisition

Feasibility Study

Cash Flow Analysis

Fiscal Integrity

Public and Private Sector Accounting

Debt Consolidation

Asset and Liability Management

Contingency Planning

Insurance and Risk Management

Interview Q&A Using Keywords

Why should we hire you, what are your strengths, and how do you see yourself contributing to our company?

You mentioned how important growth through acquisition was to your future, and I have facilitated the acquisition and integration of four small companies, consolidating production lines and warehouse space with significant expense reduction. Recently I negotiated an insurance settlement that realized $220,000 in incremental loss recovery. We have reduced audited adjustments from 40 to 4 by standardizing accounting practices. My team also saved over $600,000 in property and sales tax reduction and discovered $98,000 in double-paid charges on utility taxes.

CORPORATE ATTORNEY

Keywords

Corporate Law

In-House Counsel

Corporate Policy
Manuals

Mergers and
Acquisitions
(M & A)

Joint Ventures

Venture Capital

Start-Up Operations

Regulatory
Compliance

Employment Law

Employee Benefit
Plans

Business Contracts

Contract
Negotiations

Trade Regulations

Advertising and
Promotional Law

Food and Drug Law

Product Liability

Vendor Agreements

Customer Service
Agreements

Trademark Rights

Juris Doctor (J.D.)

Resume

Alfred Jones
9893 Valleyview Road
San Diego, California 92109
(619) 555-3589 / email@email.com

> **Corporate Attorney**
> **In-House Counsel for Fortune 500 Companies**
>
> **Mergers and Acquisitions / Joint Ventures**
> **Regulatory Compliance Specialist**

Dedicated legal professional with 15+ years of broad-based experience in multimillion-dollar corporate environments. Verifiable track record of effectively advising senior management on trade regulations and implications of their business decisions.

Core Strengths

Advertising Law	Food and Drug Law
Contract Negotiations	Product Liability
Trademark Rights	Employee Benefit Plans
Vendor Agreements	Corporate Policy Manuals

Professional Experience

JUMPSTART, INC., San Diego, California   1995 to Present

Assistant to General Counsel

Primary duties include reviewing, negotiating, and drafting business contracts. Also write all customer service agreements. Advise company management on matters of trade regulations, advertising and promotional law, employment law, food and drug law, product liability, and other areas of legal compliance. Assist with joint venture and M & A initiatives. Regularly consulted on matters of corporate policy planning.

- Completely rewrote firm's corporate policy manual.
- Selected to spearhead multimillion-dollar venture capital negotiations.
- Oversaw legal aspects of new start-up operations for Eastern Seaboard.

Education

Marquette University Law School, Milwaukee, Wisconsin
Juris Doctor, 1983

- Graduated Cum Laude
- Internship, Wisconsin Supreme Court

Interview Q&A Using Keywords

Why should we hire you, what are your strengths, and how do you see yourself contributing to our company?

As in-house counsel to several large corporations, I have excelled in the corporate law setting. I have a demonstrated record of successfully advising senior management of three Fortune 500 companies on aspects of employment law, food and drug law, and advertising law, and have prevented millions of dollars in unnecessary direct and indirect costs related to product liability. Additionally, I am particularly skilled at ensuring regulatory compliance when pursuing joint venture and merger opportunities.

CORPORATE RECRUITER

Resume

Christine Pantoya
173 Sheridan Avenue
Buffalo, New York 14216
(716) 555-1714 / email@email.com

Corporate Recruiter
Seven Years' Experience Aggressively Solving Staffing Needs

Campus Visits / Job Fair Participation
Internet Recruitment / Internship Program

Dynamic human resource professional with solid track record of finding qualified and talented technical and business personnel.

Core Strengths

Job Task Analysis	Capability Assessment
Offer Negotiation	Applicant Tracking
Succession Planning	Candidate Screening

Professional Experience

HELFER METALS, INC., Depew, New York   1992 to Present

Technical / Executive Recruiter

Oversee the full range of corporate recruitment, with emphasis on IT and management personnel. Anticipate staffing needs and forge strategic alliances with traditional and nontraditional candidate sources, including employment agencies and professional affiliations. Utilize contract and temporary personnel to eliminate overtime costs. Oversee diversity management program to insure affirmative action/EEO compliance.

- Significantly reduced turnover rate by careful and thorough reference checking.
- Designed Access database of technical and business candidates with keywords matched to companywide job descriptions.

Education

Millard Fillmore College, Buffalo, New York
Certificate in Personnel Administration, 1996

Erie Community College, Williamsville, New York
Associate in Applied Science: Business Studies, 1992
- Concentration in Human Resources

References Furnished Immediately upon Request

Keywords

Candidate Screening

Standardized Interview Forms

Job Descriptions

Diversity Management

Turnover Reduction

Campus Visits

Internship Program

Job Fair Participation

Human Resources

Job Task Analysis

Capability Assessment

Offer Negotiation

Applicant Tracking

Keyword Matching

Affirmative Action/EEO

Internet Recruitment

Corporate Recruiter

Labor Cost Reduction

Contract and Temporary Staffing

Succession Planning

Interview Q&A Using Keywords

Why should we hire you, what are your strengths, and how do you see yourself contributing to our company?

With training and development costs as high as they are, hiring and retaining the best employees is one of the most critical business practices. Our employee churn is the lowest these two years it has ever been. We streamlined recruiting process by 28% through standardized client interview forms and designed an Access database of technical and business candidates with keywords matched to companywide job descriptions. To cut fixed costs, I also utilized contract and temporary personnel to eliminate overtime costs.

COSMETOLOGIST

Resume

Carolyn Celly
45 Smith and Hale Drive
Huntington, New York 11743
(631) 555-1212 / email@email.com

Licensed Cosmetologist

Excellent business and sales skills
Strong client following

Intuitive and creative cosmetologist and skin care therapist skilled in working with women of all ages. Regional reputation for expertise with facial scar minimization.

Expertise

Consultations	Makeovers
Skin Care Regimens	Color Analysis
Scar Minimization	Moisturizers
Facials	Skin Hydration

Professional Experience

The Day Spa of Long Island, Huntington, New York   1998 to Present

Cosmetologist

Conduct consultations and provide advice on make-up application and skin care regimens in this upscale day spa. Utilize extensive dermatological knowledge to select and sell the best products to clients. Provide customized makeovers incorporating color analysis. Cross-sell other spa services.

- Increased cosmetology sales by 200% from 1998 to present.
- Cultivated relationships with local dermatologists who now refer several individuals a month for scar minimization makeovers.
- Added new services to the spa including glycolic peels, reflexology, deep pore cleansing, and scrubs.
- Developed a micronized zinc oxide sunscreen that was patented and is sold exclusively through the spa.

Education/Licensure

Rollers Institute Cosmetology School, New York, New York
  400 hours of clinical work

The Dermal Institute, New York, New York
  Certified Reflexologist

Licensed Cosmetologist; Licensed in Skin Care Therapy

References Furnished Immediately upon Request

Interview Q&A Using Keywords

Why should we hire you, what are your strengths, and how do you see yourself contributing to our company?

Besides having excellent cosmetology skills and the ability to make women feel their best, I am also quite good at selling. After having had a makeover with me, it is not uncommon for a woman to leave the spa with $100 worth of glycolic compounds, cosmetics, and moisturizers in addition to two future appointments for facials and reflexology sessions. It is this ability to cross-sell and up-sell that distinguishes me from other cosmetologists.

CREATIVE DESIGNER

Resume

Dan Schickman
67 Sacred Woods Lane
Holly Grove, California 94078
(818) 555-1122 / email@email.com

Creative Designer / Project Manager / Consultant
Specializing in Visual Communication and Virtual Reality Design

Advertising / Marketing / Corporate Identity / High-Impact Design
Media Placement / Branding and Positioning

A creative professional with 20 years of experience as a writer, designer, producer, project manager, and creative director in all media. Recognized for improving consumer perception and global market position.

Core Strengths

Digital Publishing Technology	Creative Direction
Research & Copyrighting	Production Coordination
Marketing Consultant	Multimedia Interactivity
Identity Development	Collateral Design

Professional Experience

TOP INTERNET STRATEGIES CO., Fresno, CA   1998 to Current

Creative Director

Oversee the creative end of all projects. Manage and direct teams to develop solutions using technology with a user-centered approach to interface design and content, creating meaningful connections between people, ideas, art, and technology. Provide direction to designers and production staff; liaise with sales and clients on presentations that bring technology and art together.

- Reorganized in-house advertising agency to achieve 15% savings on ad costs.
- Upgraded and managed all advertising, promotion, packaging, and cooperative programs.
- Increased sales by 200%, reduced costs by 40%.

Education

The Cooper Union for the Advancement of Science and Art, NYC
Bachelor of Fine Arts / Design and Marketing, 1983–1987

- Visual Interface Design, MIT, Boston, MA 1998
- Specialized Technology, Art Institute of PA, Philadelphia, PA 1991

References Furnished Immediately upon Request

Keywords

Design Methodology

Informatics

Virtual Reality Design

Graphical User Interface

Creative Systems Development

Project Management

Visual Communication

Collateral Design

Media Placement

Logo Identity

Branding & Positioning

Identity Development

Image

Consumer Perception

Corporate Identity

Multimedia Interactivity

Interactive Functionality

High-Impact Design

Emerging Media Technology

Digital Publishing

Interview Q&A Using Keywords

Why should we hire you, what are your strengths, and how do you see yourself contributing to our company?

My personal capabilities cover all areas relating to the development of successful twenty-first century businesses, and differentiate my value from other advertising, creative, marketing, financial, and business consultants. A specialist using emerging media technology, I will bring synergy, harmony, and interactive functionality to projects companywide that will increase productivity, improve communications, and significantly increase the organization's profitability.

CRUISE DIRECTOR

Keywords

Themed Activities

Special events
   Planning

Excursions

Entertainment

Travel

Event Coordination

Hospitality

Event Planning

Passengers

Budgeting

Big Three Cruise
   Lines

Safety

Emergency
   Preparedness

Master of
   Ceremonies

Ports-of-Call

Itineraries

Cruise

Evening Shows

Public Speaking

Foreign Languages

Resume

Gracie Holmes
2354 Mystic Street, #2
Palo Alto, California 94303
(415) 555-6859 / email@email.com

Cruise Director

Offering a combination of
hospitality, event planning, and staff management experience

Five years in increasingly responsible positions with a "big three" cruise line. Extensive ship experience spanning 75 different world itineraries and 95 ports-of-call.

Core Strengths

Special events planning	Emergency preparedness
Excursions	Budgeting
Themed activities	Life enhancement programs
Public speaking	Training and supervision

Professional Experience

P & O PRINCESS CRUISES, London, England   1996 to Present
Cruise Director (2001–Present)
Assistant Cruise Director (1997–2000)
Cruise Associate (1996–1997)

Develop and coordinate daily activities and entertainment planning for all passengers. Orchestrate safety and emergency preparedness drills for passengers and staff, ensuring procedures are carried out to exact specifications. Utilize public speaking skills while serving as Master of Ceremonies at evening shows. Hire, train, and supervise a staff of five associates.

- In 1999, conceptualized, initiated, and brought to fruition "life enhancement programming." Life enhancement programming focuses on activities with a learning component such as onboard dance and cooking classes. This initiative was so well received it has become a standard offering on Princess cruises and has also been copied by other cruise lines.

Education

Cal State University, Sacramento, California
Bachelor of Arts, Foreign Languages, 1995

References Available upon Request

Interview Q&A Using Keywords

Why should we hire you, what are your strengths, and how do you see yourself contributing to our company?

As a cruise director, I believe my role is to see that each and every passenger onboard our vessel has a pleasurable and memorable experience. To accomplish that requires a great deal of expertise, since there is so much happening on any given sailing. To be a great cruise director means, for example, that you have to know how to put on great entertainment, create themed activities, and above all, be the quintessential host or hostess. I am that person.

CUSTOMER SERVICE REPRESENTATIVE

Resume

Carol Pappas
10025 Victory Boulevard
Van Nuys, California 91405
(818) 555-4444 / email@email.com

> **Customer Service Representative**
>
> **Highly Reliable Self-Starter with Excellent Phone Skills**
> **Computer Literate... Well Organized... Attention to Detail**

Five years' experience in customer service including order entry, client relations, and general office support. Professional in work habits and appearance. Reliable with a verifiable record of punctuality and low absenteeism.

Core Strengths

Client Relations	Communication Skills
Detail Oriented	Organizational Abilities
General Office	Computer Literate
Problem Solving	Word Processing

Professional Experience

ORION INSURANCE SERVICE, Hollywood, CA   1999 to Present

Customer Service Representative

Provide customer service to insurance policy holders on phone and in person. Document conversations using Microsoft Word; maintain accurate and detailed files. Research and resolve various problems involving billing, benefits, and reimbursement issues. Assist in general office procedures as requested.

- Received numerous awards for Top Customer Service Representative.
- Reorganized filing system enabling staff to more easily retrieve information.
- Recognized by management for positive attitude and willingness to go beyond the requirements of the job.

TRIAD DISTRIBUTING, Canoga Park, CA   1997 to 1999

Customer Service / Order Entry Representative

Handled busy inbound phone inquiries regarding products sold via infomercials. Processed high volume of orders.

Education

North Hollywood High School, North Hollywood, CA
Graduated in 1999

References Furnished Immediately upon Request

Keywords

Analyze

Client Relations

Communication Skills

Computer Literate

Customer Relations

Detail Oriented

Filing

Call Center

Independence

Multitasking

Order Desk

Organizational Skills

Phone Skills

Problem Solving

Research

Self-Starter

Word Processing

Interview Q&A Using Keywords

Why should we hire you, what are your strengths, and how do you see yourself contributing to our company?

I have excellent telephone skills with all kinds of customers and like interacting with customers both in person and in a call-center environment. I have strong general office abilities including filing, organizing and word processing. You will need a self-starter that works well independently and is able to understand effectively and resolve customer problems.

DATA WAREHOUSE DEVELOPER

Keywords

E-Commerce

ERP Models

Move from Logical to
Physical Models

Data Warehouse
Processing,
Performance, and
Management

Identify, Document, and
Design Interfaces

OLAP/ETL

MIS, IT

Logical and Physical
Hardware/Software
Topology

Identify Gaps and Risks

"Single Source of Truth"
Architecture Criteria

SAP Business
Warehouse, SQL, and
Oracle Databases

BAPI/DCOM/ABAP/VB
Development and
Implementation

Web Management

B2B

B2C

CRM

Project Management

Internet

Source Systems
Limitations and Batch
Processing Windows

End-User Data Access
Performance
Expectations

Resume

Chip N. Glass
9871 North 81st Street
Wauwatosa, Wisconsin 53213
(414) 555-2447 / email@email.com

> **Data Warehouse Developer**
> **Big-picture strategist with the ability to analyze business and technical requirements at any level**
>
> **SAP Business Warehouse, SQL, and Oracle databases**

Big-picture strategist with the ability to analyze business and technical requirements at any level, to develop B2B and B2C data warehouses via SAP, SQL, and Oracle.

Core Strengths

Project management	Logical to physical modeling
Gap/risk identification	SAP Business Warehouse
"Single source of truth" architecture	BAPI/DCOM/ABAP/VB
SQL and Oracle databases	Hardware/software topology

Professional Experience

DATA STORAGE INC., Milwaukee, Wisconsin 1998 to Present

Data Warehouse Developer

Interact with management teams to analyze business and technical requirements for creating "single source of truth" architecture used in data warehouse. Develop and implement BAPI/DCOM/ABAP/VB. Identify, document, and design interfaces with existing systems. Design standard and Web-based management reporting capabilities. Document information management processes, resources, and tools.

- Designed and developed data warehouse (SAP Business Warehouse) to identify "single source of truth" architecture for retailer that specified consumer trends for marketing purposes. Included OLAP strategies and components.

Education

Marquette University, Milwaukee, Wisconsin
Bachelor of Science, Electrical Engineering, 1998

- GPA: 3.75
- Member of Tau Beta Pi Engineering Honor Society

Interview Q&A Using Keywords

Why should we hire you, what are your strengths, and how do you see yourself contributing to our company?

As a big picture strategist with the ability to analyze business and technical requirements at any level, I am confident I can develop a data warehouse that will aid your company in analyzing B2B and B2C information. My technical skills include: SAP Business Warehouse, SQL, and Oracle databases, and BAPI/DCOM/ABAP/VB development and implementation, and creating "single source of truth" architecture for retail environments.

DENTAL ASSISTANT

Resume

Claire James
2 Michelle Avenue
Kenmore, New York 14217
(716) 555-8342 / email@email.com

Dental Assistant
Extensive Background in Oral Surgery and Restorative Care

Chair-Side Assistance for Busy Dental Practice
Orthodontic and Periodontal Experience

Patient-focused dental professional with superior skills in providing pre- and post-operative care to adults and children. Earned patients' trust and confidence and contributed to expanding practice.

Core Strengths

Preventive Care	Sealant Application
Emergency Treatment	Patient Education
Insurance Processing	Community Outreach
Teeth Whitening	Infection Control

Professional Experience

AMHERST DENTAL GROUP, Amherst, New York   1989 to Current

Dental Assistant

Provide surgical and general dentistry assistance for 3 dentists in a busy general practice handling over 3000 patients of all ages. Take, develop, and interpret diagnostic x-rays and perform oral examinations. Take casts and impressions for prosthetics and restorations.

- Assist in oral surgery, periodontal surgery, advanced clinical surgery, and extractions.
- Insure safe and sanitary conditions through autoclave, ultrasound, and dry heat instrument sterilization.
- Utilize Easy-Dental Network for accurate and timely health record management.
- Present wellness lectures to area schools to promote oral hygiene and plaque control.

Education

Monroe Community College, Rochester, New York
Certificate in Dental Assisting, 1989

- Seligman Scholarship
- Dean's List

References Furnished Immediately upon Request

Keywords

Dental Assistant

Oral Examination

Patient Education

Pre- and Post-Operative Care

Appointment Scheduling

Instrument Sterilization

Diagnostic X-Rays

Emergency Treatment

Health Record Management

Insurance Processing

Casts and Impressions

Oral Hygiene and Plaque Control

Teeth Whitening

Easy-Dental Network

Infection Control

Preventive Care

Sealant Application

Oral Surgery and Extractions

Prosthetics and Restorations

Orthodontics/ Periodontics

Interview Q&A Using Keywords

Why should we hire you, what are your strengths, and how do you see yourself contributing to our company?

My experience is in assisting oral surgery, periodontal surgery, advanced clinical surgery, and extractions. I utilize the Easy-Dental Network for accurate and timely health record management. Of course, good medical practices are important to you, and I insure safe and sanitary conditions through autoclave, ultrasound, and dry heat instrument sterilization. I have also presented wellness lectures to area schools to promote oral hygiene and plaque control. Technically, I can take, develop, and interpret diagnostic x-rays and perform oral examinations.

DESIGN ENGINEER

Resume

Michael Smith
6234 La Costa Lane
Anywhere, Idaho 00000
(208) 555-0000 / email@email.com

> **Design Engineer**
> **10 Years of Demanding Engineering Testing and Development Experience**
>
> **Demonstrated Creativity, Perception, and Independent Judgment**

Expert in all aspects of experimental test techniques, including analytical, physical, and subjective evaluation of components under investigation. High level of competence in computer-aided data gathering systems.

Core Strengths

Methodical	Investigative
Rational	Creative
Analytical	Onboard Vehicle Electrical Modules
Wireless Air Interfaces	Exceptional IT Knowledge

Professional Experience

GENERAL CAR COMPANY, Clarkston, Michigan   1991 to Present

Senior Design Engineer—OnTwinkle Development

Direct the activities of a medium-sized group of engineers in defining, executing, and analyzing the highest level of experimental test scenarios and programs. Contribute to the continual improvement of product and component designs through extensive understanding of program objectives.

- Developed and implemented a GCC enterprisewide telematics strategy that replaced outdated systems.
- Improved component design in the OnTwinkle technology.
- Participated in national development of technology road maps and business models for global telematics initiatives.

Education

University of Michigan, Ann Arbor, Michigan
Master of Science Degree in Engineering; 1991

- Engineering Student of the Year, 1999
- Contributor, Student Engineering Newsletter

Keywords

Onboard Electrical Modules

Wireless Interfaces

Analog

Digital

Cellular

802.11

IT Infrastructures

Architecture Standards

Hardware

Analytical

Computer-Aided Data Gathering

Team Player

Engineering

Complex Telematics

Service Plans

Organized

Self-Directed

Evaluate

Resolve

Coordinate

Interview Q&A Using Keywords

Why should we hire you, what are your strengths, and how do you see yourself contributing to our company?

I have a thorough understanding of relationship design, build, and test cycles. I have the ability to manage, plan, and evaluate the work of others in team situations. I am highly analytical and have demonstrated technical and professional skills. I keep abreast of current product development and trends. While working for General in Detroit, I was the lead corporate representative working with communications vendors to design our new WAN technology. I have excellent knowledge of onboard vehicle electrical modules, wireless air interfaces, and working knowledge of IT infrastructures.

DIRECTOR OF MANUFACTURING

Resume

Darren C. Stevenson
1632 Tuxedo Drive
Springboro, Ohio 45458
(513) 555-0501 / email@email.com

Director of Manufacturing
Recognized Expert in Efficiency & Productivity Improvement

Multisite Operations / Just-in-Time Inventory Control
Lean Manufacturing / Continuous Improvement

Direct staff and operations of union and nonunion World-Class Manufacturing facilities. Astute management of operating budgets, emphasizing outsourcing, to achieve maximum profit & loss performance

Core Strengths

Facilities Consolidation	Technology Integration
Cost Reductions	Total Quality Management
Automated Manufacturing	ISO Certification
Union Negotiations	Training & Leadership

Professional Experience

DELPHI AUTOMOTIVE, Dayton, Ohio   1993 to Current

Director of Manufacturing

Manage multiple sites and shifts for fully automated manufacturing of shoe and brake lines for General Motors vehicles. Member of executive team guiding development and monitoring of strategic, financial, and operational plans. Introduced lean manufacturing, value-added processes, and other cost-reduction measures projected to raise plant's profitability to $10M in 2002. Increased efficiency through establishing Quality Circles.

- Increased production output to 5K pieces per line.
- Led completion of company's largest capital project.
- Restructured scheduling processes to cut production lead time 28%.
- Met $50K added labor cost without exceeding operating budget.

Education

The Ohio State University, Columbus, Ohio
Master of Science, Industrial Engineering, 1990

- Bachelor of Science, General Engineering
- Graduate GPA: 3.8; Undergraduate GPA: 3.6

References Furnished Immediately upon Request

Keywords

Facilities Consolidation

Technology Integration

Cost Reductions

Production Output

Value-Added Processes

Production Lead Time

Profit & Loss

Multisite Operations

Capital Project

Automated Manufacturing

Continuous Improvement

Operation Budget

Outsourcing

Efficiency Improvement

Productivity Improvement

Quality Circles

Just-in-Time

Inventory Control

Union Negotiations

World-Class Manufacturing

Interview Q&A Using Keywords

Why should we hire you, what are your strengths, and how do you see yourself contributing to our company?

I can help your company evolve to World-Class Manufacturing status through strengthening key areas such as automated manufacturing, inventory control, technology integration, facilities consolidation, and profit & loss performance. I have been successful in union and nonunion companies, am an expert in facilitating efficiency and productivity improvements, and am top-notch in contract negotiations. Other professional strengths that can add value to your operations are staff training and relationship management.

DIRECTOR OF MARKETING (ADVERTISING/MARKETING/PR)

Keywords

Brand Management

Product Launch

B2B and B2C

Public Speaking/
Presentations

Product
Development

Special Events
Planning

Strategic Marketing
Campaigns

Market and Product
Research

Collateral Material
Support

Focus Groups

Promotional
Programs

Corporate Identity/
Logo Development

Direct Mail and
Database
Marketing

Co-Op Campaign
Development

Creative Concepts

Signage/Package/
Support Material
Design

Budgeting/ Cost
Reduction

Client & Vendor
Relations

Marketing Strategy
& Communications

Resume

Patrick Dudash
5463 Dovelet Lane
Powell, Ohio 43065
(614) 885-1122 / email@email.com

> **Director of Marketing**
> **Driving Sales and Developing Markets within Competitive Venues**
>
> **Marketing Strategy Communications**
> **Market & Product Research • Co-Op Campaign Development**

Highly motivated marketing executive with nine years' experience building market presence and driving revenue growth within competitive product settings. Recognized as skilled public speaker and presenter.

Core Strengths

Brand Management	Corporate Logo & Identity
Product Launch	Promotional Programs &Campaigns
B2B and B2C	Budgeting/Cost Reduction
Product Development	Client & Vendor Relations

Professional Experience

Sol Rise Consultants, Brooksville, Minnesota   1993 to Current

Director of Marketing

Direct all strategic initiatives toward increasing company visibility as top provider of marketing services. Charged with planning and implementing special events, conceiving and designing creative marketing concepts, and guiding concept toward actuality. Provide design direction for signage, packaging and collateral materials. Demonstrate expertise in direct mail and database marketing; develop strategic marketing plans used on focus groups.

- Maintained 100% customer retention rate by creating customer focused initiatives.
- Generated unprecedented $5 million dollars during employment period.
- Developed innovative Web/printed material marketing plans.
- Honored with coveted "Sol Rise Ace Performance" award for three consecutive years.

Education

Miami University, Miami, Ohio
Bachelor of Arts: Business/Marketing, 1987

National Honors Society
Sigma Phi Epsilon Fraternity

References Furnished Immediately upon Request

Interview Q&A Using Keywords

Why should we hire you, what are your strengths, and how do you see yourself contributing to our company?

In our industry, competition is fierce! My extensive background in marketing strategy and communications, market/product research, and my ability to increase corporate identity through creative concepts will bring significant contributions to your company. I am also well-balanced between developing long-term strategies and shorter-term tactics that are easily tracked for effectiveness. I offer the ability to work effectively under extremely stressful environments. Whether coordinating special events for clients or building relationships with vendors, my professionalism and performance remain consistent and uncompromised.

DIRECTOR OF OPERATIONS

Resume

Elliot (E. J.) Darrow
3 Windmill Drive
Oyster Bay, New York 11771
(516) 555-4689 / email@email.com

Director of Operations

Ten years' experience in
Cross-Functional General Management and Administration

Versatile business professional adept at running a nonprofit operation. Proven talent in trimming budgets through better fiscal management. Facility in establishing excellent relationships with community representatives and outside vendors.

Core Strengths

Strategic Business Planning	Information Systems
Treasury Functions	Purchasing
Human Resource Management	Facilities Management
Policies and Procedures	Operational Efficiencies

Professional Experience

VILLAGE OF OYSTER BAY, Oyster Bay, New York   1992 to Present

Director of Operations

Oversee all facets of town government in support of service delivery for the 5000 residents and 100 business owners within this community. Manage a $2M general budget with allocations for special projects. Cultivate public and private partnerships to maximize village's ability to provide services in a cost-effective manner. Work closely with Board of Trustees on matters effecting capital expenditures and financial management. Supervise a staff of 12 civil service employees.

- Instrumental in saving the village $300,000 in waste removal fees through the adoption of a more stringent bid review process for carting companies.
- In collaboration with town attorney, successfully handled several legal challenges to the village's policies on zoning regulations.

Education

Brooklyn College, Brooklyn, New York
Bachelor of Arts, Economics, 1992

Excellent References on Request

Keywords

Information Systems

Financial Management

Human Resource Management

Administration

Capital Expenditures

Bid Reviews

Policies and Procedures

Board of Trustees

Facilities Management

Operational Efficiencies

Service Delivery

Civil Service

Legal Challenges

Treasury Functions

Cross-Functional General Management

Purchasing

Strategic Business Planning

Cost-Effective

Public and Private Partnerships

Budget

Interview Q&A Using Keywords

Why should we hire you, what are your strengths, and how do you see yourself contributing to our company?

Without wishing to appear immodest, I am proud to be able to say that in my present position as director of operations, I have turned around a village government that was headed for fiscal disaster. By implementing a traditional business model to this nonprofit arena, I was able to pull in the reins on spending, reduce waste, and perhaps most importantly institute a policy of accountability. Our operation is now a model for other local municipalities.

DIRECTOR OF PURCHASING

Resume

John H. McKinley
123 S. Fourth Street
Kewanee, Illinois 61443
(309) 555-1234 / email@email.com

Director of Purchasing / Sr. Buyer
12-Year Successful Track Record of International Procurement Services

Price Negotiations / Contract Administration / Procurement
Expertise in High-Level Contract Negotiations

Results-oriented, visionary purchasing/management professional with extensive experience in MRO Purchasing, international procurement, cost analysis, and contract conditions/terms negotiations.

Core Strengths

Contract Negotiations	Multisite Operation
Strategic Planning	Outsourcing
Cost Reduction	Vendor Negotiations
Cost Analysis	Supplier Management
JIT Purchasing	Materials Replenishment Ordering (MRO)

Professional Experience

XYZ COMPANY   1995 to Present

Purchasing Manager

Supervise, train, and mentor a staff of eight purchasing analysts in all aspects of international corporate procurement operations for a multisite company. Direct contract negotiations for all vendor services and oversee cost analysis functions. Oversee supplier management, ensure the procurement of quality materials / supplies, and secure extended terms on select items. Train and direct new purchasing agents. Direct outsourcing activities.

- Negotiated key vendor contracts, resulting in a $500,000 annual savings.
- Implemented cost analysis policies, saving $2200 in internal annual costs.
- Pioneered JIT Purchasing for national and international purchasing.
- Created and integrated a successful supplier management model.

Education

UNIVERSITY OF ILLINOIS, Collinsville, Illinois
Bachelor of Arts: Business Management/Accounting 1987

Interview Q&A Using Keywords

Why Should Our Company Hire You?

I have a proven track record of streamlining purchasing procedures for both domestic and international procurement, resulting in a significant annual cost savings. I have managed the RFP process without outside consultant support in most cases, and have implemented a wide range of effective purchasing operational procedures and programs including JIT Purchasing functions, competitive bidding, and fixed-price contracts.

EDITOR

Resume

Madison K. Nelson
123 S. Fourth Street
Kewanee, Illinois 61443
(309) 555-1234 / email@email.com

Professional Editor
Extensive Track Record of Successful Editorial Management

Media Relations / Corporate Communications / Public Relations
Multimedia and Electronic Advertising Expertise

Highly accomplished, detail-oriented, and personable editorial professional skilled in marketing communication, direct mail campaign, and electronic advertising strategies to support the corporate vision.

Core Strengths

Advertising Communications   Media Relations
Strategic Planning   Electronic Advertising
Publications Editing   Customer Communications
Creative Services   Strategic Positioning
Multimedia Advertising

Professional Experience

STRATFORD COMPANY   1997 to Current

Editorial Manager

Direct all aspects of corporate editing operations in collaborating with the marketing/public relations staff. Oversee a wide range of editing functions for multimedia advertising and supervise/train a staff of seven editors and three proofreading assistants. Ensure solid corporate, VIP, client, and management communications to reach corporate goals and deliver 100% customer satisfaction. Serve as the central point of contact in resolving editing issues.

- Negotiated effective third-party creative services contracts for graphics.
- Implemented policies to improve marketing/media relations.
- Spearheaded procedures for accurate editing of multimedia materials.
- Increased management/department communications.

Education

UNIVERSITY OF IOWA, Statesville, Iowa
Bachelor of Arts: Corporate Communications 1985

Keywords

Advertising Communications

Corporate Communications

Electronic Media

Corporate Vision

Creative Services

Customer Communications

Direct Mail Campaign

Electronic Advertising

Management Communications

Marketing Communications

Public Relations

Media Relations

Multimedia Advertising

Publications Editing

Publicity

Strategic Communications

VIP Relations

Strategic Planning

Tactical Campaign

Strategic Positioning

Interview Q&A Using Keywords

Why Should Our Company Hire You?

I have a wide range of experience in not only editing, but also media relations and marketing communications. This allows me to communicate valuable input throughout the various stages of media development. I have worked on many different kinds of work, including consumer products' marketing campaigns, fiction, and nonfiction business writing.

ELECTRICAL ENGINEER

Resume

Mark Watt
6542 Main Street
Middlefield, CT 06455
(860) 555-1122 / email@email.com

Electrical Engineer
Manufacturing and Defense Industries

High Security Clearance
Patent Holder

Electrical Engineer with background in design and testing. Experienced in manufacturing including military specifications. Able to build prototypes and develop protocols and procedures. Skilled in software applications.

Core Strengths

Design	Test Procedures
Protocols	AutoCAD 14
Cost Estimates	Installations
Research	Prototypes

Professional Experience

Sikorsky, Stratford, Connecticut   1995 to Present

Electrical Engineer

Designed electrical system for production equipment including controls, layout and components using AutoCAD 14. Developed test protocols and procedures for installations. Provided technical support, troubleshooting, and calibration for maintenance. Performed research on proposed projects creating prototypes and supplying cost estimates. Evaluated existing power supply and recommended upgrades as required.

- Patent holder for design of new wire harness in CNC machine
- Documented and wrote procedures as part of ISO 9000 team
- Assisted in design of avionics components using analog circuits
- Produced technical manual for testing protocols, reducing test time 35%

Education

University of Connecticut, Storrs, Connecticut
Bachelor of Science/Electrical Engineering 1993

- Research fellow Rensselaer Polytechnic Institute 1993–1994
- 4.0 Grade Point Average

Interview Q&A Using Keywords

Why should we hire you, what are your strengths, and how do you see yourself contributing to our company?

I have knowledge of the latest technology as well as solid skills in design and applications of electrical theory. I am able to coordinate machine and equipment installations, providing troubleshooting and other technical assistance. My strengths are in research and testing, developing protocols and procedures that streamline the process and accelerate product release while cutting production time and costs.

Resume

Deborah Davis
Route 117, Avenue B
Princeville, Illinois 61111
(309) 123-4567 / email@email.com

Elementary Teacher
Four years' experience working with children of various academic & socioeconomic levels

Intensive Phonics / Manipulatives / Literature-Based Reading
Internet & Computer-Learning Games

Resourceful and energetic teacher with a history of developing creative, hands-on activities and lessons to encourage a love of learning in students. Incorporate singing, dancing, puppets, learning centers, computer learning games, and cooperative learning groups within an inclusive classroom, and develop multiple themes across the curriculum. Commended for implementing effective discipline and class management techniques. Approach is student oriented and performance based.

Core Strengths

Student Advocate	After-School Tutoring
Creative Learning Centers	Fostering Student Self-Esteem
Literature Based Reading	Positive Reinforcement
Assertive Discipline	The Use of Brain-Compatible Techniques

Professional Experience

GARDNER SCHOOL, Princeton, Illinois   8/97 to Present

Fourth Grade Teacher

Design and teach units in spelling, cursive, math, social studies, science, and language arts, incorporating character and ethics across the curriculum in a cooperative learning environment. Implement extensive role playing, conflict resolution, Internet research, and hands-on/interactive learning projects. Collaborate with another teacher to develop stations among two rooms for various units.

- For a thematic unit on Native Americans: taught students Native American dances, demonstrated aerodynamics through the flight of an arrow for match and science, and read a short novel on Native Americans.
- Had students create a "Bill of Rights" in cooperative learning groups for social studies.
- Had students select a famous American, conduct research, write and memorize reports, and give presentations to invited guests, including community representatives, political figures, school board officials, and parents.
- Completed training and implemented "Success for All," a guided reading program to target students at all learning levels.

Education

NORTHERN ILLINOIS UNIVERSITY, DeKalb, Illinois
Bachelor of Science in Education, 5/97

Keywords

Education

Elementary Teaching

Student Advocate

Team Teaching

Self-Esteem

Manipulatives

Intensive Phonics

Literature-Based Reading

Internet /Computer Learning Games

Cooperative Learning

Hands-on Learning

Developing Themes across the Curriculum

Curriculum Development

Brain-Compatible Techniques

Performance Based

Positive Reinforcement

Assertive Discipline

Inclusive Classroom

Self-Contained Classroom

Tutoring

Learning Centers

Interview Q&A Using Keywords

Why should we hire you, what are your strengths, and how do you see yourself contributing to our company?

I'm a great believer in hands-on learning. I've developed a number of creative learning centers with themes ranging from dinosaurs and Native American to music, art, math, reading, and dance. In addition, I use positive reinforcement to foster self-esteem in children at all academic levels, and my approach is student oriented and performance based. Continuing education is also important to me. I've attended a number of seminars to stay up-to-date on various teaching strategies, including cooperative learning, assertive discipline, and the use of brain-compatible techniques.

ENVIRONMENTAL ENGINEER

Resume

Brian M. Keith
12 Pine Aire Drive
Deer Park, New York 11729
(631) 555-2099 / email@email.com

Environmental Engineer
25 years of experience in environmental construction management

Geotechnical, Foundation, Cap & Cell Construction
Local Law 11 Inspection

Broadly experienced environmental engineer with a background providing project management and compliance support on a permanent/contract basis for major industrial, commercial, and governmental clients.

Core Strengths

Project Management	Land Surveys & Mapping
Feasibility Studies	Soil Classification
Drilled Shaft Foundation	Ground-Up Facade Inspection
Proposal Development	Bids and Negotiations

Professional Experience

Enviro-Services, Inc., New York, New York   1984 to Current

Environmental Engineer

Provide first and third-party services to ensure the environmental integrity of construction sites in the areas of earthwork, electrical, concrete, drainage systems, geosynthetic material installation, petroleum cleanup, asbestos abatement, waste management, inspections, contractor relations, vendor selection, cost control, crew supervision, proposal review, regulatory compliance, and agency reporting.

- Perform ALTA, topographical, boundary, and environmental surveys.
- Supervise the Ground-Up Facade Inspection of New York landmarks.
- Led negotiations on runway, tunnel, and bridge renovation projects.
- Direct indoor air quality testing and drainage systems of train stations.

Education

Stony Brook University, Stony Brook, New York
Bachelor of Science: Civil Engineering, 1987

- **Estimating and Blueprint Reading/Development**
- **Certified Tester: Soil Pressures and Properties; Foundations**

Interview Q&A Using Keywords

Why should we hire you, what are your strengths, and how do you see yourself contributing to our company?

As an environmental engineer, I am qualified to deliver environmental solutions in areas of construction support and risk assessment. I'm confident that my experience in Quality Control, Local Law 11 inspection, architectural and computer-aided drawing, construction methods, and specialized equipment, combined with my ability to expedite the cost-effective resolve of problems and schedule delays would guide your firm in achieving its five-year plan to build six new malls across New Jersey and Connecticut.

ESTIMATOR

Resume

Donald D. Burnard
402 East Maude Avenue
Arlington Heights, Illinois 60004
(847) 555-7035 / email@email.com

**SENIOR ESTIMATOR /
GENERAL MANAGER**

*Improving Corporate Profits by Unifying Project Management,
Estimating, and Construction*

INDUSTRY EXPERT with 16 years of successful project management experience at the senior level for federal, commercial, retail, and multi-unit residential renovation and construction projects.

Core Strengths

Feasibility Studies	Contract Negotiations
Technology Surveys	Subcontractor Assessment/Selection
Pay Applications	Overview Reporting
RFIs (Request for Information)	SOVs (Schedule of Value)

Professional Experience

COOPER CONSTRUCTION, Phoenix, Arizona   1995 to Present

Senior Project Manager / Estimator

Reporting directly to the CEO, singly responsible for overseeing management of all projects, building estimates, and developing accurate and realistic schedules for a broad range of construction projects including a four-story Holiday Inn Express, Joy Medical Office Building, commercial restaurants, and multimillion-dollar renovation projects for hurricane-damaged luxury condo developments.

- Sourced and installed the innovative Quest Digital Estimating System; recruited, hired, and provided comprehensive training for two additional estimators.
- Selected by M.J. Anderson, Inc. to rescue projects worth $4.3 million in danger of degenerating into liquidated damages. Result: Reworked contracts, reversed downward trends, and completed projects profitably.

Education

University of Texas, Arlington, Texas
Bachelor of Science / Industrial Engineering, 1985

- National Merit Finalist
- College of Arts and Sciences Dean's Award for Engineering

Keywords

Project Specifications

Site Assessment

Material Procurement

Troubleshooting & Turnaround

Competitive Bidding

Value Engineering

Data Acquisition

Proposals

Budgeting

Costing/Pricing

Profit Planning

Change Orders

Feasibility Studies

Technology Surveys

Subcontractor Assessment & Selection

SOVs (Schedule of Value)

Contract Negotiations

Pay Applications

RFIs (Request for Information)

Overview Reporting

Interview Q&A Using Keywords

Why should we hire you, what are your strengths, and how do you see yourself contributing to our company?

Everything I have accomplished during my 16 years in business demonstrates my ability to add efficiency and profitability along the entire length of the construction industry value chain. I specialize in budgeting, costing and pricing, change orders, and profit planning. With a nationwide network of over 900 contractors and managers that will commit to my projects, I can ensure quality, value-driven engineering with minimum lead time preparation.

Keywords

Budget Control

Restaurant

Culinary Designs

Cultivate Relationships

Customer Relations

Diet and Nutrition

Fat-Free Generation

Food Cost Analysis

Health-Conscious

Hospitality

Kitchen Operations

Multiethnic

Public Awareness

Quality Control

Recipe Development

Signature-Style Dishes

Teach and Inspire

Team Leadership

Vendor Selection

World-Renowned

Resume

Jeffrey Bernard
Circle 6 Black Bird Road
Huntington Station, New York 11746
(631) 555-8013 / email@email.com

Executive Chef
18 years of award-winning culinary excellence

Five-Star Restaurants, Landmark Hotels / Exclusive Resorts
American, European, and Asian Cuisine

Celebrated, world-traveled chef with a flair for creating visually stimulating culinary designs and signature-style dishes. Personable with keen business management skills, and a desire to teach and inspire new chefs.

Core Strengths

Kitchen Operations

Culinary Staff Management

Customer/Public Relations

Innovative Presentations

Recipe Development

Food Cost Analysis

Quality Control

Vendor Selection

Professional Experience

La Toro Restaurant, New York, New York   1998 to Current

Executive Chef

Recruited by this 450-seat five-star restaurant, located in New York's theatre district, to whet the appetite of high-profile stars and tourists with an eclectic menu inspired by the city's multiethnic landscape. Oversee all aspects of kitchen operations in areas of culinary staff management, menu planning, purchasing, kitchen safety, customer/public relations, catering, and special events coordination, realizing annual profits of $2.7 million.

- Achieved five-star status for La Toro four years consecutively.
- Developed trademark techniques used in leading culinary institutes.
- Cultivate relationships with food critics to enhance public awareness.
- Travel globally to discover cultural-based foods and traditional recipes.

Education

Institute of America, Hyde Park, New York

Bachelor of Professional Studies: Culinary Arts, 1993

- **Member, National Restaurant Association, 1995–current**
- **Metro Restaurant Association, Best New Restaurant, 1998**

References Furnished Immediately upon Request

Interview Q&A Using Keywords

Why should we hire you, what are your strengths, and how do you see yourself contributing to our company?

In the recent decade, changes in diet and nutrition have inspired a health-conscious, "fat-free" generation, creating new challenges for the foodservice industry. I understand your organization is planning a national launch of "healthy eating" restaurants and food products. As a world-renowned chef with 18 years managing award-winning restaurants, I believe my culinary talents and business management know-how would drive this venture to commercial success.

EXECUTIVE RECRUITER, ENGINEERING

Resume

Lori Harding
9999 North Road
Bedford, Massachusetts 01730
(781) 555-1122 / email@email.com

Executive Recruiter
Mechanical, Civil, Electrical, and Computer Engineering

Fortune 1000 Companies
Defense, Aerospace, and Telecommunications Industries

High-energy recruiter with proven success in placing Project Managers and Senior Engineers in Defense, Manufacturing, and Telecommunications Industries. Skilled in Peoplesoft and other software applications.

Core Strengths

Networking	Sales
Candidate Sourcing	Screening
International Placements	Labor/Unemployment Law
Communication Skills	Recruitment

Professional Experience

Tech Recruiters Plus, Waltham, Massachusetts   1998–2002

Technical Recruiter
Identified and contacted candidates for positions in engineering. Attended job fairs and trade shows for recruitment and sales. Established contacts with colleges, military, and professional groups to create talent bank. Determined needs of company and successfully matched candidates to positions. Monitored recruitment/retention statistics for select classifications. Networked in target industries to generate new business.

- Created Web site for national recruitment, increasing talent bank 15%
- Increased sales 25% by delivering presentations at trade shows
- Tracked recruitments and hires demonstrating 92% retention rate
- Landed accounts in England opening first of many international markets

Education

Boston University, Boston, Massachusetts
Bachelor of Arts / Human Resource Management, 1996

- Graduated *Magna Cum Laude*
- Internship in Human Resources at Peabody Engineering Group

References Furnished Immediately upon Request

Keywords

Staffing
Candidate Sourcing
Project Positions
Domestic
International
Confidentiality
Discretion
Telecommunications
Emerging
  Technology
Manufacturing
Sales Skills
Defense Industry
Interviewing
Technical Recruiting
Network
Peoplesoft
Screening
Colleges
Job Fairs
Labor Law

Interview Q&A Using Keywords

Why should we hire you, what are your strengths, and how do you see yourself contributing to our company?

I utilize creative strategies in sales and candidate sourcing. Keenly aware of the need to develop new business continually, I have established contacts in hundreds of companies. I am knowledgeable in the needs of industry and can anticipate staffing requirements of companies with emerging technologies. I have a reputation of professionalism, handling issues with discretion, and maintaining confidentiality.

FINANCE MANAGER, BANKING

Keywords

Commercial Lending

Relationship
Management

Investment
Management

Asset Management

Portfolio
Management

Retail Lending

Commercial
Banking

Consumer Banking

Credit
Administration

Regulatory Affairs

Branch Operations

Securities
Management

Secured Lending

Loan Processing

Return on Assets
(ROA)

Global Banking

Foreign Exchange

Unsecured Lending

Return on
Investment (ROI)

Return on Equity
(ROE)

Resume

Anthony J. Burton
5827 Warminster Avenue
Dayton, Ohio 45472
(937) 555-2012 / email@email.com

Finance Manager—Banking
Proven Success in Expanding Scope & Profitability

Commercial Lending / Relationship Management
Investment Management / Sales & Marketing

Deliver strong and sustainable gains in revenue, fee income, and asset management. Facilitate change and revitalize organizational performance. Experience with start-up, turnaround, merger, acquisition, and growth.

Core Strengths

Portfolio Management	Retail Lending
Branch Operations	Commercial Banking
Regulatory Affairs	Credit Administration
Problem Analysis & Resolution	Organizational Reengineering

Professional Experience

NEIGHBOR'S BANK, Springfield, Ohio   1994 to Current

Vice President

Manage 17 branch operations in tristate area with focus on building relationship management programs with commercial banking customers. Responsible for expanding U.S. market reach and establishing global banking division. Ensure profitability through creating and managing strategic, financial, and operational plans. Named fourth in nation for secured lending performance and a Top 10 security investment professional.

- Increased consumer banking sales $4.5M in six months.
- Restructured operations to improve ROA 12%, ROE 20%, and ROI 24%.
- Successfully added unsecured lending to loan processing operations.
- Managed foreign exchange and regulatory affairs/compliance programs.

Education

University of Dayton, Dayton, Ohio
Bachelor of Science: Accounting, 1993

- GPA 3.9
- Top 2% of graduates

References Furnished Immediately upon Request

Interview Q&A Using Keywords

Why should we hire you, what are your strengths, and how do you see yourself contributing to our company?

I have comprehensive experience in finance and banking that includes branch operations, global banking, and investment and portfolio management. Underlying this success are key strengths, primary of which are the abilities to recognize opportunities, anticipate change, and create and sustain solid customer relationships. Drawing upon these and my broad-based experience, I can help your bank expand its market reach, increase its commercial lending, and drive profitability to new heights.

Resume

Ben A. Counter
127 Maple Street
Wethersfield, Connecticut 06102
(860) 555-1212 / email@email.com

Financial Analyst
Planning and Budget Specialist

Budgeting/Forecasting
Operations Strategist

Analytical, organized finance professional recognized for achievement in budget controls, financial reporting, and cost savings. Strong in management and operations analysis and increasing profitability.

Core Strengths

Cost Analysis	Strategic Planning
Fixed Assets	Budget Process and Implementation
Investment analysis	Pricing structures
Forecasting	Divestitures

Professional Experience

New England Corporation, Hartford, Connecticut   1989–2001

Financial Analyst

Coordinated all financial reporting and budget functions for all 15 departments of a major corporation. Oversaw month-end closings for sales and operations. Prepared and implemented annual budget with cost controls and process improvement. Recommended capital purchases and technology to trim costs and streamline operations.

- Saved $2.3MM annually through cost projections and pricing structures
- Increased profitability by 12% by streamlining operations
- Received recognition for creating expense variance reports
- Designed financial matrix for chargebacks, reducing errors and labor

Education

University of Connecticut, Storrs, Connecticut
Master of Business Administration, Finance   **1986**
Bachelor of Science, Business Administration   **1982**

Keywords

Financial Planning

Financial Reporting

Capital Projections

Annual Budget

Forecasting

Accruals

Expense Tracking

Expense Variances

Cost/Pricing
  Analysis

Audit Management

Cash Management

Investment Analysis

Technology
  Integration

Profitability

Divestitures

Asset Utilization

Strategic Planning

Financial Models

Budget
  Implementation

Fiscal Controls

Interview Q&A Using Keywords

Why should we hire you, what are your strengths, and how do you see yourself contributing to our company?

I have a proven track record of increasing profitability through sound management, financial analysis, and budget process improvement. I have had substantial results in capital areas including purchase recommendations, fixed asset management, and asset redeployment resulting in significant cost savings. I have implemented cost and budget controls resulting in, measurable decreases in expenditures. My expertise also includes long-term and short-term planning, as well as the ability to streamline operations.

FINANCIAL PLANNER

Keywords

Acquisition
Investigation

Contingency
Planning

Asset Management

Joint Venture
Analysis

Return on
Investment

Financial Reporting

Business
Development

Asset Purchase

Securities and
Investment
Banking

Feasibility Study

PowerPoint
Presentation

Cost-Benefit
Analysis

Financial Models

Equity Financing

Sales Forecasting

Risk Analysis

Market/Consumer
Research

Capital Expense
Justification

Cost Controls/Cost
Avoidance

Business
Advisement

Resume

Warren S. Michaels
155 Seventh Street
Clarence, New York 14031
(716) 555-9280 / email@email.com

Financial Planner

**Perform Risk Analysis / Secure Equity Financing
Research Launch of Product Lines**

Solid track record of implementing creative solutions to enhance market share and increase profitability. Develop financial models to situate company for aggressive expansion.

Core Strengths

Contingency Planning	Cost-Benefit Analysis
Feasibility Study	Asset Purchase
Joint Venture Analysis	Capital Expense Justification
Financial Reporting	Investment Banking

Professional Experience

HEALTH RESOURCES, INC., Buffalo, New York   1997 to Current

Vice President—Financial Planning

Provide strategic counsel to corporate executives in financial planning, new business development, and investments. Research and evaluate consumers, sales history, pricing, emerging competition, packaging, and market trends to forecast sales and profits accurately.

- Recommended acquisition of primary competitor, realizing 87% of market share.
- Initiated cost controls in production, warehouse operations, and purchasing that resulted in over $230,000 in savings.
- Provided business advisement on divestiture of poor-performing subsidiary and investment in start-up company, earning significant increase in revenues.

Education

University of Buffalo School of Management, New York
Master of Business Administration, 1984

- Phi Beta Kappa
- Magna Cum Laude

References Furnished Immediately upon Request

Interview Q&A Using Keywords

Why should we hire you, what are your strengths, and how do you see yourself contributing to our company?

As standard practice, I perform risk analysis and secured equity financing for the launch of new product lines. I also recommended acquisition of primary competitor, realizing 87% of market share. Since cost control in today's environment is so critical, I initiated cost controls in production, warehouse operations, and purchasing that resulted in over $230,000 in savings. I also provided business advisement on divestiture of a poor-performing subsidiary and investment in a start-up company, earning significant increase in revenues.

FLIGHT ATTENDANT

Resume

Phillip B. Hall
4545 Coconut Way
Honolulu, Hawaii 96818
(808) 555-5693 / email@email.com

> **Professional Flight Attendant**
> **10+ Years of Safe Flying and Superior Customer Service**
>
> **Cabin Leadership / Passenger Relations**
> **International and Domestic Experience**

A friendly, flexible, and reliable cabin safety professional. Reputation for complaint resolution techniques. As a trainer, appreciate the value of Inflight Policies and Procedures, and SOPs. Bilingual speaker of Japanese.

Core Strengths

Cabin Safety	FARs
Evacuation Procedures	In-flight Emergencies
Emergency Equipment	Crew Resource Management
Customer Service	Complaint Resolution

Professional Experience

ALL PACIFIC AIRLINES, Honolulu, Hawaii   1990 to Present

Flight Attendant

Maintain clear sense of responsibility for safety of passengers and fellow crewmembers while providing outstanding customer service aboard international flights throughout the Pacific and Asia. Jointly charged with recurrent training curriculum planning, including review of land and water evacuation procedures, water survival, first aid, emergency equipment location and use, and hijacking procedures.

- Reorganized Policies and Procedures section of flight attendant manual.
- Assisted in selecting cabin location of automatic external defibrillator.
- Achieved record $3500 in duty-free sales on single transpacific flight.
- Flight Attendant of the Year Award for superior passenger relations.

Education

University of Hawaii, Honolulu, Hawaii
Bachelor of Arts / Travel and Tourism Management, 1988

- Editor of campus travel and tourism newsletter
- Front desk internship—Royal Hawaiian Hotel

Keywords

Cabin Safety

Evacuation Procedures

Flight Attendant

Emergency Equipment

Hijacking Procedures

First Aid

Automatic External Defibrillator (AED)

Federal Aviation Regulations (FARs)

Crew Resource Management (CRM)

Cabin Leadership

Recurrent Training

In-Flight Policies and Procedures

Standard Operating Procedures (SOPs)

Air Travel

Passenger Relations

Complaint Resolution

Bilingual Japanese Speaker

International Routes

Domestic Routes

Duty Free Sales

Interview Q&A Using Keywords

Why should we hire you, what are your strengths, and how do you see yourself contributing to our company?

I have 10 years of experience with a major air carrier flying both international and domestic routes, and am a bilingual speaker of Japanese. I am a highly skilled cabin leader with particular expertise in customer service, complaint resolution, and crew resource management. Your airline will soon equip its fleet with automatic external defibrillators; I have already been trained in the use of the AED, and am qualified to teach the module during flight attendant recurrent training.

FOOD & BEVERAGE MANAGER (HOSPITALITY)

Keywords

Revenue Management

Catering

Bar & Beverage Operations

Kitchen Operations

Hospitality

Banqueting and Conferences

Food Production Technology

Customer Service

Team Building & Leadership

Planning and Organization

HACCP Standards

Purchasing Vendor Relations

Inventory Cost Control

Menu Development

Food Production Standards and Controls

Room Service

Staff Hiring & Training

Performance Management

Finance & Budgeting

Restaurant

Resume

Paul Garvey
8934 Brighton Blvd.
Columbus, Ohio 43229
(614) 716-4233

Food and Beverage Manager
Expertise in Special Events and VIP Galas...

Food Production Standards and Controls • Banquets & Conferences Bar & Beverage Operations • Food Production Technology • Purchasing Vendor Relations

---

Qualified Food and Beverage Manager with demonstrated history in empowering individuals to achieve restaurant goals. Implement cost-saving measures while utilizing resources with maximum efficiency.

Core Strengths

Revenue Management	Customer Service/Room Service
Contract Negotiations	Team Building & Leadership
Kitchen Operations	Planning and Organization
Product Knowledge	HACCP Standards

Professional Experience

Rumford Hotels, Columbus, Ohio   1997 to Present

Food and Beverage Manager

Collaborate with manager in maintaining inventory cost control, finance & budgeting, staff hiring & development, and overall performance management. Accountable for security of assets, supervision of daily operations, and ensuring guest satisfaction through excellent customer service, while increasing sales through creative menu development.

- Achieved 5% companywide food and beverage service improvement to prior year.
- Trained associates in highly important Alcohol Intervention and Life safety.
- Assisted in development and execution of highly successful sales strategy.
- Awarded annual bonus based on service and profitability.

Education

The Ohio State University, Columbus, Ohio
Bachelor of Arts, Hospitality & Tourism Management, December 2000

- GPA 3.8
- Social Director for Residence Hall, two years

References Furnished Immediately upon Request

Interview Q&A Using Keywords

Why should we hire you, what are your strengths, and how do you see yourself contributing to our company?

My qualities as a Food and Beverage Manager have been identified in areas including room service operations, banquets/conferences, and special events. The profit-centered projects upon which I've focused this past year have provided the opportunity to prove my skills in revenue management, budgeting, and cash flow, and will prove useful as a part of your management team.

FUND-RAISER

Resume

Jesse Elijah
504 49th Avenue West
Edwards, Illinois 61528
(309) 243-1111 / email@email.com

Fund-Raiser
Special Event Management / Public Relations / Capital Campaigns

Skilled in Forging Partnerships with Diverse Revenue Sources
14-Year Track Record of Organizational Development

Accomplished Fund-Raising Executive with experience managing relationships with financial contributors, boards of directors, staff, and volunteers. Track record of increasing revenues and fostering positive public and media relations. Broad base of experience in fund raising including grant writing, direct mail, annual campaigns, major gifts, telephone solicitations, and special events.

Core Strengths

Special Event Management	Public Relations/Media Relations
Capital Giving Campaigns	Budgeting
Strategic Planning	Grant Writing
Policy Development	Team Leadership

Professional Experience

HEART OF ILLINOIS LEUKEMIA FOUNDATION, Peoria, Illinois   1997 to Present

Director of Fund-Raising and Public Relations
Conceive and direct all fund-raising activities and serve as liaison to staff, volunteers, board members, the community, and the media. Responsible for strategic planning, budgeting, and reporting. Write and edit promotional materials and press releases for various events and services and give presentations to local service organizations. Recruit, schedule, motivate, train, and supervise 150+ volunteers.

- Researched and launched a grant solicitation campaign, resulting in additional revenues of approximately $100,000.
- Initiated a direct mail campaign resulting in $10,000 profit within just six months and 1000 new contributors.
- Pioneered a fashion show at an upscale area hotel, using parents and children affiliated with the foundation as models. Planned the entire event, including securing approval, recruiting and scheduling volunteers, calling on stores for donations, and selling tables to corporations. By all accounts the event was a huge success, earning a one-night $25,000 profit.

Education

WESTERN ILLINOIS UNIVERSITY, Macomb, Illinois
Bachelor of Arts in Communications, 1997

Keywords

Special Event Management

Public Relations

Media Relations

Financial Contributors

Capital Giving Campaign

Volunteer Recruitment

Nonprofit Institutions

Organizational Development

Fund-Raising

Revenue Sources

Direct Mail Campaign

Oral and Written Communication Skills

Financial Contributors

Board of Directors

Policy Development

Campaign Development

Budgeting

Grant Writing

Team Leadership

Partnerships

Interview Q&A Using Keywords

Why should we hire you, what are your strengths, and how do you see yourself contributing to our company?

My background includes the management of fund-raising operations for a nonprofit organization of 1500+ members. In that capacity, I answer directly to the Board of Directors, with broad responsibility for volunteer recruitment, budgeting, strategic planning, and staff supervision. In addition to serving as liaison to staff, volunteers, board members, and the community, I am charged with fostering a positive relationship with the media, identifying revenue sources, and conceiving and coordinating direct mail and capital giving campaigns. As a result of my efforts in the past five years, the organization's revenues have nearly doubled.

FUNERAL DIRECTOR

Resume

Clinton Worthy
200 Springview Lane
Lawrenceville, Georgia 30040
(770) 555-1212 / email@email.com

Funeral Professional
Building and holding an increasing market share
through customer support second to none.

Preneed planning specialist / Caring, comprehensive advice and counseling
Complete bereavement services / Sales and management expertise

---

Accomplished funeral professional with an MBA and 12 years' experience in funeral service. A results-oriented, success-driven leader and director with strong operational skills in finance, sales, and marketing. Initiated many strategies and programs that repeatedly added value, increased customer service performance, grew market share, and enhanced public image of the firm while meeting profit goals.

Core Strengths

Preneed and family service sales	Empathetic grief and needs counseling
Marketing & promotion to enhance our industry	Attention to detail to deliver flawless service
Operational management	Strong ethical standards

Professional Experience

Shady Rest Funeral Home, Lawrenceville, Georgia   1990 to Current

Director

Provide advice and counseling, legal documentation, assistance with administrative tasks, and the logistical management of human remains. Counsel and advise people prior to death as well as during and after bereavement. Sensitive to requirements of law, custom, and the accepted practices of the individuals and communities. Meet sales and revenue goals.

Education

University of Lowell, Lowell, Massachusetts
Bachelor of Science in Business, 1987

- *Summa cum laude*

References Furnished Immediately upon Request

Interview Q&A Using Keywords

Why should we hire you, what are your strengths, and how do you see yourself contributing to our company?

While some join the funeral industry because they think it is "recession proof," I've dedicated my entire career to serving communities and building market share. The two are related, not opposed. My strength is in providing caring, empathetic, comprehensive service that positions my organizations as the provider of choice in times of grief and sorrow. While I am an embalmer as well as a director and cemeterian, my greatest strength is in anticipating and filling final arrangement needs. What pleases me most is that most of my sales are referrals.

GENERAL MANAGER—HOSPITALITY

Resume

Roberta Alexander
208 Tallowood Blvd.
Westerville, OH 43081
(614) 555-4562 / email@email.com

> **General Manager: Hospitality**
> Able to develop strategies and follow through to impressive outcomes.
>
> **Operations Management • Human Resources Management**
> **Staff Development, Training, and Leadership**

Hotel/Resort Management professional with outstanding reputation for producing impressive results. Practical problem solver, effective when managing union staffs, and recognized for tenacity and perseverance.

Core Strengths

Guest Services	Contract Negotiations
P&L Management	Labor Cost Controls
Hotel Sales & Marketing	Convention Coordination
Labor Relations	Financial & Cost Accounting

Professional Experience

Land Paradise Resort, Honolulu Hawaii   1999 to Current

General Manager

Manage hospitality operations and guest services of 200-room resort with revenues in excess of $5 million annually. Ensure quality assurance and adherence to hotel service standard while overseeing banqueting & catering, executive housekeeping, while ensuring that front office and guest service departments operate at optimum levels. Develop and execute strategies supporting facilities planning and restaurant operation agendas.

- Successfully implemented innovative Hospitality Training System.
- Improved profit by over 25% during first year as General Manager.
- Selected as Keynote speaker at three General Managers' conferences.
- Pioneered groundbreaking "Hotel Managers Survival Camp."

Education

Cornell University, School of Hotel Administration, Ithaca, New York
Bachelor of Science: Hotel Administration, 1996

- Concentration: **Food and Beverage Management**
- Activities: **Teaching Assistant, Culinary 101**

References Furnished Immediately upon Request

Keywords

- Hotel Sales & Marketing
- Labor Relations
- Hospitality Training Systems
- Business Development
- Executive Housekeeping
- Banqueting & Catering
- Business Start-up and Turnaround
- Front Office Management
- Facilities Planning
- Financial & Cost Accounting
- Restaurant Operations Management
- Catering
- Guest Services Management
- Budget Planning and Administration
- Labor Cost Controls
- Convention Coordinating
- P&L Management/ Strategic Planning
- Quality Assurance/ Service Standards
- Staff Development, Training, and Leadership
- Contract Negotiations

Interview Q&A Using Keywords

Why should we hire you, what are your strengths, and how do you see yourself contributing to our company?

I possess talents that will contribute to your property in several key areas, the first of which will be sales and marketing. Without an increasing customer base, good service is inconsequential. Therefore, business development, despite competitive markets, must be addressed. To assure that the hotel remains first class, I will concentrate on quality in banquet/catering, convention management, executive housekeeping, and front desk service by assuring strong internal controls and building a sound associate team.

Keywords

Bridging Clients
Together

Bureau Compliance

Client Advocate

Corporate Filings

Court-Held Fraud
Cases

Database Search
Management

Domain Names

Domestic/
International
Policies

Federal Laws and
Regulations

Government
Relations

Internet Intellectual
Property

Expert Testimony

Legislative Hearings

National Speaker

Patents,
Trademarks,
Copyrights

Peer Consultation

Portfolio of Services

Tangible/Intangible
Property

Trademark
Infringement

Web Site Content

Resume

William J. Whitfield III
Coral Grove Point—Northgate Way
North Babylon, New York 11703
(631) 555-0088 / email@email.com

Government Liaison
20-Year Career Specializing in Intellectual Property

Traditional & Internet Case Management
Patents / Trademarks / Copyrights

Influential government liaison with a groundbreaking career serving as a vital link between federal agencies, patent attorneys, Internet companies, inventors, highly regarded marketing firms, and Fortune 500 companies.

Core Strengths

Government Relations	Domestic/International Policies
Client Advocate	Database Search Management
Corporate Filings	Federal Laws and Regulations
Trademark Infringement	Expert Testimonials

Professional Experience

Intellex Properties, Inc., New York, New York   1993 to Present

Government Liaison

Expedite the granting of domestic/international trademarks, patents, and copyrights specific to tangible/intangible property, Web site content, and domain names/personal names through appropriate channels. Ensure full compliance with the U.S. Patent and Trademark Office, Copyright Office, World Intellectual Property Organization, and a matrix of federal bureaus. Serve as a leading authority, case representative, and client advocate.

- Speak nationally on controversial foreign intellectual property issues.
- Provided expert testimony for clients at fraud examination hearings.
- Consult peer specialists on case analyses and legal protocols.
- Attended legislative hearings on music copyright infringements.

Education

Fordham University, Bronx, New York
Master of Arts: Political Science, 1985

- **Chairperson, World Trade Advisory Committee**
- **Member, MENSA**

Interview Q&A Using Keywords

Why should we hire you, what are your strengths, and how do you see yourself contributing to our company?

Recently, my work has centered on influencing changes in Washington on issues concerning traditional and Internet intellectual property rights. It is your organization's recent decision to expand its portfolio of services to include intellectual property that is of particular interest to me. I am confident that my expertise in this arena would prove viable in supporting this challenging initiative.

GRAPHIC DESIGNER

Resume

Patti Elliott
9911 Davidian Drive
Menlo Park, California 94025
(415) 555-9681 / email@email.com

Graphic Designer
Experienced in Freelance Graphic Design and Production

Business-to-Consumer Project Design & Management
Full-Service Graphic Design Capabilities

Nine years' experience in graphic design and project management from initial concept to finished product. Extensive experience creating corporate identity/communication packages for the technical, medical, entertainment, and retail industries.

Core Strengths

Graphic Image Manipulation	Linotronic Outputs
Multicolor Printing	3-D Packaging
Publication Design	Visual Communications Media

Professional Experience

TARGET CORPORATION, Minneapolis, MN   1993 to Current

Graphic Designer—Advertising

Develop and design creative execution of concepts for assigned projects, including (but not limited to) magazine ads, newspaper ads, outdoor advertising, collateral, catalog page layout and design, POS signing, interactive advertising, packaging, style guides, press kits, and other related projects.

- Reduced advertising/marketing budget by $80,000 over a single year by streamlining budgeting practices.
- Received awards for print design; published in multiple graphic design "best of" books including Rockport Publishers *Computer Graphics 2*.
- Designed corporate collateral and organized project archiving system.

Education

Hampton University, Hampton, Virginia
Bachelor of Arts / Fine Arts, 1993

- Graphic Artist Intern, Century Marketing, Boulder, Colorado—1992
- Graduated with *Cum Laude* Distinction

References Furnished Immediately upon Request

Keywords

Art Design

Ad Layout

Desktop Publishing

POS Signing

Electronic Pitchbook

Presentation Library

Visual Communications Media

Business-to-Consumer (B2C) Projects

Printing and Prepress Processes

3-D Packaging

Large Format Printing

Graphic Image Manipulation

Sheet-Fed Press

Web Press

Typography

Linotronic Outputs

Color Separation

Photo Retouching

Multicolor Printing

Publication Design

Interview Q&A Using Keywords

Why should we hire you, what are your strengths, and how do you see yourself contributing to our company?

With a special knack for organization, system creation, streamlining work-flow, managing projects, and solving inefficiencies, I bring proficiency in the areas of sheet-fed and web press processes, large format printing, and desktop publishing. Offering collateral value as an experienced freelance graphic specialist for design staffing services, I have nine years of experience using QuarkXPress, Adobe Illustrator, Adobe Photoshop, Adobe Pagemaker, and various other support programs and plug-ins.

GUIDANCE COUNSELOR

Keywords

Counseling

Peer Counseling

Education
Vocational/Career
Counseling

Parent and Family
Relationships

Research

Regulatory
Compliance

Intervention

Educational
Programs

Multidisciplinary
Teams

Therapists

Special Education

At-Risk Student
Populations

Student Advocate

Supportive
Colleague

Test Administration

Interactive Learning

On-Line Classrooms

Committee
Leadership

Resume

David McClosky
6738 N. Frostwood Parkway
Peoria, Illinois 61615
(309) 555-2445 / email@email.com

High School Guidance Counselor
20-year track record of helping students develop academically and socially

Career Counseling / Parent & Family Relationships / Public Relations
Expertise in the Development of Effective Student Programs for School, Career, and Family

Creative, resourceful, and dedicated Guidance Counselor with a history of identifying the needs of various student populations and leading multidisciplinary teams to develop strategies to meet those needs. Excellent communication skills in relating to administrators, teachers, therapists, and family members. Reputation as a supportive colleague and a student advocate.

Core Strengths

Intervention	Targeted Educational Programs
Vocational/Career Counseling	Interactive Learning
On-Line Classrooms	Committee Leadership
Test Administration	Peer Counseling

Professional Experience

George Washington High School, Washington, Illinois   1980 to Present

Guidance Counselor

Facilitated both personal and career counseling, and conducted vocational testing. Acted as liaison to universities and the military, and developed college financial aid and career seminars for schools, parents, and students. Conducted parent and student information sessions. Interacted extensively with teachers and administrators regarding student progress, and made college admissions and scholarship information available as needed.

- Pioneered a program with a local community college to provide classes at the high school, giving eligible juniors and seniors dual credit for both high school and college coursework.
- Developed a vocational counseling program in concert with a part-time jobs program, and served as liaison to students and employers.
- Provided leadership for the following committees: Tech Prep, Interactive Learning, and Intervention for At-Risk Student Populations

Education

ILLINOIS STATE UNIVERSITY, Normal, Illinois
M.A. in Guidance and Counseling; Administrative Endorsement, 1980
B.S. in Biology and Physical Education (Double Major), 1975

Interview Q&A Using Keywords

Why should we hire you, what are your strengths, and how do you see yourself contributing to our company?

In addition to extensive counseling with both individual students and their families, I've had the opportunity to provide leadership on a number of committees. For example, I led the project to bring interactive learning to our school district, allowing students to take college courses via on-line classrooms and receive dual credit for both high school and college. I also helped set up the tech-prep program in our school in collaboration with a local community college. In addition, I've worked closely with multidisciplinary teams of teachers, administrators, therapists, social workers, and psychologists to identify intervention strategies for at-risk and special-education students who have special needs.

HAIR STYLIST

Resume

Cindy Lawson
123 S. Fourth Street
Kewanee, Illinois 61443
(309) 555-1234 / email@email.com

> **Professional Hair Stylist**
> **12-Year Background in Professional Hair Styling and Training**
>
> **Innovative Styling Techniques / Skilled Cosmetologist Trainer**
> **Safety Training, Quality Control, and Marketing Experience**

Creative and highly accomplished expert cosmetologist with a full range of styling, management, customer relations, marketing, and training skills. Background in working successfully with high-profile clientele.

Core Strengths

Customer Relations	Customer Loyalty
Creative Styling Techniques	Quality Control
Safety Training	Marketing
Customer Satisfaction	Shaping/Trimming
Perm Techniques	Curling/Tinting

Professional Experience

THE WAVE—Chicago, IL   1995 to Current

Head Stylist

Manage styling services for top-level clients and mentor new stylists in learning various cutting, shaping, tinting, curling, and perm techniques. Implemented weekly safety and styling meetings to improve quality and reduce incidents involving safety issues. Developed highly effective marketing techniques and trained staff to up-sell accessories effectively. Selected to provide services for numerous visiting celebrities.

- Routinely train stylists on new techniques and safety compliance issues.
- Spearheaded the purchase and use of the first ergonomically efficient chairs.
- Increased customer satisfaction by implementing procedures to raise quality.
- Achieved a 20% increase in accessory sales through aggressive marketing.

Education

UNIVERSITY OF CHICAGO, Chicago, Illinois
Bachelor of Arts: Business Management 1986
Illinois State Licensed Cosmetologist 1984

Keywords

Customer Relations
Stylist
Customer Loyalty
Training
Styling Techniques
Quality Control
Safety Training
Marketing
Ergonomically
  Efficient
Beautician
Cutting Methods
Tinting
Perm Techniques
Innovative
Shaping
Hair
Trimming
Curling
Customer
  Satisfaction
Creative

Interview Q&A Using Keywords

Why should our company hire you?

I have continued to keep my skills current by attending all trade shows and training in the three-state area. In addition to my expert styling techniques, I have trained many staff members on safety, quality assurance, marketing, and customer satisfaction issues. My specialties include coloring hair, perms and multilayered cuts. I have also been selected to provide personal stylist services for high-profile clients, and once worked the set for Oprah Winfrey's guests.

HELP DESK ADMINISTRATOR

Keywords

Inbound Services
Operations

End-User Support

First-Level
Customer Service

Networking
Environment

User Support
Specialist

Troubleshooting

Escalation Skills

Problem Resolution

Data
Communications

Call Center
Environment

Team Player

Help Desk and
Hardware Support

First-Level PC
Support

Product Launch
Support

Customer Service

On-Line CRM

Network
Architecture
Support

Customer
Communications

Front-Line Help
Desk

On-Call Operations
Support

Resume

Grace Matherly
43 Murdock Court
New Brunswick, New Jersey 08901
(732) 555-1234 / email@email.com

> **Help Desk Administrator / Help Desk Coordinator**
> **Productive, high-quality inbound services operations**
>
> **End-User Support / First-Level Customer Service**
> **Stand-Alone or Networking Environments**

User support specialist experienced in troubleshooting, escalation skills and problem resolution for networking and data communications in a call center environment. Cooperative team player, able to work under pressure.

Core Strengths

Help Desk and Hardware Support   First-Level PC Support
Product Launch Support   Customer Communications
Customer Service / On-Line CRM   Escalation Resolution
Network Architecture Support   Migrations and Upgrades

Professional Experience

PHARMA BIOTECH, Princeton, New Jersey   1998 to Current

Help Desk Administrator

Front-line help desk support technician experienced in end-user computing systems and network support for 1500 personnel in U.S. headquarters for top-five international manufacturer and distributor of biotech products. First point of contact for support incidents, as well as end-user instruction.

- Ensure effective and efficient on-call operations support for product launches, data communications migrations and upgrades, and sales. Won annual company award for "Exceptional Customer Service" in 2000.
- Investigate and resolve 95% of first-level inquiries utilizing on-line knowledge base, technical knowledge, and on-line CRM system.
- Assist application users by providing prompt responses, training one-on-one and in groups, and in reactive and proactive problem solving.

Education

Rutgers University, New Brunswick, New Jersey
Bachelor of Science, Computer Science—1998

- Computer Skills: Microsoft Suite XP and 2000 products, Win NT, Win XP and 2000, PC/mainframe applications, Unix, Linux, LAN/WAN, TCPIP and Novell networks, Magic Enterprise Help Desk software.

Interview Q&A Using Keywords

Why should we hire you, what are your strengths, and how do you see yourself contributing to our company?

With four years' experience providing complex front-line help desk support in a fast-paced sales support environment, I have gained in-depth escalation skills and technical knowledge ensuring first-level customer service of the highest caliber. Utilizing on-line knowledge base tools and analytical troubleshooting abilities, I have attained a problem resolution rate of 95% for first-point-of-contact inquiries. I would like to deliver exceptional customer support services to your organization.

HIGH SCHOOL TEACHER

Resume

Mary Brown
123 Fourth Avenue
Peoria, Illinois 61615
(309) 123-4567 / email@email.com

Secondary Teacher of English
12 Years' Classroom Experience Combined with 7 Years as a Speech Team Coach

Teaching Techniques include: Writing on computer, process writing, team teaching, cooperative learning groups, role playing, and the development of thematic units.

Resourceful and energetic teacher with a commitment to fostering lifetime learning in students. Positive, outgoing, and approachable, with a talent for drawing out young people and putting them at ease. Able to communicate effectively with parents, administrators, and colleagues.

Core Strengths

Curriculum Development	Classroom Management
Mentoring Colleagues & Students	Inclusion/Team Teaching with Special Education Teachers
Identifying Learner Needs	Helping Students Develop Critical Thinking Skills
Assertive Discipline	Teaching Writing as a Process

Professional Experience

ABC HIGH SCHOOL, Peoria, Illinois   1991 to Present

English Teacher / Speech Team Coach

Taught creative writing, process writing, writing on computer, and grammar, in addition to multiple literature units on Shakespeare, Steinbeck, and Hemingway. Coached speech team members and coordinated the group's participation in tournaments in various locations throughout central Illinois.

- Developed a number of thematic units, incorporating spelling, process writing, and grammar into various literature units.
- Effectively supervised and mentored three student teachers.
- Collaborated with special education teachers to design individualized lessons for students with special needs within an inclusive environment.

Education & Credentials

Illinois State University, Normal, Illinois
Bachelor of Arts in the Secondary Teaching of English, 1990
Minor in Speech Communication

- GPA: 3.8
- Summa Cum Laude

Keywords

Higher Education

Teaching

English

Mathematics

Guidance Counseling

Performance Based

Student Oriented

Student Success

Assertive Discipline

Team Teaching

Power Writing

Process Learning

Process Writing

Writing on Computer

Thematic Units

Curriculum Development

Continuing Education

Role Playing

Mentoring

Classroom Management

Lifelong Learning

Interview Q&A Using Keywords

Why should we hire you, what are your strengths, and how do you see yourself contributing to our company?

I have employed a number of classroom teaching strategies, including process writing, writing on computer, role playing, and the development of thematic units. In addition, I have had the opportunity to mentor three student teachers and participate in curriculum development for the English department. I believe in fostering an environment that leads to student success, and that includes adapting my teaching style to meet the needs of students at multiple socioeconomic and ability levels. In addition, I am comfortable in an inclusion environment, and I have extensive experience team teaching with special education teachers.

HUMAN RESOURCES MANAGER

Keywords

Resume

Naomi Alexander
234 Cypress Street
Freehold, New Jersey 07728
(201) 555-1234 / email@email.com

> ### HUMAN RESOURCES MANAGER
> **Top-notch experience in Fortune 500 companies**
>
> **Meeting Business Needs Through Expert Management of Employee Resources**

Five years' experience with accountability for all aspects of personnel administration in a 350-person department. Key responsibilities include:

Core Strengths

Benefits Administration	Manpower Planning
Organizational Development	Performance Appraisals
Recruitment and Retention	COBRA Administration
Salary Structures and Compensation	EEO and ADA requirements

Professional Experience

JOHNSON & JOHNSON, New Brunswick, NJ   1997 to Present
Human Resource Manager (1998–Present)
Human Resource Associate (1997–1998)

Hired for the associate position and quickly promoted to HR Manager—a transition that typically takes several years. As HR Manager, direct a multitude of personnel functions for exempt and nonexempt employees with emphasis on effective staffing, training, and retention of employees. Strong knowledge of COBRA, EEO, and ADA regulations.

- Revamped recruitment strategies placing added emphasis on campus initiatives. As a result, cost-per-hire expenses fell 35% this year.
- Conducted industrywide salary surveys and subsequently realigned our salary structure to reflect market trends.
- Overhauled antiquated job descriptions to reflect current job demands.
- Spearheaded an HRIS conversion within the department.

Education

Rutgers University, New Brunswick, NJ
Bachelor of Arts, Psychology, 1997

References Furnished Immediately upon Request

Interview Q&A Using Keywords

Why should we hire you, what are your strengths, and how do you see yourself contributing to our company?

With five years of progressively responsible positions in Human Resource Management, first in generalist roles and then in various HR specialties, I have broad-based experience with the ability to handle the multitude of issues that often arise within an organization such as yours. Key needs today include employee retention and hiring the best people the first time, and our employee satisfaction surveys and churn has been the best in the company history. In my present job, in addition to the staffing, benefits, and compensation functions, I have successfully revamped our career paths, which has contributed to increased employee retention.

Resume

Jane Smart
45-454 East King Street
Honolulu, Hawaii 96815
(808) 555-7873 / email@email.com

Image Consultant
Personalized Fashion Guidance

Wardrobe Analysis and Planning / Fashion Makeovers
Nonverbal Communications and Business Etiquette Authority

Dedicated professional seeking consultative position with mid- to large-size firm. Background includes 10 years' image design experience, 50+ corporate workshop presentations.

Core Strengths

Corporate Dress	Business Casual Dress
New Image Design	Closet Overhaul
Long-Term Wardrobe Planning	Shopping Skills Development
Color Analysis	Mannerisms

Professional Experience

IMAGINE THIS, Honolulu, Hawaii   1992 to Present

Proprietor / Image Consultant

In-person coaching of over 700 individuals to maximize their personal and professional image potential. Select clients include sports professionals, corporate senior management, and lawyers. Key areas of guidance include professional and casual dress, often requiring complete wardrobe overhaul.

- Helped rookie salesperson with wardrobe color analysis. New look contributed to 30% hike in personal sales volume.
- Designed fashion makeover for laid-off 48-year-old middle manager—business and casual dress. Boost in confidence helped client land better-paying, more responsible position within a month.

Education

San Diego State University, San Diego, California
Bachelor of Arts / Marketing, 1986

- 4.0 GPA
- Who's Who Among American College Students

References Furnished Immediately upon Request

Keywords

Corporate Dress

Professional Dress

Business Casual

Casual Dress

Dress for Success

New Image Design

Wardrobe Analysis

Long-Term
  Wardrobe Planning

Closet Overhaul

Fashion Makeovers

Shopping Skills
  Development

Personal Shopping

Color Analysis

Hair

Mannerisms

Nonverbal
  Communications

Business Etiquette

In-Person
  Consulting

Corporate
  Workshops

Wedding Planning

Interview Q&A Using Keywords

Why should we hire you, what are your strengths, and how do you see yourself contributing to our company?

I have a 10-year track record of advising individuals on dress-for-success techniques, significantly heightening their professional potential. I am an experienced workshop presenter, and will advise and guide your workforce on basics of image design, including professional dress, wardrobe color analysis, and long-term image planning. I am also an expert at teaching essential nonverbal communication and business etiquette skills, enhancing your company's professionalism in the mind of your customers.

INSURANCE CLAIMS ADJUSTER

Resume

Sharon Tamiya
72801 Robin Lane
Ojai, California 93023
(805) 555-1122 / email@email.com

Claims Adjustor
Independent Contractor

Automobile
Collision / Theft / Personal Injury

Independent Claims Adjustor—nine years
representing major automobile insurers and underwriters
California insurance adjuster's license #C5551212
Arizona insurance adjuster's license #A5558888

Core Strengths

Site Investigations   Communications/Interviews
Estimating   Interviewing
Project Management   Remaining Calm in Emergencies

Professional Experience

Claims Adjuster / Independent Contractor   **1991 to Current**
Investigating, estimating, and resolving motor vehicle collision claims. Conduct crash site investigation. Take statements from witnesses. Assess damage (property, theft, or personal bodily injury). Photograph and document site. Analyze police and witness reports for inconsistencies. Reinterview if warranted. Determine liability after consideration of uninsured motorist and third-party involvement. Make repair/replace recommendations. Submit Xactimate estimates in final report submitted to field office.

- Mobile Office Capability: 2002 Chevy 4X SUV with laptop computer, GPS, mapping software, printer, cell, and digital camera.

Education

Insurance Institute of America, Malvern, Pennsylvania
Associate in Claims (AIC) / 2001
Registered Professional Adjusters, Inc., Napa, California
Registered Professional Adjuster (RPA)

References Furnished Immediately upon Request

Interview Q&A Using Keywords

Why should we hire you, what are your strengths, and how do you see yourself contributing to our company?

I offer a combination of critical claims adjusting and project management skills in addition to industry licenses and certifications. With adjuster's licenses for both California and Arizona, I can extend my operations over a greater area. With my high-tech, mobile office you get 24/7 accessibility and state-of-the-art electronic communications. I prepare my reports in the field and submit them electronically, while on my way to our next job.

Resume

Stephen Gallegos
456 Kelley Road
Dallas, Texas 75240
(214) 555-1122 / email@email.com

SUCCESSFUL INSURANCE SALESMAN
with more than 13 years of outstanding achievements

2001 Company Salesman of the Year
$14 million in annual sales

Proven track record of success in the sales of life and health insurance with recognition for new market start-ups, increasing annual sales from $6 million to $14 million in six years, and consistently exceeding quotas.

Core Strengths

Unique prospecting techniques	Interfacing with senior executives
Developing long-term relationships	Securing referrals from clients
Strategic marketing	New product introductions
Strong presentation skills	Excellent customer service

Professional Experience

L & H INSURANCE COMPANY, Dallas, Texas   1995 to present

District Sales Representative

Prospect for new clients, make formal presentations, and close sales in the North Texas District. Focus on small to medium-size businesses as well as individuals, analyze their needs and recommend the appropriate products to build their confidence and trust. Develop and implement strategic marketing and advertising plans. Provide excellent service to all clients to generate repeat business and referrals.

- Opened three new markets and generated $1 million in the first year.
- Increased annual territory sales to $14 million in 2001.
- Secured a Fortune 100 company with $3 million in annual premiums.
- Received the Top District Sales Award in all four quarters of 2001.

Education

Baylor University, Waco, Texas
Bachelor of Business Administration Degree; 1995
GPA: 3.8
Dean's List in every semester

References Furnished Immediately upon Request

Keywords

Insurance Sales
Increased Sales
Exceeded Quotas
Sales Awards
Prospecting
Presentations
Closing Skills
Relationships
Repeat Business
Referrals
Customer Needs
Customer Service
Interface
Licensed
Insurance Products
Product Introductions
Territory
Strategic Plans
Forecasting
Client Base

Interview Q&A Using Keywords

Why should we hire you, what are your strengths, and how do you see yourself contributing to our company?

I have more than 13 years of outstanding achievements in the sales of life and health insurance generating as much as $14 million annually. My strengths include the ability to secure new clients, interface with senior executives, and develop strong relationships resulting in long-term repeat and referral business. I believe my excellent prospecting, presentation, and closing skills will produce outstanding sales results that will contribute greatly to the continued growth and success of your company.

INTERIOR DESIGNER

Resume

Margaret West-Hafford, ASID
12 Linden Court
Southampton, New York 11968
(516) 555-8787 / email@email.com

INTERIOR DESIGNER

Focused on creating comfortable yet innovative interior spaces

---

Over 10 years' experience helping a wide variety of clients surround themselves with beautiful, functional environments. Skilled in all aspects of space planning for residential, commercial, and industrial projects.

Core Strengths

Traditional, Old World, & Contemporary Design	Floor Plans
Construction & Renovation Projects	Space Planning
Budgeting	Architectural Elements
Design Trends	Accessories

Professional Experience

INTERIOR DIMENSIONS, Southampton, New York   1990 to Present

Interior Designer

Work collaboratively with clients from initial consultation to completion of interior design projects. Utilize strong drafting skills to create detailed floor plans to assist in construction and renovation phases. Provide input on architectural elements and select and purchase furnishings/accessories. Frequently visit New York City showrooms keeping abreast of design trends to offer maximum options to clientele.

- Won first place design award for *Most Inviting Master Bedroom*, Muttontown Interior Designers Showcase, November 2001.
- Designed and commissioned a one-of-a-kind faux finish to replicate an old world plaster effect for the Oheka Castle renovation.

Education

New York University, New York, New York
Bachelor of Fine Arts, Art History, 1985
Metropolitan Institute of Interior Design, Plainview, New York
Diploma, Interior Design, 1999

Affiliations

Professional Membership, American Society of Interior Designers

References Furnished Immediately upon Request

Keywords

- Residential
- Commercial
- Industrial
- Trends
- Space Planning
- Floor Plans
- Drafting
- Architectural Elements
- Budgeting
- Consultations
- Traditional
- Old World
- Contemporary
- Construction
- Faux Finishes
- Renovations
- Furnishings
- Showrooms
- Accessories
- Interior Design Showcases

Interview Q&A Using Keywords

Why should we hire you, what are your strengths, and how do you see yourself contributing to our company?

I'd like to think that what sets me apart from other interior designers is the flexibility I bring to each project. Though like most professionals in this field, I have strong preferences in what I consider truly beautiful, I remain entirely open and adaptable to the wants and styles of my clients. For example, I've had clients recommend me to friends and in the process called me a contemporary design specialist, while others just weeks later have referred to me as a traditional designer. I get a real kick out of that.

INVENTORY CONTROL MANAGER

Resume

John E. Davis
925 Grand Avenue South
St. Paul, Minnesota 55104
(651) 555-3498 / email@email.com

> **Inventory Control Manager**
> **18-Year Career Complemented by MRP and CIRM Credentials**
>
> **Broad Materials Management Experience ...**
> **Industry Networking / Multisite Global Operations**

A keen eye for improving efficiency while controlling costs. Consistently able to identify problems and implement solutions. Track record of achieving order accuracy, trimming fulfillment costs, reducing capital asset deployment, and cutting spoilage/loss and shrinkage.

Core Strengths

Contract administration	Acquisition management
Identification and tracking	Automatic data capture
Real-time inventory	Supplier management
Cost control and reduction	Inventory protection

Professional Experience

BENSON INDUSTRIES, St. Paul, Minnesota   1995 to Current

Inventory Control Manager

Manage daily operations of a 54-person inventory control division with both union labor and support personnel. Manage $68 million inventory. Enhance real-time features: inventory receipts, withdrawals, availability, commitments, and customer service information. Direct acquisition management function responsibilities for over $1 billion in annual expenditures. Oversee contract administration, negotiation, and rebid functions for over $200 million in annual subcontracts. Established inventory protection programs for components and subcontractors.

- Implemented an automatic data capture network system using bar codes and radio frequency.
- Reduced raw-material inventory by 38% in first year, without write-outs or stock-outs.
- Achieved 2000 material cost savings of 39%, and 28% during 2001.
- Integrated a supplier management model based on partnership strategies and visions.

Education

St. Cloud State University, St. Cloud, Minnesota
Bachelor of Science: Business Management, 1984

- Inventory & Materials Management Diploma, St. Cloud Technical College, 1981
- 3.78 GPA

References Furnished Immediately upon Request

Keywords

- Certified Integrated Resource Manager (CIRM)
- Material Requirements Planning (MRP) Certification
- Industry Networking
- Inventory Planning and Control
- Materials Management
- Contract Administration and Negotiation
- Real-Time Inventory
- Acquisition Management
- Multisite Operations
- Cost Control and Reduction
- Improved Efficiency
- Supplier Management
- Global Locations
- Inventory Document Development
- Item Identification
- Inventory Protection Programs
- Leadership Strengths
- Item Tracking
- Cycle Counts
- Automatic Data Capture

Interview Q&A Using Keywords

Why should we hire you, what are your strengths, and how do you see yourself contributing to our company?

As an 18-year veteran in inventory control and planning, I will ensure improved efficiency with controlled costs. I have directed globally located, multisite operations, and managed multiyear supply agreements as large as $60 million. My CIRM and MRP credentials are backed by significant real-time inventory and automatic data capture experience. I have a track record of applying innovative, state-of-the-art concepts in cycle counts, item identification, and tracking. My expertise in developing inventory protection programs, documents, and contracts has resulted in industry networking.

Resume

Susan Stafford
98765 Writers Lane
Dallas, Texas 75252
(469) 555-1122 / email@email.com

HIGHLY PUBLISHED JOURNALIST
with 10 years of outstanding accomplishments

Newspapers, Magazines, and Trade Journals
Dallas "Writer of the Year" in 2001

Creative and analytical journalist who constantly comes up with story ideas, conducts research, utilizes various resources, and is technology savvy, to develop well-written and interesting articles.

Core Strengths

Excellent writing skills	Investigative/factual information
Multiple projects	Always meets specified deadlines
Disciplined/detail-oriented	Editing and proofreading
Journalism degree	Electronic publishing

Professional Experience

STAFFORD & ASSOCIATES, Dallas, Texas   1992 to present

Independent Journalist

Constantly seek out newspapers, magazines, and trade journals that welcome creative and factual articles. Present story ideas to publishers and editors and determine specific deadlines. Conduct research, utilize resources, organize materials, and use excellent writing skills to develop well-written and interesting articles. Edit and proofread all articles before submitting for publication.

- Six articles published in the *Texas State Newspaper* in 2001.
- Guest columnist in the *Wall Street Bulletin* in July of 2001.
- Selected from among 25 Independent Journalist to create a weekly home improvement column in the *Texas Home and Garden Magazine*.
- 2001 "Writer of the Year" Award presented by the Dallas Writers Club.

Education

Texas Tech University, Lubbock, Texas
Bachelor of Arts Degree; Major: Journalism; 1991
GPA: 4.0
Member of Phi Kappa Beta Honor Society

References Furnished Immediately upon Request

Keywords

Writing Skills

Creative

Analytical

Ideas

Research

Interviewing

Investigative

Factual Information

Utilize Resources

Editing

Proofreading

Meets Deadlines

Magazines and
Journals

Multiple Projects

Creative Writing

Fiction

Journalism Degree

Communication
Skills

Nonfiction

Electronic
Publishing

Interview Q&A Using Keywords

Why should we hire you, what are your strengths, and how do you see yourself contributing to our company?

I am a creative and analytical journalist who has been published in several major newspapers, magazines, and trade journals since 1992. I continually work on multiple projects, including interviewing, organizing materials, conducting research to obtain factual information, and using my excellent, detail-oriented writing skills. I always meet specified deadlines. I can contribute greatly to your company by always coming up with story ideas and utilizing various resources to develop well-written and interesting articles.

LAB TECHNICIAN

Resume

Eleanor M. Salerno
2 Pennsylvania Way
East Brentwood, New York 11717
(631) 232-5555
email@email.com

Laboratory Technician
10 years of experience in medical and clinical laboratory settings

Specimen analysis and reporting / Clinical data processing
Instrument calibration and maintenance

Cross-trained in broad areas of medical laboratory procedures including hematology, microscopy, chemistry, serology, and bacteriologic testing. Organized and analytical with exceptional time management, error reduction, and outcome reporting skills.

Core Strengths

Hematology/Phlebotomy	Specimen Handling
Blood Bank	Infection Control
Equipment Care	Medical Waste Removal
Quality Assurance	Northern/Western Blot Analyses

Professional Experience

ALL SAINTS HOSPITAL, West Islip, New York   1996 to Present

Laboratory Technician
Work collaboratively with a medical technologist to maintain a compliant department that strictly adheres to regulatory guidelines. Interface with all concerned throughout multiple hospital units. Perform laboratory tests, routine preventive maintenance, and quality control procedures. Analyze, interpret, record, and communicate test results, and ensure the integrity of computerized systems and high-end equipment functionality.

- Coordinate in-service training programs for new clinical assistants.
- Continue to reduce the annual error rate for specimen testing by 20%.
- Participate in audits to ensure regulatory compliance and state funding.
- Render off-site phlebotomy services across the medical community.

Education

Suffolk County Community College, Brentwood, New York
Associate in Applied Science: Medical Laboratory Technology, 1992

- **New York State Certified Phlebotomist**
- **Member, American Association for Clinical Chemistry**

References Furnished Immediately upon Request

Keywords

Analysis and Reporting

Bone Marrow Slides

Chemistry

Clinical Data Processing

Coagulation

Cross-Trained

Customer Care

Fire and Safety

Hematology/ Phlebotomy

Infection Control

In-Service Training

Inventory Control

Medical Laboratory Procedures

Medical Waste Removal

Northern/Western Blot Analyses

Quality Assurance

Specialized Equipment Care

Specimen Handling

Urinalysis

Venipuncture

Interview Q&A Using Keywords

Why should we hire you, what are your strengths, and how do you see yourself contributing to our company?

As an evening shift laboratory technician of 10 years, I am recognized for my ability to prioritize, coordinate, and perform tasks concurrently during periods of limited staffing and supervision. I offer cross-trained experience in areas of hematology, phlebotomy, blood bank, urinalysis, coagulation, chemistry, bone marrow slides, vital signs, venipuncture, and fire and safety. I am confident that my technical, clinical, and administrative abilities would ensure the integrity of your hospital's laboratory functions in areas of quality assurance, clinical data processing, and specialized instrument/equipment care management.

<table>
<tr><td>

</td><td>

Resume

Rachel Oster
6738 N. Frostwood Parkway
Peoria, Illinois 61615
(309) 555-2445 / email@email.com

School Librarian
Fostering a love of learning in young people of all ages for 15 years

Children's Librarian / Reference Librarian
Forging Links with Children, Parents, and Educators to Enhance Learning

Information and resource specialist with a background in the development of numerous after-school programs. Excellent research and organizational / cataloguing skills combined with the ability to communicate effectively with people at all levels and provide first-class service.

Core Strengths

Tutoring	Promoting Literacy
Reader's Advisory	Internet Research
Cataloguing	Multiple Disciplines (languages/social sciences/literature)
On-Line Circulation	Providing Positive Customer Service

Professional Experience

FORBES SCHOOL SYSTEM, Forbes, Illinois   1990 to Present

Librarian

Oversee all operations for a library serving four schools, elementary through high school, with responsibility for the hiring, scheduling, and supervision of part-time student staff. Serve as reference librarian to students of all ages. Collaborate with teachers to coordinate library time and training for various classes, and direct multiple after-school programs.

- Conducted a thorough assessment of the information systems of other school libraries, both through personal visits and via telephone with librarians, and updated the Forbes Library to incorporate many of their features.
- Implemented specialized catalogues and indexes, making research materials more accessible.
- Setup a "Computer Day" one Saturday each month to teach Internet research to interested students.

Education

UNIVERSITY OF ILLINOIS, Urbana, Illinois
Master of Library Science (MLS), 1989
Bachelor of Science in French; Minor in Spanish, 1986
Bachelor of Science in Human Relations; Minor in English Literature, 1983

</td></tr>
</table>

Interview Q&A Using Keywords

Why should we hire you, what are your strengths, and how do you see yourself contributing to our company?

Of course, I have an MLS from an ALA Accredited University. In addition, I have extensive coursework in multiple disciplines including history, psychology, French, and Renaissance literature. But I believe that all the knowledge in the world isn't very helpful to a librarian who doesn't possess good customer service skills, so I have always tried to be very sensitive to the needs of our patrons. In that regard, I've developed a number of activities and events to reach multiple populations, including an adult literacy program, and an after-school tutoring and homework-help program.

Resume

Andrew Bankwell
24-680 Waikiki Boulevard
Honolulu, Hawaii 96818
(808) 555-3265 / email@email.com

> **Professional Chauffeur**
> **Enhancing the Limousine Experience**
>
> **Airport Transfers / Special Events / City Tours**
> **Courteous and Professional**

Expert driver with detailed knowledge of island roads and sight-seeing points of interest. Experienced with stretch limos and luxury SUVs. Hold current commercial driver's license.

Core Strengths

Customer Service	Customer Loyalty
Itinerary Planning	VIP Handling
City Tours	Sight-Seeing Destinations
Entertainment Destinations	Special Occasions

Professional Experience

STRETCH OF THE IMAGINATION LIMOS, Honolulu, Hawaii   1995 to Current

Limousine Driver / Chauffeur

Primary activities include client/VIP airport pick-up for area businesses. Also drive for variety of exclusive events, including weddings, birthdays, and graduations. Accountable for light cleaning and minor maintenance of vehicles. Ensure adequate supply of convenience items (newspapers, magazines, and drinks) and proper functioning of cellular phone, CD player, and television. Teach quarterly safety training class for new chauffeurs.

- Regularly receive positive letters of commendation from satisfied local and international clients.
- Received *Chauffeur of the Year 2001 Award* for customer loyalty.
- Researched and wrote circle-island limousine tour script.

Education

Kapiolani Community College, Honolulu, Hawaii
Associate of Science / Hospitality Management, 1991

- Internship at Royal Hawaiian Hotel

References Furnished Immediately upon Request

Keywords

Chauffeur

Stretch Limousines

Luxury SUVs

Airport Transfers

Special Occasions

Weddings

Birthdays

Bachelor Parties

Graduations

City Tours

Business Client Pick-Up

VIPs

Commercial Driver's License

Safety Training

Customer Service

Customer Loyalty

Convenience Items

Itinerary Planning

Entertainment Destinations

Sight-Seeing Destinations

Interview Q&A Using Keywords

Why should we hire you, what are your strengths, and how do you see yourself contributing to our company?

As a limousine driver, I will contribute to your profitability through my ability to create loyal customers. I am a reliable, courteous, and detail-oriented driver. I skillfully anticipate the needs of my passengers. I have driven for literally hundreds of special occasions, from birthdays to wedding anniversaries, and conscientiously set the appropriate atmosphere for each. In addition, my island-wide tour itineraries have become somewhat legendary—clients love them and regularly refer friends to me.

Keywords

Resume

Ryan Smith
309 Main Street
Albany, New York 06548
(518) 555-1122 / email@email.com

Mortgage Loan Officer / Originator
Prime & Subprime Markets

Top-Producing Loan Officer
Expert in Mortgage Banking, Training, Sales, and Finance

Loan officer with extensive experience underwriting multifamily and commercial real estate loans and providing lending products in branches of a bank having the highest rate of growth in the state.

Core Strengths

Loan Origination Programs	FHA, VA, and Conventional Products
Desktop Underwriting	Preapproval Programs
Point-of-Sale Systems	Financial Services Reporting Software
MS Business Administration	Conventional A thru D Paper

Professional Experience

Norwest Financial, Albany, New York   1998 to Present

Senior Loan Officer

Reporting directly to the director of the branch, manage eight loan officers with responsibility for $288 million in production, plus full responsibility for training. In addition to personal account management and sales responsibility, recruited to design point-of-sale systems and preapproval programs to boost market share in a highly competitive market.

- Closed over $30,000,000 in FHA, VA and conventional products since 1998.
- Established eight new locations nationwide.
- Increased loan volume by 50% resulting in $18,000,000 in new revenue.
- Established equity loan products including primary and secondary trust deeds.

Education

University of Michigan, Ann Arbor, Michigan
Masters in Business Administration/Finance, 1997

- Member, National Association of Mortgage Brokers
- MS Word 1997, Excel, Access, and WordPerfect

References Furnished Immediately upon Request

Interview Q&A Using Keywords

Why should we hire you, what are your strengths, and how do you see yourself contributing to our company?

As a senior loan officer with more than five years of successful service, I offer extensive experience in both prime and subprime lending markets. You will find that I have a verifiable track record of success for meeting and exceeding sales objectives, and will consistently deliver strong revenue and profit contributions through aggressive account management and superior customer service initiatives.

LOSS PREVENTION MANAGER

Resume

Joel S. Lawson
3 Bradford Drive
Bristol, CT 06010
(860) 555-1212 / email@email.com

> **Loss Prevention Manager**
> **12 years' experience with nationally recognized retailers**
>
> **Proven expertise in reducing retail losses through proactive measures**

Driven to achieve substantial reductions in profit losses through leadership, vigilance, and planning and execution of top-notch loss prevention strategies.

Core Strengths

Asset protection	Policies and procedures
Fraud training	Electronic surveillance
Auditing	Undercover operations
Security reports	Internal theft investigations

Professional Experience

COACH, Inc. New York, NY   1990 to Present
Loss Prevention Manager (1994–Present)
Loss Prevention Associate (1990–1994)

Oversee activities pertaining to loss prevention in 300 stores across the United States. Review audits of store inventory and assess discrepancies. Consult with company executives regarding inventory inconsistencies. Formulate and administer company policies with regard to antitheft procedures at the store level. Train store personnel in proper procedures for interacting with customers engaged in dishonest activity.

- Achieved a 40% reduction in shrinkage from 1996 to 2001.
- Researched, evaluated, purchased, and implemented state-of-the-art surveillance equipment for all stores. New equipment, prominently displayed, is credited with a reduction in store theft.
- Instituted undercover operations using store detectives posing as sales staff. To date informants have identified 10 company employees involved in theft of merchandise.

Education

Long Island University, C.W. Post Campus, Brookville, NY
Bachelor of Arts, Criminal Justice, 1990

References Furnished Immediately upon Request

Keywords

Asset Protection

Inventory Shortage Analysis

Electronic Surveillance

Security Operations

Industrial Security

Stolen Property

Store Detectives

Undercover Operations

Auditing

Security Breaches

Employee Integrity Interviews

Policies and Procedures

Revenue Loss

Security Reports

Informants

Internal Theft Investigations

Physical Inventory

Shrinkage

Chargebacks

Fraud Training

Interview Q&A Using Keywords

Why should we hire you, what are your strengths, and how do you see yourself contributing to our company?

There are many similarities between the challenges your company has and the ones present in the company I am with now. As I see it, the number of stores, the type of items sold, and even the typical customers, are strikingly similar. As such, I can offer my ability to hit the ground running. I am confident that my full knowledge of asset protection including physical inventory monitoring, fraud training, and security reporting will provide the answers to any difficulties you have in this area.

Keywords

Decision Making/ Analysis

Accounting

Budget Control

Staff Training & Development

Cost and Quality

Business Taxation

Customer Service

Forecasting and Analysis

Operations Management

Process Management

Business Development/ Administration

Organizational Leadership

Team Building & Leadership

Problem Solving

Budget Development & Administration

Sales & Marketing

Relationship Building

Goal Setting/ Incentive Programs

Organizational Leadership

Profit and Loss

Resume

Justin Coury
3452 Broman St.
Cincinnati, Ohio, 45327
(513) 555-4567 / email@email.com

Management
Combining organizational leadership with profit & loss experience

Decision Making/Analysis • Staff Training & Development
Business Development/Administration • Budget Development

Extremely motivated entry-level management professional offering formal education in management as well as hands-on management experience within fast-paced retail settings.

Core Strengths

Accounting	Customer Service
Budget Control	Forecasting and Analysis
Cost and Quality Theory	Process/Operations Management
Business Taxation	Team Building & Leadership

Professional Experience

FOOTPROOF, Cincinnati, Ohio   2000 to Current

Manager

Ensure performance of daily operations within fast-paced shoe retail store ranked third in region. Accountable for proactive sales and marketing of store items as well as developing problem-solving strategies that address profit and loss issues. Provide excellent customer service, and focused on expanding referral base by building relationships with repeat customers.

- Increased store profits by 35% within only three months of employment.
- Successfully implemented new goal setting/incentive programs.
- Recipient of "Golden Foot" for consistently exceeding store goals.
- Decisively replaced lagging employees with goal-driven individuals.

Education

Klipplinger College of Business, Boulder, Colorado
Bachelor of Science, Management, 2000

- Young Professionals student chapter, vice president
- Honors Society, member

References Furnished Immediately upon Request

Interview Q&A Using Keywords

Why should we hire you, what are your strengths, and how do you see yourself contributing to our company?

I have paid for nearly 90% of my education while serving as a sales associate in a retail setting. Promoted to a management position, I have been afforded the opportunity to gain hands-on experience in profit/loss, staff hiring/development, and business development processes. Reinforcing my professional experience is a formal education in business management, which added to my knowledge in budget development and administration, forecasting/analysis, and operations management, will produce successful results.

MANUFACTURER'S REPRESENTATIVE

Resume

Mark Williams
3443 Sandy Hill Drive
Birmingham, Alabama 35201
(205) 555-1212 / email@email.com

> **Manufacturer's Representative (A vested partner in your success)**
> **Building and keeping OEM sales high—at the lowest cost of sales**
>
> **Compiling, tracking, and using comprehensive customer databases**
> **to great advantage**
> **Maintaining steady territory presence**

An experienced, "hungry" sales professional with an in-depth knowledge of a rich and developing territory. A master at finding and using competitive intelligence to put us inside your competitors' sales decision cycles.

Core Strengths

Closing	Anticipating specific customer needs
Selling related, but not competitive, products	Making every call a relationship call
Building or recovering distributor networks	Finding emerging markets

Professional Experience

Vulcan General Manufacturing, Birmingham, Alabama   1992 to Current
Manufacturer's Representative

Manage a large territory effectively and efficiently. Find and cement lasting relationships with purchasing decision makers. Develop, implement, and continually improve marketing and sales strategies that match our corporate strengths with our customers' ever-changing needs. Increase the number of SKUs sold to each account

- Reignited a distributor network that had been neglected for years. Sales up 22%.
- Captured an account that had relied upon a traditional sales rep. for five years. Revenue from this account exceeds $250K annually.
- Increased add-on sales last quarter at the highest rate ever recorded for our company.

Education

University of Alabama, Birmingham, Alabama
Bachelor of Science in Marketing, 1990

Keywords

Manufacturing

Construction

Metals and Raw Materials

Fabrication

Consulting Services

Customer Database

Decision Cycle

Emerging Markets

Entrepreneur

Increasing the Number of SKUs

Independent Marketing Partners

Market Niche

OEM Business

Product Knowledge

Qualified Dealer Network

Recover and Build a Distributor Network

Related but Not Competitive Products

Relationship Calls

Field Sales

Steady Territory Presence

Interview Q&A Using Keywords

Why should we hire you, what are your strengths, and how do you see yourself contributing to our company?

You should put me on your team if you want to minimize the cost of sales and maximize your return on investment. I could never have been successful as a manufacturer's rep. without the polished skills that come with years of solid performance as a sales professional. Add to that credential a detailed knowledge of your territory, a permanent presence before your customers, and relationships that let me exploit industry trends faster than ever-changing sales forces and we have a solid foundation for a mutually profitable arrangement. Remember, because you don't pay me a base salary, I must sell in order to live.

Keywords

Project Management

Brand Recognition

Market Share

Collateral Material

Direct Marketing

Communication Strategies

Media Relations

Press Releases

Intranet

Web Site

Distribution Channels

Product Offerings

New Product Launch

Quark XPress, FrontPage, Flash, Java, HTML

Vendor Sourcing/ Outsourcing

Talent Management

Competition, Market, Trend Analysis

Consumer Relations

Marketing Plan Development

Strategic Planning

Resume

Robin Claterbaugh
736 Marquette Avenue
Milwaukee, Wisconsin 53202
(414) 555-1492 / email@email.com

Marketing Manager

Creative, innovative marketing manager with expertise in creating sales collateral, direct marketing, and communication strategies to drive revenue, product offerings, and new marketing opportunities.

Core Strengths

Project management	Media relations
Web marketing and e-solutions	Trend/market analysis
Talent management	Strategic marketing plans
Brand recognition	New product launch

Professional Experience

MORGAN BANK, Milwaukee, Wisconsin   1998 to Present

Marketing Manager, Insurance Division

Administer a $2 million marketing budget. Create sales collateral, direct marketing, and communication strategies to drive revenue, grow product offerings, and identify new marketing opportunities for this $300 million division. Identify methods to market strategically and drive sale and distribution of insurance products through distribution channels. Keep abreast of competition and trends. Manage vendor relationships.

- Strategized and collaborated with SJ Bank to develop communication program, including page of Morgan Bank's Intranet, regarding its acquisition. Coordinated media relations for coverage of acquisition.
- Created and developed pages for Major Bank Insurance Group's intranet. Project involved converting policies/procedures into HTML, creating electronic access to newsletter, site navigation testing, and more.

Education

University of Wisconsin-Milwaukee, Milwaukee, Wisconsin
Bachelor of Business Administration: Marketing, 1995

- Member of the American Marketing Association—Student Chapter

Interview Q&A Using Keywords

Why should we hire you, what are your strengths, and how do you see yourself contributing to our company?

As an innovative, results-oriented marketing manager, I am experienced with creating and developing sales materials/collateral, direct marketing, and communication strategies to drive revenue, grow product offerings, and identify new marketing opportunities. In one project, I utilized HTML to convert polices, procedures, and product information for our company Web site, which significantly increased sales and market share. I have also had a tour in sales, which enables me to understand that both sales and the end customer are my two customers.

Resume

Ross Johnson
123 S. Fourth Street
Kewanee, Illinois 61443
(309) 555-1234 / email@email.com

Media Buyer
Highly Skilled in Branding Strategies within International Markets

Experienced in Multimedia Technology and Strategic Positioning
Solid Purchasing and Marketing Experience

Talented media buyer and marketing professional with a unique balance of hands-on experience. Thorough understanding of strategic positioning, buy analysis, multichannel media distribution, and negotiation techniques.

Core Strengths

Corporate Communications	Print Advertising
International Markets	Imaging Technology
Client Relations	Electronic Media
Branding Strategies	Purchasing
Buy Analysis	Quality Assurance

Professional Experience

MEDIA NOW TECHNOLOGIES—Hamond, IL   1999 to Current

Assistant Media Buyer

Manage 10 top-level key accounts in directing all aspects of international media buying. Collaborate with top-level client management teams to review branding strategies, negotiate purchasing terms, and ensure strategic positioning by selecting quality electronic, print, and television media. Oversee client relations, quality assurance, corporate communications, and contracts for additional creative services.

- Negotiated major media buys for all 10 clients with $22.5 million to profits.
- Played a key role in three clients' breaking into international markets.
- Reengineered internal buy analysis strategies, increasing accuracy by 30%.
- Created six national and four international brand management campaigns.

Education

UNIVERSITY OF ILLINOIS, Collinsville, Illinois
Bachelor of Arts: Marketing 1998
Bachelor of Arts: Corporate Communications 1987

Keywords

Marketing

Purchasing

Buying

Corporate Communications

Multimedia Technology

Strategic Positioning

Buy Analysis

Print Advertising

Television

Imaging Technology

International Markets

Negotiation

Multichannel Media Distribution

Client Relations

Quality Assurance

Advertising Communications

Brand Management

Creative Services

Electronic Media

Branding Strategies

Interview Q&A Using Keywords

Why Should Our Company Hire You?

Because I have held both buying and marketing positions, I know the business from both sides. I have a thorough understanding of media marketing, brand management, and strategic positioning from my previous experience, which better equips me to buy media effectively for my clients. I also have solid Corporate Communications and Marketing credentials, along with hands-on experience in print advertising and television.

MEDICAL BILLING SUPERVISOR

Resume

Karen Odom
789 White Boulevard
Dallas, Texas 75240
(972) 555-1212 / email@email.com

MEDICAL BILLING SUPERVISOR
with 14 years of diversified experience

Consistently commended for accurate transactions
and a low percentage of delays in payments

A dedicated medical billing supervisor with experience in fast-paced environments with Dallas-based healthcare companies focusing on streamlining procedures to maximize productivity and profitability.

Core Strengths

Managed care experience
Rapid processing of claims
Low delays in payments
Team environment of employees

Employee-Assisted Programs (EAP)
Accurate transactions and coding
Resolve patient problems quickly
Excellent reports and statistics

Professional Experience

DALLAS MEDICAL PRACTICE, Dallas, Texas   1990 to present

Medical Billing Supervisor

Supervise a team of six employees in the daily verification of insurance, patient eligibility, coding, and processing of claims. Ensure that accurate transactions are entered as fast as possible and research any billing problems to eliminate "explanation of benefits notices" and delays in payments from insurance companies. Prepare weekly and monthly reports and statistics for the Clinical Director and Chief Financial Officer.

- Managed the successful processing of 20,000 billings/claims in 2001.
- Maintained a 96% to 98% accuracy rating of all transactions.
- Increased employee productivity by revising job responsibilities.
- Implemented new medical billing software and trained all employees.

Education

Richland College, Richardson, Texas
Associate of Arts Degree; 1987
Major: Accounting
GPA: 3.75

References Furnished Immediately upon Request

Interview Q&A Using Keywords

Why should we hire you, what are your strengths, and how do you see yourself contributing to our company?

I have 14 years of medical billing supervisory experience with Dallas-based healthcare companies. My supervisors have consistently commended me for accurate transactions, coding, and processing of claims with a low percentage of delays in payments. I have also built a team of dedicated employees who concentrate daily on resolving problems and providing excellent service to all patients while maintaining strict confidentiality. My outstanding accomplishments are proof of how I will contribute greatly to your company.

NATIONAL ACCOUNT SALES

Resume

Tonya Stevens
815 Carmack Way
Tipp City, Ohio 45371
(937) 555-3396 / email@email.com

National Account Sales
Dynamic Career in Sales, Management, & Marketing in fiercely competitive, high-growth businesses. Expert in managing top-producing organizations.

New Product Launch / Profit & Loss Control / Key Account Management
Strategic, Sales, & Business Planning / Marketing & Advertising

---

Outstanding presentation, negotiation and sales-closing skills. Ability to merge cross-functional teams. Consistently achieve objectives, even during periods of increased competition & economic downturns.

Core Strengths

Teaming & Leadership	Consultative Sales
Direct & Indirect Sales	Global Marketing
Revenue & Profit Growth	Multichannel Distribution
Time Management	Attention to Detail

Professional Experience

PITNEY INDUSTRIAL SALES   1987 to Current

National Accounts Manager

Direct nationwide group of sales professionals serving manufacturing industry. Fully responsible for profit & loss of 12 sites with annual sales of $150M. Direct supervision of 12 managers; indirect responsibility for 200 people. Recognized for achieving highest sales increase and lowest attrition rate in corporate network. Consistently received performance-based promotions to company's key management team.

- Increased 2002 sales 22% first quarter; repeat sales grew 12%.
- Led organization to first place for international sales.
- Received company's most prestigious profit award last three years.
- Named *Top Accounts Manager* seven years in row.

Education

Miami University, Oxford, Ohio
Bachelor of Science, Organizational Management, 1992

- GPA: 4.0
- Class Valedictorian

References Furnished Immediately upon Request

Keywords

Account Development

Account Management

Account Retention

Competitive Analysis

Consultative Sales

Customer Loyalty

Customer Satisfaction

Direct Sales

Indirect Sales

Global Markets

Key Account Management

Product Launch

Multichannel Distribution

Negotiations

Profit & Loss

Sales Closing

Solutions Selling

Team Building/ Leadership

Profit Growth

Revenue Growth

Interview Q&A Using Keywords

Why should we hire you, what are your strengths, and how do you see yourself contributing to our company?

I came up through the ranks, so I understand the problems that every sales representative faces, every day, to keep the company strong in tough markets. My strength lies in consultative selling that provides solutions for customers. Most sales people have a difficult time developing and nurturing relationships with large accounts, and approaching them strategically. I excel in developing, managing, and retaining highly profitable accounts by looking at the larger picture from the customer's perspective. As a member of your sales management team, I can take a leadership role in advancing your direct, indirect, and global sales efforts. I can also handle new product launches, from planning to putting them in the customers' hands.

NETWORK ARCHITECT

Keywords

LAN/WAN

TCP/IP Networking
Protocols

Cisco VPN Solution

Technical Support/
Documentation

Analytical Problem
Solving

Client/Server
Programming

Routing

Configuring,
Debugging,
Programming at
Network Level

Windows NT/2000

Novell

SQL, Oracle

Communication
Skills

Team Player

Cisco Certified
Network Associate
(CCNA)

Network Security

Multisite Exposure

Budget
Development/
Compliance

Purchasing

Project Management

Disaster Recovery
Plans

Resume

Vernon P. Schultz
1982 Grafton Street
Grafton, Wisconsin 53024
(262) 555-1122 / email@email.com

Cisco Certified Network Associate
Eliminates downtime through LAN/WAN design and administration

Configuring, programming, and debugging at network level
Communicates solutions and provides technical support

Innovative network architect with expertise configuring, programming, and debugging Windows NT/2000 and Novell LAN/WAN, including client/server programming, to eliminate downtime.

Core Strengths

Project management	Technical Support
Hardware/software purchasing	Budget development/compliance
Multisite environments	TCP/IP networking protocols
Client/server programming	Cisco VPN Solution

Professional Experience

NETWURX UNLIMITED, Waukesha, Wisconsin   1998 to Present

Network Architect, CCNA

Support global Microsoft server infrastructure in a global company with business efforts in 50 countries. Support, administer, and design NT, Novell, and OS/2 systems and networks. Install hardware for Windows NT and OS/2 workstations. Set up Distinct, Rumba, Cisco Secure, and Ethernet configurations. Provide technical support to more than 2500 internal users at all levels. Travel nationwide to resolve system issues or set up/install new systems, applications or upgrades. Source vendors to purchase complete systems.

- Coordinated installation of 28-site frame relay supporting AS/400 5394 and 5494 controllers, terminals, and printers for key manufacturer. Tied project into AT&T frame and Internet Security utilizing Cisco's PIX firewall.
- Directed Novell-to-NT server migration.

Education

Milwaukee School of Engineering, Milwaukee, Wisconsin
Bachelor of Science, Computer Science, 1995

- GPA: 3.5
- Member of Tau Beta Pi Engineering Honor Society

Interview Q&A Using Keywords

Why should we hire you, what are your strengths, and how do you see yourself contributing to our company?

As a Cisco Certified Network Associate, I possess broad-based server and network experience including hardware, software, and network configuration, programming, troubleshooting, and repair, as well as user training. Additionally, I possess experience working with third-party vendors and negotiating favorable terms to purchase complete systems, hardware, software, and services. With this expertise, I can virtually eliminate downtime and keep your network operating smoothly.

NETWORK ENGINEER

Resume

Connie Connect
888 Current Way
San Jose, California 95112
(408) 555-1122 / email@email.com

> **Network Engineer**
> **Five years' experience in Communications Engineering**
>
> **Certified Network Engineer**

Certified network professional adept in latest technology. Strong installation, troubleshooting, and administration skills. Able to meet and exceed expectations in quality and rollout. Expertise in routing protocols.

Core Strengths

TCP/IP	Cisco
Windows NT	Novell NetWare
Installation	Troubleshooting
Remote access	Extranet

Professional Experience

ConnectNet, San Jose, CA   1995 to 2001

Communications Engineer
Responsibilities:
Planned, built, and managed computer network infrastructures. Integrated new hardware and software into existing networks. Created new local and wide area networks. Designed wire line and wireless linkages for simple and complex systems. Provided technical support and troubleshooting for installations and maintenance phases of project.

- Installed remote access system for global company of 15,000 employees
- Piloted design of broadband system
- Designed Virtual Private Network using public network transport
- Developed security access controls including sign-on, filters, firewalls

Education

Stanford University, Palo Alto, California
Bachelor of Science / Communications Engineering, 1994

- California Institute of Technology, Pasadena, California
- Certified Network Engineer 1995

References Furnished Immediately upon Request

Keywords

TCP/IP
Unix
Windows NT
Local Area Network, LAN
Wide Area Network, WAN
Internet
Routing Protocols
Troubleshooting
Servers
Telecommunications
Cisco
Circuit Design
Installation
Integration
Firewalls
Remote Access
Extranet
Network Design
Infrastructure
Novell NetWare

Interview Q&A Using Keywords

Why should we hire you, what are your strengths, and how do you see yourself contributing to our company?

I am an experienced Certified Network Engineer with excellent customer service and communication skills. I utilize the latest technology to customize system solutions that exceed customer expectations. Coordinating vendors, coupled with tenacious problem solving and troubleshooting, allows me to bring the project in ahead of schedule. I took the initiative to upgrade my skills in security and designed a virtual private network. I describe myself as a self-starter, attentive to detail, and cost conscious.

NONPROFIT PROGRAM DIRECTOR

Keywords

After-school Programs

Agency Relations

Board Elections

Budget Planning

Caseload Management

Curriculum Development

Day Care Center Inspections

Early Childhood Development

Exit Conferences

Federal Funding

Health and Safety

High-Scope Trainer

Individual Education Plans

Nonprofit Fund Raising

Program Evaluation and Analysis

Regulatory Compliance

Requests for Funding Proposals

Research Studies

Student Advocate

Teacher Training

Resume

Carolyn Freeman
90-A Gillespie Avenue
Ozone Park, NY 11418
(718) 555-2222 / email@email.com

Nonprofit Program Director
30-year career in education and program management

Preschool and School-Aged Day Care Centers
Early Childhood Development Programs

Dedicated, accomplished program director with a career ensuring the quality of education with a focus on the planning, development, and implementation of educational programs for early childhood development.

Core Strengths

Program Evaluation	Curriculum Development
Agency Relations	Requests for Funding Proposals
Budget Planning	Regulatory Compliance
Facilities Inspection	Board Elections

Professional Experience

High Bridge Learning Center, New York, New York   1989 to Current

Program Director

Guide the evaluation of early childhood development programs, and determine programmatic and facility ratings based upon curriculum content, staffing, regulatory compliance, facility conditions, and health and safety guidelines. Plan budgets, prepare requests for funding proposals, and confer with Board of Education and agency officials on a range of educational, budgetary, and regulatory issues.

- Cochair Board elections; hold Certified Parents Association meetings.
- Manage a caseload of 150 preschool and school-aged day care centers.
- Conduct weekly Exit Conferences to present findings of evaluations.
- Serve as a High-Scope trainer, and advocate for special needs students.

Education

Education, Queens College, Flushing, New York
Master of Science: Education, 1985

- **New York State Certification, Nursery through Sixth Grade**
- **Administration Training for Educational Directors**

References Furnished Immediately upon Request

Interview Q&A Using Keywords

Why should we hire you, what are your strengths, and how do you see yourself contributing to our company?

I have a strong interest in your early childhood development program, and believe my experience as a classroom teacher and program director overseeing similar programs would be of value. I offer strengths in areas of day care and after-school program evaluation and analysis, proposal development, curriculum and Individual Education Plan development, educational facilities inspection, federal funding, health and safety compliance, teacher training, research studies, and Board elections.

NURSE

Resume

Louise Lamarr
2858 Fir Street
Ventura, California 93003
(805) 555-1122 / email@email.com

Registered Nurse (RN-BSN)
Nursing Home and Convalescent Care Management

Skilled Diagnostics and Treatment Planning
Quality through Compassionate, Managed Care

Ardent communicator with over 14 years of providing medical services to geriatric patients in state licensed, long-term care facilities.

Core Strengths

Resident Assessments   Acute Care / Long-Term Care
Treatment Plan Development   Diagnostic Models
Case Management   Patient Education

Professional Experience

SEAVIEW GERIATRIC CARE CENTER
Ventura, California

Charge Nurse—Registered Nurse (RN II)   *1995 to Current*

Direct the admission, treatment, and discharge of patients in this 120-bed nursing home. Consult with interdisciplinary team members regarding patient treatment and implementation of patient care plans. Instructed patient and family diagnosis, prognosis, and in-residence care.

- Resident expert and staff trainer in the Resident Assessment Instrument and the Minimum Data Set.
- Initiated and conducted a series of practice RAI/MDS audits. Seaview has earned 100% compliance on all inspections since 1998.
- RAI/MDS Facilitator certification expected in September 2002.

Education

California State University at Northridge, California
Bachelor of Science, Nursing (BSN) / 1994

References Furnished Immediately upon Request

Keywords

Registered Nurse (RN)

Long-Term Care

Managed Care

Health Care

Case Management

Prognosis

In-Residence Care

Patient Admissions and Discharge

Treatment Plans

Rehabilitation Plans

Patient Care Plan

Problem Solving

Clinical Intervention

Diagnostic Models

Minimum Data Set (MDS)

Resident Assessment Instrument (RAI)

Nursing Homes

Communications Skills

Patient Education

Life Support Monitoring Equipment

Interview Q&A Using Keywords

Why should we hire you, what are your strengths, and how do you see yourself contributing to our company?

During my entire 14-year nursing career in state-licensed nursing homes, I have been an advocate of compassionate care and efficient treatment for my patients and their families. While high costs accompany quality care, my expertise in the use of rapid and accurate intake and discharge assessment tools such as the Resident Assessment Instrument and the Minimum Data Set can not only ensure that the facility meets its regulatory requirements, but also help eliminate unnecessary stays and treatments.

119

NUTRITIONIST

Keywords

Integrative Care

Meal Plans

Dietetic & Nutrition Services

Treatment Plans

Metabolic Typing

Chelation Therapy

Intravenous Vitamins & Minerals

Immunology

Therapeutic Skin Care Analysis

Biochemistry

Metabolic Nutrition

Enzyme Nutrition

Rehabilitation Services

Nutrition

Natural Allergy Treatment

Client Consultation/ Analysis

Holistic Approach

Diet, Exercise, & Lifestyle

Vitamin Supplementation

Nutrient Depletion

Resume

Janice Scott, CN
123 S. Fourth Street
Kewanee, Illinois 61443
(309) 555-1234 / email@email.com

> **Certified Nutritionist**
> **Highly Skilled in Holistic Approaches to Health and Fitness**
>
> **Natural Allergy Treatment / Therapeutic Skin Care Expertise**
> **Integrate Various Diets, Supplement Protocols, and Enzyme Approaches**

Results-oriented, enthusiastic, and highly accomplished certified nutritionist with a solid track record of assisting patients at all age levels in overcoming various health problems including diabetes, ADD, allergies, and weight issue.

Core Strengths

Metabolic Typing	Integrative Care
Metabolic Nutrition	Biochemistry
Rehabilitation	Well Family Guidance
Natural Allergy Treatment	Therapeutic Skin Care
Patient Analysis	Treatment Plans/Meal Plans

Professional Experience

NUTRITION PLUS—Janesville, IL   1992 to Current

Director of Nutrition

Spearhead and manage various nutritional outreach programs for this thriving organization providing services to hospitals, nursing homes, clinics, and other large entities/corporations. Supervise, train, and mentor a staff of eight in all aspects of performing client consultations/ analysis, introducing vitamin and mineral supplementation, and reinforcing a holistic approach involving the nutrition, exercise, and lifestyle changes needed to obtain optimum health.

- Pioneered a highly successful Family Wellness Guidance program.
- Increased annual revenues through new programs by 60%.
- Recruited and hired new staff members to assist in managing new business.

Education

STATE UNIVERSITY OF ILLINOIS—Mercer, Illinois
Bachelor of Science in Nutrition/Biochemistry (1988)
Certifications: **Certified Personal Trainer (1990)** • **Illinois State Certified Nutritionist (1989)** • **Certified in Hair Analysis (1989)**

Interview Q&A Using Keywords

Why Should Our Company Hire You?

I believe in a holistic approach to health because health is much more than just the absence of disease. Optimum health is to thrive in a state of vitality. The way I accomplish this is through proper client analysis and the implementation of vitamin supplementation, diet, exercise, and lifestyle changes, enzyme nutrition, chelation therapy, natural allergy and skin care treatments, and the integrative care methods. This balanced and whole body approach has proven highly effective because it is a multisided approach and brings on a more rapid achievement of positive results.

PARALEGAL/LEGAL ASSISTANT

Resume

Tina Vitou
4230 Dove Drive
Citrus Heights, California 95621
(916) 555-1122 / email@email.com

> **Certified Paralegal**
>
> *Dedicated to providing superior, uninterrupted administrative support to legal and nonlegal staff.*

Confident, articulate, and results-oriented legal support professional offering a strong foundation of education and experience. Creative and enthusiastic with a proven record of success in prioritizing and processing heavy workflow without supervision. Superior organization and communication skills, committed to personal and professional growth.

Core Strengths

Client/Trial Preparation
Research & Support
Domestic Relations
Exhibits/Witness Lists

Subpoena & Affidavit Preparation
Motion & Order Preparation
Discovery/Client Interviewing
Memoranda of Law

Professional Experience

County Attorney's Office—Fremont, CA   1995 to Present

Paralegal
Conduct in-depth research and summarize depositions, declarations, and memoranda of law. Organize documents for trial, and assist with jury instruction. Provide litigation support by assisting with case presentation including independent preparation of motions, affidavits, pleadings, and subpoena responses.

- Promoted above peers to paralegal position after serving as intern.
- Repeatedly noticed by senior attorneys for accuracy and precision handling of documents in time-critical and key litigation cases.
- Formally recognized for superior performance by the state government of California.

Education

Sullivan College, San Francisco, CA
Associates of Science Degree, Paralegal Studies

- Magna Cum Laude distinction
- Commissioned Notary Public at Large

Keywords

Litigation Support
Paralegal/Legal Assistant
Deposition
Pleadings
Declarations
Memoranda of Law
Trial Preparation
Subpoena/ Subpoena Response
Affidavit
Jury Instructions
Case Investigations
Civil/Criminal
Domestic Relations
Motions
Orders
Research/Discovery
Power of Attorney
Exhibits
Complaints
Witness List Preparation
Client Interviewing

Interview Q&A Using Keywords

Why should we hire you, what are your strengths, and how do you see yourself contributing to our company?

I am committed to the highest standards of performance, and am looking for a long-term employment relationship. My areas of specialty are civil law, domestic relations, research and discovery, client interviews, and document preparation, which, as I understand your requirements, make me a perfect match for your position. I will be able to provide the support you require immediately without further training, and am ready to begin when you are!

PEOPLESOFT CONSULTANT

Resume

Lin Chin Wong
18-A Kissena Blvd.
Flushing, New York 11355
(718) 555-2220 / email@email.com

> **PeopleSoft Consultant**
> **20-year career leading HRMS projects into production**
>
> **PeopleSoft HR/ADP Payroll Interface/Base Benefits**
> **Financials/Distribution/Manufacturing**

Functional and Technical PeopleSoft Consultant with a verifiable record of success in guiding the mass deployment of multimodule PeopleSoft HRMS implementation projects for government and Fortune 1000 clients.

Core Strengths

Project Management	Team Leadership
Planning and Development	Needs Assessment/Consultation
Self-Serve Technology	Vendor Management
Technical Writing	Development Life Cycle

Professional Experience

GROELGER-PARAMUS, New York, New York   1992 to Current
PeopleSoft Consultant
Spearhead multiple PeopleSoft HRMS projects in charge of planning, developing, and implementing task-specific, customized modules. Develop self-serve Internet architectures in response to requirements for Web-based technology. Conduct fit gap analyses to gauge labor productivity and data integrity throughout the development life cycle.

- Led firm to compete on a global scale for eight consecutive years
- Successfully lead multimillion-dollar government contract negotiations
- Cost-effectively strengthen teams through train-the-trainer programs
- Author technical and user manuals for companywide distribution

Education

Queens College, Flushing, New York, 1988
Bachelor of Arts: Mathematics

- PeopleSoft V5.10-8.0, Oracle, Unix, ERP, SAP
- SQL7, Sybase, Informix, COGNOS

References Furnished Immediately upon Request

Interview Q&A Using Keywords

Why should we hire you, what are your strengths, and how do you see yourself contributing to our company?

As an accomplished PeopleSoft consultant with a notable career, I bring to the table an expertise in business systems implementation, change analysis, design, and management of PeopleSoft HRMS projects for government sectors and Fortune 1000 clients. Your organization's recent acquisition of similar business models will no doubt require these strengths to ensure the seamless integration of an Internet architecture with customized business solutions and self-serve technology.

PERSONAL TRAINER

Resume

Susan Quinn
35 Memorial Boulevard
Newark, NJ 07104
(973) 443-5555 / email@email.com

Personal Trainer

Helping clients achieve fitness and weight-loss goals

**Certified Personal Trainer / B.S. in Exercise Science
High client referral rate**

Certified Personal Trainer/Fitness Specialist with five years' experience at an upscale fitness club. Skilled at motivating clients to achieve goals. Book 30% more clients on average than other trainers at the facility.

Core Strengths

Fitness evaluations	Communication skills
Goal Setting	Muscle conditioning
Customized program design	Motivating clients
Interpersonal skills	Fitness software

Professional Experience

HIGHTOWER SPORTS CLUB, Cleveland, OH   1997–Present

Personal Trainer

Train a client base of up to 40 members per week. Perform fitness assessments including body-fat analysis. Set and modify goals in consultation with clients. Use fitness software to maintain accurate records. Train clients on use of equipment, including Nautilus and free weights. Develop professional weight-training and cardiovascular programs. Perform introductory consultations and book new clients.

- Top trainer as measured by number of referrals booked
- Developed professional programs based on exercise science
- Helped clients achieve weight-loss and strength-improvement goals
- Developed successful incentive programs to keep clients motivated

Education

University of Maine, Orono, ME
Bachelor of Science in Exercise Science 1997

- First Aid certified
- CPR for the Professional Rescuer

References Furnished Immediately upon Request

Keywords

Fitness Specialist

Certified Personal Trainer

Fitness Instructor

First Aid Certified

CPR for the Professional Rescuer

Health and Wellness Programs

Exercise Science

Evaluations

Assessments

Setting Goals

Modify Goals

People Skills

Body Fat Assessment

Muscle Conditioning

Stretching and Flexibility

Program Design

Weight Room Management

Fitness Assessments

Communication Skills

Organizational Skills

Interpersonal Skills

Fitness Software

Interview Q&A Using Keywords

Why should we hire you, what are your strengths, and how do you see yourself contributing to our company?

I have been highly successful in helping clients achieve their fitness goals. My four-year academic training in exercise science has given me a solid knowledge base from which to design safe, workable, and successful personalized fitness programs. I am a "people person" who is able to keep clients motivated. My ability to increase participation in personal training programs can enhance revenues for a fitness facility.

PHARMACEUTICAL SALES REPRESENTATIVE

Resume

Marci J. Leonard
77 Main Street
East Brunswick, New Jersey 08816
(732) 555-1234 / email@email.com

Pharmaceutical Sales Rep
Award-Winning Territory Sales Producer

Clinical Selling Skills / Hospital Territory Management
Pharmaceutical Direct Sales to Key Accounts

Pharmaceutical sales professional and former registered nurse with track record of success in sales and client relationship management dealing with "hard-to-see" key customers and managed care account directors.

Core Strengths

Direct and Indirect Sales	Medical Terminology/Processes
Hospital Territory Sales	Customer-Focused Selling Strategies
Key Physician Accounts	Revenue/Market Share Gain
Therapeutic Knowledge	Market Leader/Product Positioning

Professional Experience

PHARMA PRODUCTS, INC., Princeton, New Jersey   1997 to Current

Pharmaceutical Sales Representative

Market multiple classes of pharmaceutical products to hospital accounts and key physician contacts. Closely manage marketing budget (5% under) and monitor competitor products to deliver persuasive clinical sales presentations. Use customer needs assessment, as well as pharmaceutical market and managed care contracting knowledge to achieve medical sales.

- Consistently overachieved sales quota and increased market share in major product groups. Won top sales achievement awards in hospital territory sales for four consecutive years (1999–2002).
- Teamed with three field representatives to triple dollar volume and boost market share 45% in highly competitive northern New Jersey territory.
- Delivered strong results for secondary products in hospital territory, doubling sales year over year. Selected as sales training advisor and medical information resources provider for sales and marketing team.

Education

State University of New York, Buffalo, New York
Master of Science, Nursing Education
(cum laude)—1988
Bachelor of Science, Nursing (summa cum laude)—1986

Interview Q&A Using Keywords

Why should we hire you, what are your strengths, and how do you see yourself contributing to our company?

With demonstrated pharmaceutical direct sales success and therapeutic knowledge gained as a registered nurse, I combine an aggressive, results-oriented approach to hospital territory management with finely honed clinical sales presentation skills. This proactive approach utilizes customer needs assessment, key account sales strategies, and product positioning to win market share. May I have the opportunity to put my pharmaceutical knowledge and clinical selling skills to use for you?

PHARMACEUTICAL TECHNICIAN

Resume

Camille Roberts, CphT
6234 La Costa Lane
Anywhere, Michigan 00000
(208) 555-0000 / email@email.com

Certified Pharmacy Technician
Seven Years of Pharmaceutical Experience
Experienced in Handling Radioactive Pharmaceuticals

Strong science, chemistry, and health care background. Comprehensive knowledge of medical terms and medications. Precise handling of radioactive pharmaceutical products. Currently learning pharmaceutical robotic machine programming.

Core Strengths

Health Physics   Nuclear Chemistry
Organic Chemistry   Pharmacy Law
Organization   Alert/Responsible
Quality Control   Ability to Decipher Difficult Handwriting

Professional Experience

PHARMACEUTICAL COMPANY, Walled Lake, Michigan   1995 to Present

Certified Pharmacy Technician

Input and track patient data, transcribe pharmacy orders, and accurately fill orders according to unit dose system. Check in supplies and inventory. Compound IV solutions, fill cassettes, order entry, billing, and handle narcotics. Establish and maintain patient profiles, prepare insurance claim forms, and stock and take inventory of prescription and over-the-counter medications. Assemble 24-hour supplies of medication for in-home patients. Verify accuracy and completeness of prescriptions.

- Employee of the Year, 2000.
- Secured in a $2 million annual contract from a local government agency.
- Presenter, National Conference of Pharmaceutical Technicians.

Education

Ferris State College, Big Rapids, Michigan
Bachelor of Science Degree in Organic Chemistry, 1990

- Mentor for Freshmen Chemistry students
- Volunteer, Big Rapids Hospital, six years

Keywords

Dispensing

IV Compounding

Radio-
    pharmaceutical

Cassette Fill

Order Eentry

Billing

Narcotic Handling

Pyxis

Unit Dose

Sterile Techniques

Measure

Independent

Communication

Meticulous

Mathematics

Health Physics

Pharmaceuticals

Health Care

Drugs

Prescription

Interview Q&A Using Keywords

Why should we hire you, what are your strengths, and how do you see yourself contributing to our company?

As a Certified Pharmacy Technician, I have a thorough understanding of dispensing and compounding techniques, computer procedures, and billing procedures. I am knowledgeable in radiological half-life concepts and working with radiopharmaceutical products. I work well with or without supervision. My personal traits include being accurate, meticulous, detailed, and thorough. My experience includes working as a health physicist in a radioisotope laboratory. I am conscientious, a team player, customer service oriented, and quality control conscious.

PHARMACIST

Resume

Angela Woodstone
19 Ashland Avenue
St. Paul, Minnesota 55102
(651) 555-1138 / email@email.com

> **Highly Qualified Licensed Pharmacist/Consultant**
> **15-Year Background in Government & Hospital Settings**
>
> **Licensed by the Minnesota and Wisconsin State Boards of Pharmacy**
> **Effectively Balance Protocol Management and Relationship Building**

Extensive background in administering government and hospital programs. Skilled in developing maintenance systems and creating in-service programs. Recognized for consulting, counseling, and interface expertise with the medical community and its customers.

Core Strengths

Record-keeping & patient profile systems	Consulting and counseling
Regimen review	Third-party systems
OBRA & VBRA 40 regulations	In-service training programs
Chemical compounding	Inventory control

Professional Experience

MINNESOTA DEPARTMENT OF HEALTH—St. Paul, Minnesota   1995 to Current

Pharmacist, Industrial Rehabilitation Center: Worker's Compensation

Order and distribute medications to clients and provide client counseling on medication dosages, adverse effects, and general usage. Develop and implement wean schedules for clients, helping them to reduce and eliminate medication use. Maintain well-controlled inventory, including legally handling and storing controlled substances. Trained staff regarding laws and newly marketed medications. Consulted with private physicians and intuitional staff on medications. Develop record-keeping and patient profile systems. Oversee high-volume dispensing.

- Received *Client Interface* recognition from the American Pharmaceutical Association, 1999
- Created protocol for contingency cabinet, eliminating unwarranted use
- Implemented new unit dose medication system, expediting medication delivery
- Established physician signature card process, reducing physician approval delays by 35%

Education

University of Minnesota, Minneapolis, Minnesota
Master of Science: Pharmacy Administration, 1987

- Benjamin M. Cohen Memorial Scholarship recipient (financial need and academics)
- Research assistant for Paul Schaef, Pharm.D., Associate Professor, Antibiotic Resistance

Interview Q&A Using Keywords

Why should we hire you, what are your strengths, and how do you see yourself contributing to our company?

I can bring to the table 15 years' combined pharmacy administration experience in government and hospital programs. As a seasoned licensed pharmacist, I have served as consulting pharmacist to various medical staffs on medication issues. As an in-service trainer, I have mentored multilevels of healthcare staff in remaining proactive on pharmacy issues. My client interface and counseling skills have been recognized by the American Pharmaceutical Association. Combined expertise with pharmaceutical law and technology ensure well-controlled inventory and dispensing. An extensive background with third-party systems, OBRA, and VBRA 40 foster effective processing and protocol.

PHOTOGRAPHER

Resume

Robarra Cicchalone
7231 Ventura Boulevard
Ventura, California 93003
(805) 555-1122 / email@email.com

> **Photographer**
> **Industrial—Documentary—Digital Portraiture**
>
> **Corporate Image Building & Repair through**
> **Inspired Photojournalism**

Core Strengths

- Proven program management and analytical skills coupled with the photographic eye
- Excellent communicator with the ability to earn subjects' trust and cooperation quickly
- Working experience with an impressive range of camera, lenses, film, formats, sizes, and computer graphics software...35 millimeter, video, digital, panoramic, SLR, automatic, Quark, Dreamweaver, Flash, Adobe Photoshop...*See Photographic Skills Addendum, attached...*

Professional Experience

Freelance Photographer   1997 to Current
Corporate/industrial clients include: *The Los Angeles Times*, Mobil Oil, AT&T, IBM, American Express IDS, Turner Broadcasting, Ciba-Geigy Pharmaceuticals, *Sunset Magazine*, *TV Guide Magazine*, Norton Simon Museum, Los Angeles Museum of Modern Art, and numerous others...
View my Web portfolio at http://www.dock.net/~myportfolio.

Plan and produce photography, Web, and graphic design projects consistent with corporate vision. Assess clients and products for compatibility with corporate intent. Consult with public relations department on target audience and media selection. Present proposals to board members. Coordinate and shoot executive portrait sessions within program budget and schedules.

- International Film Channel Award for Best Documentary about the Los Angeles Museum of Modern Art—2002

Education

California Institute for the Arts, Valencia, California
Bachelor of Fine Arts in Photography—1997
Associate of Arts in Computer Graphics—1995

References Furnished Immediately upon Request

Keywords

Analytical and Problem-Solving Ability

Strong Oral and Written Communications Skills

Program Management and Coordination

Creativity (e.g., Have the "Photographic Eye")

Public Relations

Computer Graphics

Fine Art

Photographer

Marketing

Advertising

Digital Photography

Documentary

Image Building

Portraiture

Industrial Photography

Photojournalism

Single Lens Reflex (SLR)

Videography

35 Millimeter to Panoramic

Name Specific Equipment and Formats in Photographic Skills Addendum

Interview Q&A Using Keywords

Why should we hire you, what are your strengths, and how do you see yourself contributing to our company?

As an award-winning industrial photographer and videographer, I can help you develop positive, visual marketing messages for your company through probing executive portraits and work site documentaries that reflect your business image and ethics. Awards and formal training in digital photography, computer graphics, and fine art portraiture round out my success story.

PHYSICAL THERAPIST

Keywords

Injury Prevention

Workplace Wellness Education

Progress Charting

Strength Analysis

Functional Capacity

Daily-Living Activities

Rehabilitation Services

Hydrotherapy

Respiratory Efficiency

Injury Management

Treatment Planning

Cross Training

Funding and Contract Development

PTA Clinical Supervision

Assistive Technology and Supportive Devices

Therapeutic Massage

Range of Motion

Uniform Standards of Patient Care

Human Anatomy and Physiology

In-Service Training

Resume

Kim Tynan, PT
133 Park Lane, Unit 3
Orchard Park, New York 14127
(716) 555-6932 / email@email.com

Physical Therapist
**Seasoned Professional Providing Injury Management /
Rehabilitation Services**

Clinical Supervision / Training of PTAs

Licensed physical therapist with six years' experience working with patients ranging from school-age children to older adults. Specialize in addressing women's health issues.

Core Strengths

Strength Analysis	Treatment Planning
Therapeutic Massage	In-Service Training
Daily-Living Activities	Sports Physical Therapy

Professional Experience

HEALTHY WOMEN CENTER, Amherst, New York   1996 to Current

Physical Therapist

Utilize extensive knowledge of human anatomy and physiology to evaluate functional capacity and develop treatment plans. Assist patients in improving range of motion, agility, strength, and respiratory efficiency. Chart progress and create follow-up home exercise programs. Break down tasks into manageable components, ensuring positive outcomes. Utilize hydrotherapy and assistive technology.

- Developed workplace wellness education programs to prevent back, neck, shoulder, and wrist injuries.
- Established referral contracts with local Employee Assistance Programs.
- Implemented cross training and initiated uniform standards of patient care, enabling collaborative treatment and reduced labor costs.
- Secured funding for arthritis education and exercise program.

Education

Russell Sage College, Troy, New York
Bachelor of Science: Physical Therapy, 1996

New York State Department of Education
Licensed Physical Therapist, 1996

References Furnished Immediately upon Request

Interview Q&A Using Keywords

Why should we hire you, what are your strengths, and how do you see yourself contributing to our company?

My areas of specialty include orthopedic support and spinal correction. My group, under my lead, developed workplace wellness education programs to prevent back, neck, shoulder, and wrist injuries. I have established referral contracts with local Employee Assistance Programs (EAP) and secured funding for a community arthritis education and exercise program.

PHYSICIAN'S ASSISTANT

Resume

Margaret Bradford
789 Wilson Boulevard
Dallas, Texas 75287
(972) 555-2121 / email@email.com

> **PHYSICIAN'S ASSISTANT**
> **with 10 years of diversified experience**
>
> **Internal Medicine, Pediatric, Family Practice**
> **Clinics, Hospitals, and Nursing Homes**

Extensive experience assisting physicians with minor injuries, suturing, splinting, and casting, along with performing and analyzing x-rays, and diagnostic, therapeutic, and laboratory tests.

Core Strengths

Diversified health care experience	Excellent service to all patients
Tremendous asset to physicians	Accurate analysis of various tests
Counseling patients	Comprehensive reports/progress notes
Dedicated and reliable	Commendations and staff awards

Professional Experience

PHYSICIANS NETWORK, Dallas, Texas   1996 to present

Physician's Assistant

Assist internal medicine, pediatric, and family practice physicians in a fast-paced environment. Gather medical history from patients, and perform and analyze x-rays and a variety of other tests necessary for treatment. Order supplies and/or equipment for patients, prepare comprehensive reports and progress notes, and ensure that the best possible service is provided to all patients.

- Assisted physicians with over 5000 patient appointments in 2001.
- Performed and accurately analyzed more than 2500 tests in 2001.
- Completed 1000 sutures, 500 splints, and 250 casts on patients.
- Recognized as the "Physician Assistant of the Year" in 2001.

Education

Baylor University, Dallas, Texas
Bachelor of Science Degree; Major: Health Care; 1990
GPA: 3.5
Dean's List twice in 1989 and once in 1990

References Furnished Immediately upon Request

Keywords

Health Care Services
Internal Medicine
Pediatrics
Family Practice
Clinics
Hospitals
Nursing Homes
Physician's Assistant
Diagnostic
Therapeutic
Laboratory Tests
X-Rays
Minor Injuries
Suturing
Splinting
Casting
Medical History
Progress Notes
Supplies/Equipment
Reports

Interview Q&A Using Keywords

Why should we hire you, what are your strengths, and how do you see yourself contributing to our company?

I have more than 10 years of experience providing health care services to internal medicine, pediatric, and family practice patients in clinics, hospitals, and nursing homes. I gather medical history as well as perform and analyze x-rays; diagnostic, therapeutic, and laboratory tests; and assist physicians with minor injuries, suturing, splinting, and casting. I will be a tremendous asset to your company because of my extensive experience and dedication to providing the best possible services to all patients.

POLICE OFFICER—MILITARY CONVERSION

Keywords

Community Outreach

Crises Response

Emergency Planning & Response

Interrogation

Investigations management

Law Enforcement

Personal Protection

Public Relations

Safety Training

Surveillance

VIP Protection

Tactical Field Operations

Security Operations

Asset Protection

Electronic Surveillance

Emergency Preparedness

Corporate Fraud

Corporate Security

Industrial Espionage

Industrial Security

Resume

Johnathan P. Kemper
708 Worthington Avenue
Kettering, Ohio 45429
(937) 555-1773 / email@email.com

Police Officer—Military Conversion
Seven Years of Experience as Law Enforcement Officer

Investigations Management / Corporate & Industrial Security
Emergency Planning & Response / Crisis Response

Comprehensive knowledge of law enforcement directing surveillance, VIP protection, and Tactical Field Operations teams to protect military, government, and private facilities. Honesty. Integrity. Excellent leadership.

Core Strengths

Riot Control	Domestic Disturbances
Terrorist Threats	Drug Investigations
Security Operations	Hostage Negotiations
Analytical Thinking	Creative Problem Solving

Professional Experience

U.S. AIR FORCE   1990 to Current

Desk Sergeant / Patrolman

Advanced from field patrol to investigations management. Provide asset protection, surveying, and securing of multiple installations. Member of crisis response team resolving hostage situations. Lead VIP personal protection teams guarding top-ranking officials. Set up electronic surveillance systems around base perimeters. Selected to represent Air Force police at community outreach and other public relations events.

- Led investigations of domestic disturbances, thefts, assaults, and DUIs.
- Conducted electronic and field surveillance for crime investigations.
- Monitored National Air Intelligence Center's computerized systems.
- Arrested and interrogated suspects; processed prisoners.

Education

Community College of the Air Force
Bachelor of Science, Criminal Justice, 2001

- GPA: 3.7
- Minor in Spanish

References Furnished Immediately upon Request

Interview Q&A Using Keywords

Why should we hire you, what are your strengths, and how do you see yourself contributing to our company?

I can use my military law enforcement training to help your organization meet its service goals. I moved through numerous areas of law enforcement to an area that I find most interesting, and one in which I excel—investigations management. I have put together teams that incorporate strengths in all areas, such as electronic and field surveillance, corporate and industrial espionage, and tactical field operations to handle expertly all phases of investigations. I can do the same for you.

PRODUCTION MANAGER

Resume

Charles W. Morgan
1400 North Avenue
Atlanta, Georgia 30040
(770) 555-1212 / email@email.com

> **Production Manager**
> **The ability to translate your corporate vision into profits**
>
> **Guiding complex production teams to success**
> **Systems view of production that creates synergy between**
> **people and capital investment**

A credible, profit-oriented leader known for skill in recruiting, motivating, and retaining teams of production professionals dedicated to continuous manufacturing improvement.

Core Strengths

Optimal capacity planning	Yield improvement
Cost avoidance	On-demand customization
ISO 9000 series certification	Inventory control

Professional Experience

TransKing Corporation, Norcross, Georgia   1996 to Current

Rail Program Manager

Responsible for design and manufacture of bus, truck, trailer, container, and rail temperature controls for a company with $1B sales annually. Build enduring business "alliances" with vendors that produced "win-win" situations even in niche production. Guided the renovation of a 28,000-square-foot plant without interrupting the two-shift operation required to meet customer demand.

- Got 32 demanding subcontractors (from our competitor!) under control. Mapped nearly 1,100 tasks to guide team one day at a time. Profits 16% above forecast.
- Helped negotiate then managed complicated, fast-track $1.5M program. Profit level: 22% (10% projected). Cut delivery times in half.
- In six months, routinely cut 800 defects per rail car—a record in our company.

Education

State University of New York
Associate of Applied Science in Automotive Technology and Engineering, 1981

- Inducted into national engineering honor society
- Dean's List every quarter

Keywords

Capacity Planning

Cell Manufacturing

Cost Avoidance

Cross-Functional Teams

Cycle Time Reduction

Facilities Consolidation

Inventory Control

ISO 9000 Standards

Just-in-Time (JIT)

Manufacturing Integration

Materials Replenishment Systems (MRP)

On-Demand Customization

Operations Reengineering

Operations Start-Up

Outsourcing

P & L Management

Productivity Improvement

Technology Integration

Turnaround Management

Yield Improvement

Interview Q&A Using Keywords

Why should we hire you, what are your strengths, and how do you see yourself contributing to our company?

If you could "design" your next project manager, would the following be good enough to meet your specs? Worldwide, "hands-on" experience with every aspect of design and production in your industry, encyclopedic knowledge of compliance law, and credibility that only comes from broad experience. You will find a dozen specific examples of performance in my resume—they illustrate the kinds of contributions I can make to your bottom line. As you read them, I hope my personal standards become apparent. First, I must earn people's trust before I can deliver results. Second, I must prove my competency at every level, every day—from shop floor to boardroom. Finally, I must deliver quality to the customer *and* profits to my company.

PROJECT MANAGER

Keywords

Single/Multifamily

Price Ranges

Lot Size

Design

General Contractor

Specifications

Estimating

Purchasing

Scheduling

Material Delivery

Material Costs

Labor Costs

Architects

Subcontractors

Supervising

Quality Control

Customer Service

Warranty

Construction Defects

Maintenance

Resume

Michael Cunningham
16151 Arapaho Boulevard
Dallas, Texas 75287
(972) 555-2211 / email@email.com

> **CONSTRUCTION PROJECT MANAGER**
> with more than 20 years of experience
>
> **Single and Multifamily Homes**
> **$100,000 to $3 million price range**

Extensive experience in the custom design, cost estimating, scheduling, and overall management of home construction projects. Focus on quality control and completing all projects on time and within budget.

Core Strengths

Working with architects	Design and specifications
Supervising subcontractors	Tracking material and labor costs
Cost estimating and purchasing	Scheduling and material delivery
Excellent service to home buyers	Warranty/maintenance work

Professional Experience

NORTH TEXAS HOME BUILDERS, Dallas, Texas   1985 to present

Construction Project Manager

Manage all aspects of the construction of single and multifamily homes in north Texas. Work directly with architects in the custom design, specifications, cost estimating, and scheduling. Secure and supervise subcontractors, and continually track material and labor costs. Focus on quality control, providing excellent service to home buyers, and completing all projects on time and within budget.

- Started and finished the construction of 10 single and 15 multifamily homes in 2001, generating more than $25 million in revenues.
- Developed a new tracking system that reduced labor costs by 30%.
- Created a Warranty Department for scheduling and making repairs.
- Commended by the President for consistent, outstanding work.

Education

University of Texas, Austin, Texas
Bachelor of Arts Degree; 1981
Major: Construction Management
Minor: Business Administration

References Furnished Immediately upon Request

Interview Q&A Using Keywords

Why should we hire you, what are your strengths, and how do you see yourself contributing to our company?

I have more than 20 years of experience in the overall management of the construction of single and multifamily homes with price ranges from $100,000 to $3 million. I work directly with architects in the custom design, specifications, cost estimating, and scheduling. I also secure and supervise subcontractors, and continually track labor costs. I will contribute greatly to your company by focusing on quality control, providing excellent service to home buyers, and completing all projects on time and within budget.

PROPERTY MANAGER

Resume

Richard Land
6543 Beretania Street
Honolulu, Hawaii 96826
(808) 555-9999 / email@email.com

On-Site Property Manager
Seasoned Community Association Manager

Residential Properties / Multisite Administration
Particularly Skilled at Tenant Relations

12+ years' experience in various residential real estate settings.
Cost-conscious administrator adept at designing preventative maintenance strategies.
Expertly facilitate owner/tenant relationships.

Core Strengths

Condominiums
Luxury Properties
Project Scheduling
Complaint Investigations

Apartments
Facilities Maintenance and Repair
Cash Flow Management
Contractor Oversight

Professional Experience

ASSET MANAGERS, INC., Honolulu, Hawaii 1995 to Present

On-Site Property Manager

Responsible for 120-unit luxury apartment building. Supervise staff of nine, ensuring safe and properly maintained property. Monitor pool cleaning, painting, and security contract personnel. Act as liaison between board of directors and owners. Accountable to asset property manager.

- Raised tenant retention rate by 50% through enhanced owner/tenant communication efforts. Created biweekly newsletter distributed to owners and residents.
- Saved over $25,000 per year since 1997 by implementing comprehensive preventative maintenance program.
- Directed $3 million landscape renovation project.

Education

University of Hawaii at Manoa, Honolulu, Hawaii
Bachelor of Arts / Business Administration, 1980

- Graduated with honors
- Chosen *Most Creative Businessperson* by campus business club

Keywords

Residential Properties

Multisite Management

Condominiums

Apartments

Luxury Property

Community Associations

Complaint Investigation and Resolution

Tenant Retention

Tenant Relations

Preventative Maintenance

Facilities Maintenance and Repairs

Maintenance Record Auditing

Project Scheduling

Property Security

Contractor Oversight

Renovations

Board of Directors Liaison

Rent Collections

Cash Flow Management

Asset Property Manager

Interview Q&A Using Keywords

Why should we hire you, what are your strengths, and how do you see yourself contributing to our company?

My background is very broad, including administration of apartments, condominiums, and luxury properties. I have a demonstrated ability to cut costs. This is accomplished through aggressive maintenance record audits, followed by implementation of comprehensive preventative maintenance initiatives. Through this process I ensure the safe, smooth, and economical operation of properties. I investigate and resolve complaints without delay. This improves tenant relations, satisfying both residents and owners.

PUBLIC RELATIONS DIRECTOR

Keywords

Program
  Management

Public Relations

Crisis Management

Image Development

Market Analytics

Media Relationships

Speech and Script
  Writing

Press Releases

International
  Markets

Interview and Crisis
  Management
  Coaching

Publicity Campaigns
  Development

Public Information

Presentations

Leadership

Media, Print,
  Television, and
  Radio

Support Service
  Networks

Strong Oral and
  Written
  Communications
  Skills

Journalism, English,
  Communications,
  or Business Degree

Graphic Design

Analytical and
  Problem-Solving
  Ability

Resume

Barbara Weaver
10200 Wilshire Boulevard
Los Angeles, California 90024
(213) 555-1122 / email@email.com

Public Relations Director
Celebrity Image & Personal Marketing Consultant

Publicity Campaign Development
Crisis Management

Highly consulted by Celebrities and Fortune 500 companies to design and direct high-visibility or politically sensitive publicity campaigns and industry promotions. Known for sizzling communication strategies that sell people to people, business to business, in print, television, radio, or on the Web. National and international media and support service networks.

Core Strengths
- Celebrity image development
- Interview and crisis coaching
- Media relationships
- Market analytics
- Communications skills

Professional Experience

Universal Studios, Burbank, California   2001 to Present

Public Relations Director / Marketing Consultant

Assess celebrity clients for studio image and compliance with public information policies. Provide interview and crisis management coaching to client. Conduct market analytics to target best audiences and media choices. Review staff recommendations on scripts, speeches, press releases, presentations, graphic design and Web site content. Develop and manage program budget and schedules. Consult with legal and marketing departments in areas of international communications (especially censorship and royalty agreements).

- Guided senior PR specialists in research, design, and launch of a major celebrity's music video—2001.
- Past President, Public Relations Society of America: 2000–2001

Education

California State University at Los Angeles, California
Master of Science, Business Administration—1994
Bachelor of Arts, Communications—1987

References Furnished Immediately upon Request

Interview Q&A Using Keywords

Why should we hire you, what are your strengths, and how do you see yourself contributing to our company?

As a public relations director, I have managed high-visibility publicity campaigns with annual budgets of up to $10 million that delivered the clients huge profits. I ensure that both my target markets and the effectiveness of the selected media are evaluated through demographics, polls, and other analytics. My media contacts range from local news channel and newsprint to Capitol Hill and around the world, ensuring that our message gets to those who can do the most good for our cause.

QUALITY ENGINEER

Resume

Amanda Hershkowitz
1973 78th Street
Memphis, Tennessee 37000
(901) 555-1212 / email@email.com

Quality Engineer
A decade of leading companies to quality and customers to value

Continuous quality improvement / Metric systems that work for people
Value-added processes in manufacturing and sales

A highly-trained quality systems executive with the communications skills, drive, and vision to infuse a quality culture throughout your organization. Solid track record of producing world-class quality.

Core Strengths

Anticipating drags on quality processes
Reengineering WIP for greater ROI
Obtaining ISO 9000 certifications

Managing vendor quality systems
Translating trend data into quality guidelines
Administering responsive QA programs

Professional Experience

Arista Corporation, Norcross, Georgia   1992 to Current

Vice President for Quality Management

Formulate QA practices consistent with master production plans. Providing QA reports for the review and approval of management. Reviewing adequacy of QA/QC processes and standards as part of an overarching QA framework. Reduce risk and improve organizational performance. Reviewing testing and providing for general awareness of QA/QC requirements and values. Business process improvement. Recommending acceptance of deliverables from vendors as being within scope and contract. Ensuring that RFP and contracts have appropriate terms and conditions to assure a quality product.

- Topped 15 tough competitors to win the Tennessee Quality Award (2002)
- Reduced scrap rate by 22% in just one quarter
- Overhauled task groups and process analysis to reignite TQM. QA measures soared.

Education

University of Lowell, Lowell, Massachusetts
Bachelor of Science in Business, 1987

- *Summa cum laude*

References Furnished Immediately upon Request

Keywords

Continuous Quality Improvement

ISO 9000 Certification

Process Analysis

Quality Assurance and Control

Quality Circles

Quality Culture

Rejection Rate

Scrap Rate

Task Groups

Total Quality Management

Trend Information

Value-Added Processes

Vendor Management

WIP (Work in Progress)

World-Class Quality

Zero Defects

Interview Q&A Using Keywords

Why should we hire you, what are your strengths, and how do you see yourself contributing to our company?

Do not hire me unless you demand quality as a way of life from every team member. My strengths are straightforward: I have gone beyond mastering the art and science of engineering quality into products. My track record reflects a knack for having people adopt a world-class quality outlook and think that my suggestions are their own good ideas. My contributions may be a mix of technical and leadership skill, but the outcomes for our company is enduring market domination.

RADIO DISC JOCKEY

Keywords

Pleasant Voice

Articulate

Recording Stars

Recording Groups

Recording Equipment

FCC Licensing

Control Board

Tape Decks

Vinyl Records (45s and 78s)

CD Players

Archiving

Sports

Live and Recorded

Mixing

Commercials

News

Talk Shows

Sponsors

Remote Location

Equipment Set-Up

Resume

Peter H. Harris
735 College Road
South Portland, Maine 04106
(207) 555-0000 / email@email.com

> **Radio Disc Jockey**
> **Varied Talk Show Host**
>
> **Total Sound Room Set-Up / Unique Mixing Style**
> **Recognized for Diversity in Broadcasting Special Events**

Well-rounded disc jockey with the proven ability to wear many hats in his position while succeeding in keeping the full attention of his audience through the microphone and the radio. Recognized for exceptional talents in his field and for having devoted many hours in promoting many charitable organizations through fund raisers, marathon broadcastings, and personally hosting related talk shows.

Core Strengths

Excellent Voice Projection	Industry Knowledge (20 Years)
Excellent Library of Recordings	Total Technology Emersion

Professional Experience

WABC—1010AM Radio, Portland, Maine	1982–1992
WJRK—93.5FM Radio, South Portland, Maine	1992–Current

Radio Disc Jockey

Accept phone requests; provide live and prerecord music to suit various audiences. Research archives for requests and return when done. Maintain archives while monitoring inventory. On occasion, write advertising copy and produce voice-overs. Ensure that airing of commercials is timely. Host shows live, when necessary. Perform creative mixing and dubbing as needed. Conduct frequent telephone and mail surveys to assure airing and proper mix.

- Trained other disc jockeys in effectively researching archives.
- Conceptualized frequent comedy skits and won an award for creativity.
- Created several new characters "on the air" to increase overall ratings.
- Selected as "Disc Jockey Who Introduced the Most Hit Records in 2000".

Education

Bates College, Lewiston, Maine
Studied Political Science   Completed two years, 1980–1982

- Managed campus radio station WRBC—91.5FM.
- Recognized for candid interviews with several visiting dignitaries.

Interview Q&A Using Keywords

Why should we hire you, what are your strengths, and how do you see yourself contributing to our company?

As a veteran disc jockey of 20 years, my experience has taken me through several generations of recording stars in addition to major changes in media presentations, equipment, quality of sound, and overall radio and recording technology. Currently enjoying the total evolvement of the industry to present—working with state-of-the-art equipment in a computerized industry that produces the quality and sounds that could only be imagined 20 years ago on the radio. Peripheral involvement through the years has included hosting varied talk shows and on- and off-site special promotions.

RADIOLOGIST

<table>
<tr><td>

Resume

Robert C. Scooner, M.D.
689 Beltline Drive
Dallas, Texas 75240
(214) 555-8888 / email@email.com

CERTIFIED RADIOLOGIST
with more than 15 years of experience

Specializing in
MRIs, CT Scans, and Ultrasounds.

American Board of Radiology Certified Radiologist who has performed over 15,000 radiographic examinations, interventional procedures, diagnostic overreads, and plain film interpretations.

Core Strengths

Arthrograms	Venograms
Barium Studies	Flouroscopy Screens
X-Rays	MRIs, CT Scans, Ultrasound
Mammography	Biopsies, IVPs

Professional Experience

RADIOLOGY ASSOCIATES, Dallas, Texas   1986 to present

Full-Time Radiologist

Perform radiographic examinations of patients' internal structures and organ systems, diagnose results, and recommend treatments to primary care physicians and surgeons using interventional procedures and plain film interpretations. Assigned the major city of patients requiring MRIs, CT scans, and ultrasounds.

- Increased the company's annual revenues by $300,000 by developing a marketing campaign to secure patients requiring interventional procedures.
- Recognized by the American Board of Radiology for outstanding work on extensive barium studies involving patients from 1999 to 2001.
- Featured in *Radiology Magazine* in June of 2001 for interventional procedures.

Education

University of Texas Southwestern Medical Center at Dallas
Doctor of Medicine; Major: Radiology; 1985
University of Texas at Austin
Bachelor of Science Degree; Major: Medicine, 1980

</td><td>

Keywords

Board Certified

Treatments

X-Ray

Flouroscopy

Biopsy

MRI

CT Scan

Mammography

Ultrasound

IVPs

Radiology

Radiographic
    Examination/
    Substances

Internal Structures

Physician

Radioisotopes

Interventional
    Procedures

Plain Film
    Interpretations

Barium Studies

Arthrograms

Venograms

</td></tr>
</table>

Interview Q&A Using Keywords

Why should we hire you, what are your strengths, and how do you see yourself contributing to our company?

I am a Certified Radiologist who specializes in Interventional Procedures, MRIs, CT scans, and ultrasounds. I have performed over 15,000 tests, including mammograms, arthrograms, venograms, flouroscopy, and barium studies. I believe I can be an outstanding addition to your physician team due to my diversified experience in diagnostic overreads, interventional procedures, plain film interpretations, excellent peer reviews, and my focus on ensuring superb quality of service to all patients.

REAL ESTATE BROKER

Keywords

Licensed Real Estate Broker

Purchase & Sale (P&S) Transactions

Relocation

Closing Skills

Negotiation Skills

Prospecting

Networking

Lead Generation

Competitive Market Analysis

Customer Service

Overcoming Objections

Meeting and/or Exceeding Goals

Chairman's Club / President's Club

Buyer's Agent / Seller's Agent

Marketing

Promotional Activities

Advertising

Strategic Market Planning

Mortgage

Value-Added Services

Resume

Robert K. Beaton
495 Peregrine Point
Marblehead, MA 02478
(617) 555-1212 / email@email.com

Real Estate Broker
More than $8 million in annual sales for 10 years in up and down markets

Top 3% in field of 2000 brokers / Specialize in high-end properties
Developing and implementing creative marketing strategies

High-powered, top-performing sales professional with 10 years' experience selling high-end properties for a national leader in residential real estate sales. Ahead of the curve in using technology to drive sales results. Initiatives in value-added customer service have earned the business referrals and loyalty of both home buyers and home sellers.

Core Strengths

Prospecting	Strategic marketing
Negotiation skills	Communication skills
P&S transaction oversight	Networking
Promotional activities	Customer service

Professional Experience

RE/HOMES Northshore, Marblehead, MA   1992–Present

Real Estate Broker

Sell properties in the oceanfront communities on Boston's North Shore. Develop marketing strategies. Prospect for leads, build client relationships, and show properties. Negotiate terms and support P&S transactions. Manage personal Web site as a marketing tool. Develop advertising and promotional strategies. Experienced in acting both as seller's agent and as buyer's agent.

- Top Producer Award in 1999 for the Northeast Region
- Ranked in the top 3% of brokers nationally for last three years
- Chairman's Club seven consecutive years ($4 million+)
- First to use a laptop computer with clients for on-the-spot comparables

Education

University of New Hampshire, Manchester, NH
Bachelor of Arts: Sociology, 1992
Graduate of the Gaines School of Real Estate, Concord, NH, 1991
Licensed Real Estate Broker, 1991

References Furnished Immediately upon Request

Interview Q&A Using Keywords

Why should we hire you, what are your strengths, and how do you see yourself contributing to our company?

I have ranked in the top tier of brokers within a national real estate company throughout my career. My personal sales have ranged from $8 million to $12 million annually in a competitive, high-end residential market. I am known for superior customer service and personal integrity. I have strong networking, lead generation, and closing skills. My competitive drive coupled with across-the-board real estate sales skills have consistently resulted in exceptional revenue generation for my company.

RECEPTIONIST

Resume

Rachael Anne Howard
Crestview Estates—#34
Lewiston, Maine 04240
(207) 555-1122 / email@email.com

> **Senior Corporate Receptionist**
> **PBX Administration / Domestic & Foreign Communications**
>
> **Multilingual Communication Skills**
> **Proven Executive-Level Business/Support Skills**

Seasoned senior-level receptionist with an ability to spill over into public relations and administrative support. Outstanding personality and professional manner. State-of-the-art equipment/technology trained (telephony & computer).

Core Strengths

Top Management Interaction	PBX Familiarity
Articulate (Presentations)	Detail Oriented
Administrative Assistant	Bilingual, French
Notary Public	Financial Accounting

Professional Experience

MACROSOFT INC., Silicon Valley, California   1992 to Present

Corporate Receptionist

Oversee total operation of a 100-line PBX telephone system and a staff of four; greet clients, screen, and direct calls to 400 (plus) in-house extensions. Trained individuals to manage the PBX area enabling time to assist (part of the day) in the executive office area. Provide French translations of "in" and "outgoing" messages via telephone, fax, and email. Provide varied secretarial and desktop publishing assistance.

- Developed a procedural manual for the PBX area.
- Screen, hire, and train PBX operators.
- Developed a system which allows tracking of corporate credit card expenses.
- Schedule and track all corporate-related travel for six individuals.

Education

University of Maine, Orono, Maine
Bachelor of Arts: Business   **Office Automation, 1990**

- Dean's List Student, four Years / GPA—3.8
- Recipient, Margaret Chase Smith Scholarship Award

Keywords

Professional Environment
PBX Skills
Articulate
Multitask Capabilities
Fast-Paced Environment
Word Processing
Spreadsheet Applications
Bilingual (French)
Detail Oriented
Public Relations
Presentation Skills
Call Screening
Message Taking
International Calls
Travel Arrangements
Hotel Reservations
Expense Accounts
Professional Appearance
Commissioned Notary Public
PBX

Interview Q&A Using Keywords

Why should we hire you, what are your strengths, and how do you see yourself contributing to our company?

As a qualified corporate receptionist with 10-plus years of experience in a professional setting, I feel confident that I could perform and surpass your expectations. With a focus on international relations and utilizing (daily) exceptional executive-level administrative assistant skills, I have developed the ability to "switch gears" very effectively while juggling multiple tasks. I am familiar with a variety of different phone systems and PBX. Computer knowledge includes word processing, spreadsheet applications, desktop publishing, and database management.

139

REGULATORY AFFAIRS COUNSEL

Resume

Helen Kramer
333 San Pedro Street
Los Angeles, California 90012
(213) 555-1122 / email@email.com

Regulatory Affairs Counsel
Telecommunications Policy Expert

Case-Winning Negotiator
Audit Planning and Review

Expert policy advisor to emerging technology, especially on government and trade association standardization forums. Dual degrees in both Information Technology and Corporate Law.

Core Strengths

Advising new starts	Strategic operational assessment
Policy formulation	Integrating objectives
Audit planning and execution	FCC compliance
Negotiation	Trade lobbyist

Professional Experience

Bates & Bates, LLP, Los Angeles, California   1995 to Current

Regulatory Affairs Counsel

Technical advisor to emerging telecommunications companies regarding regulatory policy formulation, antitrust investigation, and legislative matters. Assess initial strategic operational plans for Federal Communications Commission (FCC) and regional compliance regarding broadband, privacy, network security, access, and domain name competition. Integrate compliance actions with corporate objectives.

- Key negotiator for the postponement of the FCC's auction of the 700-megahertz band spectrum until 2003. This will allow emergency services to acquire interference-free transmission.
- High-visibility as an expert witness and lobbyist to Congress regarding fair competition practices for industry and nonprofit organizations.
- Appointed to the Federal Telecommunications Accessibility Advisory Committee (1999–2000).

Education

University of California at Los Angeles, California
Bachelor of Science / Information Technology, 1996
Juris Doctor / Corporate Law, 1992

References Furnished Immediately upon Request

Interview Q&A Using Keywords

Why should we hire you, what are your strengths, and how do you see yourself contributing to our company?

My life is dedicated to facilitating rapid growth and universal accessibility in the industry by interpreting standards and streamlining regulatory compliance activities for new business. My broad experience in regulatory compliance has included FCC complaints and policy proceedings, mergers and acquisitions, e-commerce, privacy, and broadband. I will use my connections and negotiation skills to spot and resolve any roadblocks to a successful venture; for example, securing the 700-megahertz auction postponement.

RESTAURANT MANAGER

Resume

Jan Scott
1090 Encore Ave.
Columbus, Ohio 43229
(614) 555-1122 / email@email.com

Restaurant Manager
Controlling costs and ensuring profitability...

Staff Training/Development • Food Standards & Controls
Budget Planning/Administration • Customer Service Management

Seasoned management professional offering nearly 10 years' experience in fast-paced, high-volume food service/bar environments. Maximizing staff potential through excellent leadership and organizational skills.

Core Strengths

Inventory/Cost Control
Food & Beverage Operations
Facilities Management/Sanitation
Menu Development

Purchasing/Vendor Relations
Accounting/Payroll
Team Building and Leadership
Business Development

Professional Experience

Worthington Woods Resort, Columbus, Ohio   2000 to Present

Restaurant Manager

Coordinate all marketing and promotions, operations management, budgeting, weekly sales reporting, vendor relations, customer service. Accountable for profit & loss, total quality, and cash management operations. Consult with general managers, F&B directors, and support staff for strategic planning purposes.

- Grew operating profits by 8.4% within first year.
- Coordinated and supervised $500,000 restaurant renovation.
- Marketed restaurant benefits and features that attracted high-profile travelers.
- Strategically designed highly creative menu that became standard for all hotels.

Education

The Ohio State University, Columbus, Ohio
Bachelor of Science, Hotel Administration, 1992

- Concentration: Food and Beverage Management
- Study Abroad: èn-Provence, France, Spring 1991

References Furnished Immediately upon Request

Keywords

Inventory/Cost Control
Food & Beverage Operations
Facilities Management/Sanitation
Menu Development
Purchasing/Procurement
Team Building & Leadership
Budget Planning/Administration
Profit & Loss Management
Banquets/Catering
Accounting/Payroll
Customer Service Management
Total Quality Management
Sales and Promotions
Business Development
Cash Management/Deposits
Vendor Relations
Staff Hiring/Training/Development
Operations Management
Food Production Standards & Controls
Cash Management

Interview Q&A Using Keywords

Why should we hire you, what are your strengths, and how do you see yourself contributing to our company?

Whether in high- or low-volume restaurants, I have consistently identified root problems for lagging sales. The need for a qualified and enthusiastic staff cannot be overstated. It would be my first priority to assess the existing staff and if necessary, rehire, train and ensure continued development for new employees. My natural leadership style in addition to my extensive experience in inventory/cost control, food/beverage operations, profit/loss, and customer service management will prove highly beneficial to your vision of excellent hospitality service.

RETAIL SALES MANAGER

Keywords

District Sales

Customer Loyalty

Business
  Development

Low Employee
  Turnover

In-Store Promotions

Loss Prevention

Pricing

Inventory Control

Merchandising

Security Operations

Retail Sales

Employee Retention

Stock Management

Warehousing
  Operations

Product
  Management

Continuous Process
  Improvement

Customer-Driven
  Management

Margin
  Improvement

Customer Service

Credit Operations

Resume

Seth Miller
123 S. Fourth Street
Kewanee, Illinois 61443
(309) 555-1234 / email@email.com

Retail Sales Manager
11-Year Background in Performance and Process Improvement

Customer-Driven Management / Margin Improvement Skills
Start-Up and Turnaround Management Experience

Driven and experienced retail sales management professional with proven skills in cost reduction and business development. Successful background of implementing highly profitable in-store promotions.

Core Strengths

Loss Prevention	Merchandising
Strategic Planning	Stock Management
Margin Improvement	Customer Service
Business Development	Inventory Control
Retail Sales Training	Cost Reduction

Professional Experience

STUFF-MART, Centerville, IL   1999 to Current

Retail Sales Manager

Recruited to boost retail sales and improve merchandising strategies for this highly successful merchandising warehouse operation. Implemented effective stock management policies, created profitable in-store promotions, and turned focus to a customer-driven management style. Directed customer service and warehousing operations. Achieved significant margin of improvement and led efforts to increase customer loyalty.

- Increased district sales by $60,000; achieved highest margin of improvement.
- Drove sales for credit operations by training staff in up-selling techniques.
- Implemented highly effective management strategic planning sessions.
- Pioneered security operations to reduce inventory loss.

Education

Wisconsin University, Jasper, Wisconsin
Bachelor of Arts: Business Management, 1990

Interview Q&A Using Keywords

Why Should Our Company Hire You?

I am a highly enthusiastic management professional with a customer-driven management style. One key element to successful retail management is employee retention. One key strength I possess is selecting and retaining good retail employees. My track record reflects record-breaking district sales. I have successfully designed and implemented cutting-edge in-store displays, and I have played a key role in start-up operations and strategic planning.

RISK MANAGEMENT

Resume

Steven H. Nash
177 Linden Boulevard
Snyder, New York 14226
(716) 555-6954 / email@email.com

> **Risk Management**
> **Seasoned Professional with Expertise in Investigating**
> **Loss History/Trends to Predict and Avoid Future Risk**
>
> **Perform Insurance Analysis, Determine Severity and**
> **Frequency Potential, and Minimize Financial Impact**

Direct risk management staff overseeing $4 million in credit exposure. Instill performance-based culture by allocating responsibility and accountability. Develop programs to maximize loss control.

Core Strengths

Health and Safety Programs	Carrier and Broker Selection
Operational and Risk Reporting	Self-Insurance and Noninsurance
Fidelity, Surety, and Liability	Program Development

Professional Experience

HELFER INDUSTRIES, LTD., Buffalo, New York   1982 to Current

Risk Management Specialist

Research and analyze corporate products and operations and determine appropriate coverage levels. Negotiate contracts based on hazard identification and risk exposure. Conduct health and safety audits and report results to senior management. Utilize PowerPoint to graphically demonstrate ways to implement loss control.

- Reengineered processes resulting in $1.2 million loss avoidance/risk reduction in 1 year.
- Reversed $745,000 in annual losses and broke-even in $1\frac{1}{2}$ years.
- Implemented comprehensive risk-management strategic plan.
- Saved $500,000 annually through renegotiation of information contracts.

Education

Canisius College School of Management, Buffalo, New York
Bachelor of Science: Business Administration, 1982

- Milton Seligman Business Scholar
- Who's Who in American Colleges and Universities

References Furnished Immediately upon Request

Keywords

Insurance Analysis
Financial Impact
Fidelity, Surety, Liability, and Property Coverage
Program Development
Loss Control
Workers' Compensation, Group Life, Pension, and Medical Plans
Health and Safety Programs
Carrier and Broker Selection
Severity and Frequency Potential
Operational and Risk Reporting
Strategic Plan
Avoidance and Transfer
Minimization, Reduction, and Prevention
Self-Insurance and Planned Noninsurance
Credit Exposure
Negotiation and Renegotiation
Hazard Identification
Performance-Based Culture
Risk Management
Loss History and Trends

Interview Q&A Using Keywords

Why should we hire you, what are your strengths, and how do you see yourself contributing to our company?

At Helfer, I reengineered processes resulting in $1.2 million loss avoidance/risk reduction in one year. We reversed $745,000 in annual losses and took broke even in one-and-a-half years. Overall responsibilities include directing a risk management staff overseeing $4 million in credit exposure. Here, we implemented a comprehensive risk management strategic plan and saved $500,000 annually through renegotiation of information contracts.

SALES/CORPORATE TRAINER

Keywords

Human Resources Management

Program Development

Training

Curriculum Development

Budget Preparation and Control

Adult Learning

Certification Programs

Educational Needs Assessment

Employee Training

Career Development Counseling

Executive Development Programs

Employee Assistance Programs (EAP)

Facilitator Training Programs (Train-the-Trainer)

Time Management / Project Management

Motivational Training

Team Building

Supervisory Skills

Communications Skills

Multicultural Workforce

Corporate Ethics

Resume

Patricia Capizzi
1188 Bedford Drive
Camarillo, California and 93010
(805) 555-1122 / email@email.com

> **Corporate Trainer**
> **Committed to the educational needs of American industry**
>
> **Executive Development / Adult Learning**
> **Human Resources Management**

An energetic and success-driven education and human resources leader with a 15-year history of turning marginally performing employees into top producers.

Core Strengths

Educational needs assessment	Curriculum development
Executive development	Motivational training

Professional Experience

Procter & Gamble Paper Product Division   2000 to Current
Oxnard, California 93030

Director of Corporate Training

Recruited as a "troubleshooter" to identify educational needs and develop training programs for the next millennia's executive and technical workforce. Implemented training plans within corporate business plans, budget, and schedules.

- Originated an educational incentive program that provides bonuses for earning career-related certifications and subsidizes recertification costs.
- Adapted selected executive development program courses (such as time/program management, supervision, and team building) to lower-level employees. Improved year-end production was attributable to better employee attendance and awareness of management goals.
- Incorporated courses such as ethics, success training, and career-life balance into all employee training plans to encourage a healthy workforce.

Education

University of California at Santa Barbara, California
Masters degree in Adult Education / 1990
Bachelor of Science degree in Psychology / 1986
Certified Job & Career Transition Coach
Member, American Counseling Association

References Furnished Immediately upon Request

Interview Q&A Using Keywords

Why should we hire you, what are your strengths, and how do you see yourself contributing to our company?

My expertise in corporate training stems from a solid education—degrees in Adult Education and Psychology, backed by a career counseling certification and practical work in several motivational training techniques. Additionally, I am gifted with the ability to assess correctly and meet the present and future educational needs of industry managers and a technical workforce. Above all else, I really care about people's development and helping to make them successful.

Resume

Gary Sloan
495 Belmont Avenue
Belmont, MA 02478
(617) 555-1212 / email@email.com

> **Sales Representative**
> **Four-year track record of revenue enhancement**
>
> **Presentation & closing skills / Opening up new markets**
> **Consistently exceeding sales quotas**

Outgoing, aggressive sales professional with four years of part-time experience selling in competitive markets. Outperformed four full-time rental agents while earning B.S. degree. Conversational Spanish.

Core Strengths

Prospecting	Organizational Skills
Presentation Skills	Communication Skills
Closing Skills	Networking
Strategic Market Planning	Customer Service

Professional Experience

BOSTON CITY RENTALS, Boston, MA   1997–Present

Rental Agent / Sales Representative

Manage the Beacon Hill and Jamaica Plain territories. Prospect for leads, show properties, build customer relationships, present customized selling points, close sales, and provide after-sales customer service. Build networks of relationships with city landlords. Develop strategic market plans for market penetration. Create sales collateral. Develop advertising placements and strategies.

- Ranked #1 in rental sales for the last three years
- Gained 10% market share in the saturated Back Bay market
- Opened up a territory that represented $100K in new 2002 revenue
- Launched the first corporate Web site to offer real-time rental data

Education

Boston University, Boston, Massachusetts
Bachelor of Science: Business Administration, 2001

- Completed degree in 3.5 years
- Paid own way through school with sales earnings

Keywords

Sales
Prospecting
Account Management
Closing
Consultative Sales
  Approach
Sales Engineering
Presentation Skills
Closing Skills
Networking
Competitive Analysis
Customer Service
Overcoming
  Objections
Territory
  Management
Opening Up New
  Territories
Market Penetration
Gaining Market
  Share
Meeting and/or
  Exceeding Sales
  Target
Meeting and/or
  Exceeding Quotas
Persuasive
  Communication
  Skills
Cold-Calling
Strategic Market
  Planning
Customer
  Relationship
  Building
Alliance Building

Interview Q&A Using Keywords

Why should we hire you, what are your strengths, and how do you see yourself contributing to our company?

I have demonstrated an ability to be highly successful in exceeding sales quotas, opening up new territories, and gaining market share in competitive markets. I am adept at researching and prospecting to identify a customer's needs. Then I would develop key selling points, tailoring them to the customer's needs, and closing the sale. My communication and interpersonal skills have enabled me to excel in building relationships with existing and potential customers. What separates me from others is the intensity of my commitment to growing revenues and providing superior customer service.

SALES SUPPORT/COORDINATOR

Keywords

Advertising Experience

Multimedia Advertising

Available to Travel

Internet Advertising

Computer Skills

Key Account Management

Marketing Strategies

Appointment Scheduling

Travel Arrangements

Printing/Typesetting Knowledge

Newsletter Creation

Itinerary Management

Sales Promotions

Product Knowledge

Co-op Advertising

Presentation Preparation

Trade Shows

Ad Design & Layout

Promotional Materials Handling

Resume

Joan C. Millani
13 Pleasant Street
Sabattus, Maine 04280
(207) 555-2222 / email@email.com

Sales Support/Coordinator
Multimedia Specialist

Trade Show Coordinator and Presenter
Promotional Materials Selection and Management

Highly energetic individual who is driven by the challenges presented in sales, marketing, and promoting new products. Outstanding team player who thrives on supporting the efforts of a successful sales team.

Core Strengths

Multimedia Advertising	Newsletter Creation and Distribution
Marketing Strategies	Printing/typesetting Expertise
Co-op Advertising	Ad Design & Layout
Internet Research	Business Support Skills

Professional Experience

Shad's Advertising Company, Auburn, Maine   1997–Present

Sales Support/Coordinator

Provide sales and clerical support to a sales team of eight serving a tri-state area. Assist in maintaining communications with key accounts. Help select and prepare for shipping all promotional materials for presentations and trade shows. Recommend products for special promotions and advertising. Help design ads, provide copy, and prepare layout for final approval. Coordinate printing with printer to assure quality and meeting deadlines.

- Instrumental in acquiring several major accounts through presentations.
- New accounts generated an additional $1.5 million in sales in 2001.
- Recouped $20,000 in co-op advertising dollars in last six months.
- Created a new and more efficient system in preparing proposals.

Education

Andover College, Portland, Maine   1995–1997
Associates Degree in Marketing / Focus: Advertising

- Selected by Faculty to Design Cover of Yearbook
- GPA / 4.0

Interview Q&A Using Keywords

Why should we hire you, what are your strengths, and how do you see yourself contributing to our company?

I feel confident that I could prove to be an asset to your organization. My past experience has been very heavily focused in advertising with sales support as a major part of my responsibilities. Support skills have included the need for much travel while creating and preparing promotional materials and assisting at trade shows. Most of the coordination work I have done is through the Internet and the use of varied in-house software programs. In addition, your company could benefit from very diversified hands-on secretarial support skills.

Resume

Cythina "Cindy" Matthews
2020 McLean Drive
Auburn, Alabama 36830
(334) 555-1212 / email@email.com

Sales Support Engineer
Positioning your company as the "sole source"

Relationship & consultative selling / Presentation skills at the engineering level
Customer needs analysis

A driven sales professional with all the engineering experience needed to uncover and fill market niche needs—even those your customers aren't yet aware of. Totally dedicated to the idea that customer support always equals sales support. More than seven years as an industrial engineer and more than five years as sales support engineer.

Core Strengths

Matching customers' needs with our products   Consultative selling
Leveraging market intelligence   Troubleshooting
Spotting industry trends   Mastering production procedures

Professional Experience

Railtor Packing Equipment Company, Auburn, Alabama   1998 to Current

Sales Support Engineer

Responsible for the sales process from lead generation to delivery to comprehensive follow-up. Collaborate closely with our engineering, marketing, and sales departments to match or modify our 215-item product line to customers' requirements. Work closely with customers to develop best practices—often on site. Develop and qualify new leads for a company with $375M annual sales.

- Used customer's requirements to spin off new product line that generated $200K in sales.
- Helped a customer find better ways to use our legacy equipment. Sold upgrade worth $350K.
- Found an improved method to capture second-level leads by establishing relationships with purchasing professionals

Education

University of Alabama, Birmingham, Alabama
Bachelor of Science in Industrial Engineering, 1985

References Furnished Immediately upon Request

Keywords

Engineering Sales

Technology

RFP

Consultative Selling

WAN

Data Sales

Network Design

Pricing

Semiconductor

Computers

Software

Hardware

Programming

LAN

Cisco Certified

OEM

IP

Nortel

Special Pricing

Router

Network
  Architecture

Interview Q&A Using Keywords

Why should we hire you, what are your strengths, and how do you see yourself contributing to our company?

I am your link to the most influential buying decision makers in your market: engineers. I do a lot more than speak "engineering-ese" fluently. I know how to spark engineers' desire to make a very smart buy—and avoid triggering their powerful aversion to being "sold." And what I sell is more than our products. I sell the confidence that guides companies to think of us as their sole source for capability that drives their own profits. I want every sale I make to be the first of many.

SAP ANALYST

Resume

Michael Smith
25 Tulip Avenue
East Floral Park, New York 11201
(516) 555-2220 / email@email.com

SAP Analyst
Fast-track career providing ERP solutions across multiple industries

Supply Chain Management / Sales and Distribution
Materials Management / Customer Relationship Management

Award-winning IT professional with 18 years of experience leading Fortune 500 clients through global system changes to meet the functional and technical demands of ERP business solutions and SAP requirements.

Core Strengths

Project Management	Supplier Relationships
Systems Analysis	ERP Business Solutions
Visibility Portals	Performance Measurement
Seamless Integration	Networking Capabilities

Professional Experience

INTEGRATED SOLUTIONS, New York, New York   1994 to Current

SAP Business Systems Analyst

Continually measure the performance of ERP business solutions designed to promote the seamless integration of networking capabilities and visibility portals. Define functional requirements to support the transition from a linear, sequential supply chain to an adaptive supply chain network. Equally effective at strengthening supply chain management, customer relationships management, and improving business processes.

- Led an award-winning SAP team in the management of ERP projects
- Built industry-specific modules integrating R/3, APO, and Extricity
- Enhanced supplier relationships and realized profitability by $20 million
- Optimized supply chain networks and planned capacity allocations

Education

Stony Brook University, Stony Brook, New York
Bachelor of Science: Computer Science, 1993

- Certification in SAP APO DP
- Certification in SAP Retail R/3 Module

References Furnished Immediately upon Request

Interview Q&A Using Keywords

Why should we hire you, what are your strengths, and how do you see yourself contributing to our company?

With an 18-year career spearheading large integration projects for parallel business models, specifically Supply Chain Management, I am uniquely positioned to manage your organization's critical ERP implementation projects on both the technical and functional sides. I believe my ability to lead, mentor top-gun SAP teams, and translate business objectives into actionable plans, will prove vital in the development of a highly flexible technology infrastructure to run your business operations.

SCHOOL PRINCIPAL

Resume

Joseph Saunders
123 11th Avenue South
Metamora, Illinois 61111
(309) 123-4566 / email@email.com

Secondary School Administrator
Offering 20+ years in education, with a proven commitment
to creating a nurturing culture

Foster teamwork among educators and effectively mentor teachers
to promote student advocacy.
Expertise in Curriculum Development/Instruction &
Supervision/Consulting & Collaboration

Resourceful and visionary education administrator widely experienced in program development, grant writing, curricula development, school consolidation, computer education, staff development, budget management, strategic planning, and community / media relations. Excellent written and oral communication skills.

Core Strengths

Fostering Student Engagement   Promoting Authentic Assessment
Encouraging Lifelong Learning   Designing Courses / Curriculum Planning
Textbook Review   Mentoring Educators
Consulting/Collaboration   Evaluation of Learning Goals & Objectives

Professional Experience

ROSS GAMBLE HIGH SCHOOL, Delaware, Illinois   8/84 to Present

Principal

Oversee all operations, providing personnel development and related services to a staff of 40 teachers, aides, and counselors. Administer programming, long-range planning, and policy development, and ensure compliance with state regulations.

- Built a reputation as a first-class source for information, with cutting-edge teaching techniques and an up-to-date resource library for staff.
- Utilized compression planning process to develop needs assessment for at-risk students.
- Implemented Scientific Literacy Project in collaboration with Southern Illinois University, that was ranked one of the best in the state.

Education

Bradley University, Peoria, Illinois
Master of Science in Education Administration, 5/84
University of Illinois, Urbana, Illinois
Bachelor of Science in History, 5/76

Keywords

Education
School Principal
Lifelong Learning
Program Development
Grant Writing
Educational Administration
Cooperative learning
Classroom Management
Course Design
Curriculum Planning
School Consolidation
Student Advocate
Textbook Review
Mentor
Vocational Education
Staff Training and Development
Teamwork
Consulting / Collaboration
Evaluation of Learning goals and Objectives

Interview Q&A Using Keywords

Why should we hire you, what are your strengths, and how do you see yourself contributing to our company?

I believe in promoting a nurturing culture that fosters student engagement, but to do it effectively requires a combination of strategies. I mentor individual teachers and make myself available to them, and I try to create a teamwork environment. After all, there's no room for competition, because we're on the same side; we're all student advocates. I've brought a number of seminars to the school to promote staff training and development. I've also worked with counselors and teachers to identify authentic assessment techniques to ensure that we have a good measure of the needs of our students and to help us design targeted learning goals and objectives.

SENIOR BUSINESS CONSULTANT

Keywords

Business Consulting

Sales Channel
Distribution

Business Process
Reengineering

Competitive Market
Position

Corporate Culture
Change

Change Management

Corporate Image/
Vision/Mission

Cross-Functional
Team Leadership

Financial
Management/
Restructuring

Accelerated Growth
Strategies

Operating Leadership

Organizational
Development

Deliverables

Performance
Improvement

Quality Improvement

Advanced
Technologies

Merger/Acquisition
(M&A) Integrations

Initial Public Offering
(IPO) Management

Efficiency
Improvement

Crisis Management/
Disaster Recovery

Resume

Tim Thompson
10 East 14th Street, Apt. 3D
New York, NY 10003
(212) 555-1122 / email@email.com

Finance and E-Business Specialist
Fortune 500, Start-up, and Global Strategic Business Consulting

Broad International Experience—Europe, Pacific Rim, Latin America
M.B.A. in Finance and M.A. in International Affairs from Wharton

---

Develop innovative business, finance, and e-commerce strategies that deliver impressive bottom-line impact. An acknowledged global thought leader, bringing cross-cultural business expertise to every assignment.

Core Strengths

Business Process Reengineering	Corporate Culture Change
Financial Management	Organizational Development
Performance / Quality Improvement	Advanced Technologies
Accelerated Growth Strategies	Disaster Recovery

Professional Experience

Gunther, Reaburn, & Batson Consulting   1996 to Current

Managing Consultant, Global Practice

Collaborate with management teams of globally aligned companies and start-ups in all industries to provide concrete guidance in business development, business reengineering, competitive market positioning, change management, corporate image / mission / vision restructuring, operating leadership, M&A integrations, IPO management, efficiency improvement, disaster recovery, and crisis management.

- Raised over $40 million funding for successful Dutch telecom start-up.
- Built Hong Kong's first e-commerce solution, still in business today.
- Brought public / launched (12 nations) the first non-U.S. microbrewery.
- Hold board positions with two Fortune 1000 firms.

Education

The Wharton School, University of Pennsylvania, Philadelphia, PA
M.B.A.: Finance, 1990 / M.A.: International Affairs, 1985
Georgetown University, Georgetown, VA
Bachelor of Science: International Affairs, 1983

References Furnished Immediately upon Request

Interview Q&A Using Keywords

Why should we hire you, what are your strengths, and how do you see yourself contributing to our company?

Immediate contribution is my hallmark—I quickly assess your business situation and deliver short-term impacting solutions while delving deeper into the details to develop solutions-based action plans that achieve management and staff buy-in. Using fluency in three languages and an understanding of diverse cultures' business practices, I can improve your global business practices.

Resume

Theresa Mascagni
24 Aubrey Court
Princeton Junction, NJ 08550
(609) 555-1122 / email@email.com

> **Senior-Level Sales Management Professional**
> **20 Years' Sales and Marketing Leadership**
>
> **Multi-Million-Dollar Achievements in Revenue Gain**
> **Deliver Sustained Business Growth and Solid Alliances**

Transform corporate goals into profits by cross-functional teaming to develop speed-to-market strategies, by constructing innovative sales programs, and by managing dynamic, solutions-based sales teams.

Core Strengths

National Account Oversight	Market Evaluation and Strategy
Short- and Long-Term Goals	Sales Organization Restructuring
Sales Program Development	Sales Force Motivation and Training
Profit & Loss Oversight	C-Level Relationship Management

Professional Experience

Med Solutions, Philadelphia, PA   1998 to Current

Senior Vice President of Sales

Member of core management team directing restart for this leading manufacturer of EMS-related medical devices. Redefined and restructured company, achieving 25% annual growth. Used market and product evaluation, strategy, and competitive analysis to rebuild distribution channels, create lean yet effective sales budgets, develop new accounts, and negotiate joint partnerships for multichannel distribution.

- Took business from $54 million to $80 million in under three years.
- Revitalized market position, bringing to fifth in industry from tenth.
- Reduced turnover to 10% less than industry comparables.
- Created systems to address difficulties caused by accelerated growth.

Education

Rutgers University, New Brunswick, NJ
Bachelor of Science: Mathematics, 1982

- Development program in leadership, Harvard Law School, 2001
- Development program in mentoring, University of Michigan, 2000

References Furnished Immediately upon Request

Keywords

Market/Product Evaluation and Strategy

Consultative Sales Techniques

Relationship Management

Core Management Team

P&L Oversight

Sales Organization Restructuring

Short- and Long-Term Sales Goals

Vice President

National Account Oversight

Sales Program Development

Sales Force Motivation/ Training

Competitive Analysis

Sales Budgets

Strategic Plans

Speed-to-Market Strategies

Cross-Functional Teaming

Solutions-Based Sales

Multiteam Sales management

Multichannel Distribution

C-Level Relationship Building/ Negotiations

Interview Q&A Using Keywords

Why should we hire you, what are your strengths, and how do you see yourself contributing to our company?

An experienced senior sales leader, I direct regional and national programs and sales teams serving Fortune 100 companies. We grow new and core business in corporations and entrepreneurial companies, using strategic plans and breakthrough positioning to gain competitive advantage and convert visions into results. I believe in consultative sales combined with calculated risk, and encourage my team to develop and deliver innovative solutions that build business, generate profits, and solidify customer relationships.

Keywords

Crisis Intervention

Behavior Management

Personality Disorders

Adult Services

Casework

Community Outreach

Diagnostic Evaluation

Chronic Substance Abuse

Social Functioning

Independent Living Skills

Human Services

Mainstreaming

Protective Services

Treatment Planning

Youth Training Program

Vocational Rehabilitation

Client Placement

Group Counseling

Domestic Violence

Coping Mechanisms

Resume

Julie P. Rackley, LSW
123 Main Street
South Portland, Maine 04106
(207) 555-9999 / email@email.com

Social Worker / Child Protection Advocate
Licensed Social Worker

Selected to Develop Relevant Programs and Instruct Other Caseworkers
Expertise in Autism and Pervasive Developmental Disorders
Formed Varied Support Groups for Parents

Diversified Caseworker with an innate ability to access, evaluate, and make decisions pertaining to children (or adults) relevant to their safety and the possible need for treatment or rehabilitation. Many need relocation or protection from dysfunctional home environments, surroundings, and guardians.

Core Strengths

Lead Group Counseling Sessions	Diagnostic Evaluation
Oversee Child Guidance Clinics	Investigate Home Conditions
Evaluate Personal Characteristics	Behavior Modification Programs

Professional Experience

Department of Human Services, Augusta, Maine   1992–Present

Child Protective Caseworker

Counsel individuals or family members regarding behavior modification, rehabilitation, social adjustments, financial assistance, vocational training, childcare, or medical care. Lead group counseling sessions to provide support in such areas as grief, stress, or chemical dependency. Serve as liaison between student, home, school, family service agencies, child guidance clinics, courts, protective adoptive home, or to protect children from harmful environment.

- Developed a program to train other caseworkers to better understand Autism.
- Assisted in the founding of a new outreach hotline for runaways.

Education

University of New England, Biddeford, Maine
Bachelor of Science Psychology / Concentration, Mental Health, 1992
Master in Social Services / Spring, 2003

- Psychology National Honor Society, PSI CHI
- Current GPA/3.8

Interview Q&A Using Keywords

Why should we hire you, what are your strengths, and how do you see yourself contributing to our company?

As a candidate for my Master's in Social Work, I also offer 10 plus years of experience in crisis intervention working with people of all ages and with varying issues. In addition, I have trained other caseworkers and community providers regarding child abuse and neglect, among other areas. I believe your organization could benefit from such diversity while benefiting from my capability to help your organization expand its services in the community.

SOCIAL WORKER

Resume

Naomi Bridges
402 West Adams Street
Pekin, Illinois 61111
(309) 555-1111 / email@email.com

Human Services Professional
Social Services / Case Management / Staff Management

Strong qualifications facilitating cooperative partnerships
in both the private and public sector.
Excellent communication, team leadership, and crisis management skills.

Licensed social worker with extensive experience in the development and management of specialized programs targeting the needs of multiple patient populations. Combine team leadership experience with a solid background in counseling and therapy. Confident and focused under pressure; exercise prudent judgment in decision-making areas.

Core Strengths

The Prevention of Teen Pregnancy	Vocational Education
Management/Administration	Policy and Planning
Regulatory Compliance	Mental Health Assessments
Research	Counseling/Group Therapy

Professional Experience

FAMILY SERVICES AGENCY, Peoria, Illinois 1996 to Present

Team Leader / Case Manager
Direct all aspects of programming and client services for a private agency providing service to children and families throughout three counties. Also manage a busy caseload, with responsibility for identifying client needs and structuring treatment plans in collaboration with an interdisciplinary team of social workers, nurses, therapists, and physicians, with an emphasis on behavioral change and lifestyle goals.

- Launched a six-week high-risk teen pregnancy group incorporating childbirth and parenting education. Solicited the donations of bassinets and layettes to use as incentives to motivate expectant mothers to attend all six meetings; attracted 20+ participants.
- Initiated and delivered a number of educational seminars and workshops including "Close the Gap—Current Challenges of Adolescence," which was sold out within a week. Elected to serve on Peoria's Adolescent Consortium as a result of the success of this program.

Education

UNIVERSITY OF ILLINOIS, Urbana, Illinois, 1996
Master of Social Work
BRADLEY UNIVERSITY, Peoria, Illinois, 1991
Bachelor of Science in Social Services

Keywords

Substance Abuse and Addiction

Vocational Education

Adult and Youth Populations

Childbirth and Parenting Education

Counseling

Management / Administration

Policy and Planning

Regulatory Compliance

Mental Health Assessments

Case Management

Daily Living Skills

Parenting Skills

Behavioral Change

Lifestyle Goals

Facilitating Support groups

Research

Grant Writing

Grant Administration

Public & Private Partnerships

Group Therapy

Interview Q&A Using Keywords

Why should we hire you, what are your strengths, and how do you see yourself contributing to our company?

I began as a case manager and counselor for substance abuse and additional clients from both adult and youth populations, and I progressed to the management of a growing agency. In that capacity, I have forged a number of public and private partnerships with government and public agencies, as well as leaders in the business community. I've also written and administered numerous grants. I believe I offer a unique balance of skills, ranging from clinical social work (developing mental health assessments, helping patients develop effective parenting and other critical skills, and the facilitation of therapy groups) to full administration, including budgeting, research, regulatory compliance, and policy and planning.

SOFTWARE ENGINEER

Keywords

C

C++

Visual Basic

Java

Fortran

Pascal

MCF V++

Infrastructure
  Planning

Design

Development

Engineering

System
  Functionality

System Stability

Innovative

Self-Starter

Independent

Team Player

Programming

Needs Assessment

Customer
  Requirements

Resume

Deborah Neal
5635 Katchina Lane
Anywhere, Idaho 00000
(208) 555-0000 / email@email.com

> **Software Engineer**
> **17 years of successful experience in designing and developing**
> **sophisticated software systems**
>
> **Expert Software Engineer**
> **Outstanding Programming Techniques**

Proficient in a number of programming languages. Efficient analytical, problem-solving, and decision-making skills. Able to solve complex problems and provide working solutions. Can assist others in utilizing productive programming techniques. Work well under pressure.

Core Strengths

Multidiscipline Engineering	System Functionality
MCF VC++	Embedded Kernal OS
Infrastructure Planning	C and Assembler
Software Design/Development	System Implementation

Professional Experience

AMI SEMICONDUCTOR, Lincoln, Idaho   2001 to Present

Software Engineer

Design, develop, test, and maintain real-time embedded software for proofing devices. Design, develop, test, and maintain DSP, and MCF VC++ application software. Experience in design, development, testing, implementation, and maintenance of systems software written in C and Assembler running in a real-time environment. Experience with version control and cross-platform development tools and procedures.

- Completed a 12-month project in under 9 months—received $2500 award.
- Lead the Software Engineering Team in a project that resulted in a $30,000 savings to the customer.

Education

North Idaho College, Couer d'Alene, Idaho
Bachelor of Science Degree in Engineering. Minor: Information Technology. 1999.

- Selected as team leader in development of a new Microsoft game client.
- Awarded Student Innovation Scholarship.

Interview Q&A Using Keywords

Why should we hire you, what are your strengths, and how do you see yourself contributing to our company?

I am organized and capable of self-management. I am a proactive team player. I have excellent programming and functionality skills. I am innovative, creative, and take initiative to get the job done. I can handle stress and unpredictable workloads, conflicting deadlines, and interruptions, and most importantly, have strong interpersonal skills with coworkers. I have outstanding design and development skills. I meet all qualifications described in the posting. I earned a Bachelor of Science degree in Computer Science.

SPEECH THERAPIST

Resume

Cynthia Janis Miller
137 East Longwood Drive
Miller Place, New York 11764
(631) 555-9080 / email@email.com

Speech Therapy
Eight years' experience in speech-language pathology

Screenings, Evaluations, and Recommendations
Early Intervention / Kindergarten–Secondary Education

Credentialed speech-language pathologist experienced providing speech-language therapy to children, adult, and geriatric speech-impaired clients throughout clinical, hospital, educational, and homecare settings.

Core Strengths

Screenings and Evaluations   Program Development
Auditory Processing Deficits   Early Intervention
Language Acquisition   Standardized Testing
Augmentative Communication   Cochlear Implants

Professional Experience

St. Augustine Catholic School, Brentwood, New York   1997 to Current

Speech-Language Pathologist
Manage the development and implementation of speech and language therapy for children with receptive and expressive language delays, neurological auditory processing deficits, articulation/phonological disorders, and oral motor feeding impairments. Perform diagnostic screenings and evaluations, develop Individual Education Plans, and attend Committee on Special Education Annual Review meetings.

- Advise parents/teachers on educational and communication strategies.
- Conduct weekly support groups for parents of speech-impaired children.
- Developed "Hear Me Out," a socially structured after-school program.
- Coplanned the school's first interactive Web site, "Kids Talk."

Education

Northwestern University, Evanston, Illinois
Masters of Science: Speech-Language Pathology, 1992

- **New York State Licensed Speech-Language Pathologist**
- **New York State Certificate of Clinical Competence**

Keywords

After-School Programs

Auditory Processing Deficits

Augmentative Communication

Children, Adult, Geriatric

Clinical, Educational, Homecare

Cochlear Implants

Committee on Special Education

Communication Strategies

Early Intervention

Feeding Impairments

Individual Education Plans

Language Acquisition

Phonological Disorders

Planning and Development

Receptive and Expressive Delays

Screenings and Evaluations

Small-Group Speech Therapy

Speech-Impaired

Standardized Tests

Support Groups

Interview Q&A Using Keywords

Why should we hire you, what are your strengths, and how do you see yourself contributing to our company?

As a speech-language pathologist with a background working in clinical and educational settings, my strengths include diagnostic screenings, evaluations, and therapies for speech-impaired client populations, specifically children. Combined with a commitment to fostering communication between parents, students, and professional teams, I am confident that I would be an asset to your school district.

SPORTS AGENT ATTORNEY

Keywords

Athlete Contract
Negotiation

Good Faith
Negotiation

Arbitration

Representation
Contract

Signing Bonus

Right Not to be
Traded

Performance
Incentive Clause

Endorsements

Fluent in Spanish

JD

Westlaw, Lexis Nexis

Free Agent

First-Round
Selection

Research, Structure
Contracts

Multimillion,
Multiyear
Contracts

Media Relations

Severance

Meticulous
Preparation

Commitment to
Community

Philanthropy

Resume

Bianca L. Freeman
1134 Holmgren Way
Green Bay, Wisconsin 54303
(920) 555-1122 / email@email.com

Sports Law Attorney
Negotiate multimillion, multiyear contracts for professional athletes

Recognized in *Sports Business'* "100 Most Powerful People Behind the Scenes"
Represented 20+ first-round selections in football's free-agent draft

---

With partner, successfully negotiated more than $1 billion in athletic contracts. In addition to athlete contract negotiation, provides wealth management, endorsement, media relations, and philanthropy services.

Core Strengths

Contract research, structure	Player representation
Multimillion contract negotiation	NBA, NFL
Endorsements	Wealth management
Media relations	Commitment to community

Professional Experience

SMITH & FREEMAN, S.C., Appleton, Wisconsin   1993 to Present

Sports Law Attorney, Partner

Research, structure, and negotiate multiyear, multimillion contracts for athletes. Negotiate and draft endorsement contracts. Assist with media relations. Represent clients during NFL or NBA grievances, hearings, or appeals. Recommend wealth management programs, including financial planners and accounting services. Collect career-ending/disability proceeds. Obtain termination and severance pay.

- Negotiated a $150 million, eight-year contract for NBA forward, Stilts Tully.
- Negotiated a $4.2 million, two-year contract for NFL Green Bay Packer tight-end, Fred Mertz.
- Named to *Sports Business'* "100 Most Powerful People."

Education

Marquette University, Milwaukee, Wisconsin
Juris Doctor, 1990

- Editor, Marquette Sports Law Review
- President, Sports Law Society

Interview Q&A Using Keywords

Why should we hire you, what are your strengths, and how do you see yourself contributing to our company?

Recognized as one of *Sports Business'* "100 Most Powerful People Behind the Scenes in Sports," I am skilled with negotiating multimillion, multiyear contracts for football and basketball athletes. In addition to successful athlete representation, I assist my clients with wealth management, endorsement, and workers compensation services. I have a commitment to philanthropy and won't work with clients unless they agree to give back to their community.

SPORTS COACH

Resume

Paul Macca
3439 Fastbreak Lane
Denver, Colorado 80212
(303) 555-9523 / email@email.com

Intercollegiate Basketball Coach
Successful Athletic Administrator—NCAA Division 2

Turnaround Management / Team Building
Academic Standards

Results-oriented leader with excellent skills in instructing, guiding, and motivating college-level basketball players. Effectively employ group and one-on-one training and development programs. Member of National Association of Basketball Coaches.

Core Strengths

Team Building	Team Image
Nutrition and Fitness	Skills and Conditioning
Recruiting	Scouting

Professional Experience

THE ROCKIES UNIVERSITY, Denver, Colorado   1995 to Current

Head Coach

Lead 12-man basketball squad with emphasis on sportsmanship, personal development, life-long learning, and academic success. Oversee staff of three assistant coaches, providing guidance on scheduling, travel planning, and equipment inventory issues.

- Improved program graduation rate from 78% to 95%. Team GPA skyrocketed to 3.6.
- Led team to winning season five of seven years.
- Established cross-sport summer fitness camp, boosting enrollment by 350% within four years.
- Upgraded off-court dress code, boosting team's professional image.

Education

University of Denver, Denver, Colorado
Master of Arts/Sports Psychology, 1988

- Vice President, College Leadership Guild
- GPA 3.9

Keywords

NCAA Division 2

Athletic Administration

Turnaround Management

Recruiting

Scouting

Team Building

One-On-One Training and Development

Player Development

Team Scheduling

Travel Planning

Team Image

Leadership Training

Sportsmanship

Lifelong Learning

Skills and Conditioning

Nutrition and Fitness

Off-Season Camps

Academic Standards

Equipment Inventory

National Association of Basketball Coaches

Interview Q&A Using Keywords

Why should we hire you, what are your strengths, and how do you see yourself contributing to our company?

In seven years of coaching in the college ranks, I have proven myself to be a superior athletic leader. My focus is on individual player development, both on and off the basketball court, as the basis of team cohesiveness and success. I contribute to the positive image of the school by stressing the value of sportsmanship, ongoing learning and development, and academic effort. My aggressive scouting and recruiting program attracts noteworthy talent as the foundation for team achievement and school visibility.

SURVEYOR

Resume

Nancy Salisbury
119 South 100 East
Anywhere, Idaho 00000
(208) 555-0000 / email@email.com

Surveyor
Land and Airspace

Proven Senior-Level Surveyor
Professional Land Surveyor's License

Seasoned senior-level surveyor with ability to perform a variety of functions and support. Outstanding skills using state-of-the-art instrumentation and equipment.

Core Strengths

Extremely precise	Experienced in fieldwork
Proficient use of GPS/GIS equipment	Project oriented
Enjoys outdoors, walking, climbing	Goa oriented
Team builder and player	Excellent technology skills

Professional Experience

MOUNTAINVIEW ENGINEERING, Idaho Falls, Idaho   1988 to Current

Senior Surveyor

Plan and oversee a variety of field work including land and airspace distance and direction measuring. Interpret GPS and GIS data, verify accuracy of data, prepare plots and maps, and write reports. Research evidence of previous boundaries, analyze data to determine location, and record results. Create plats for subdivisions. Utilize electronic distance-measuring equipment. Provide expert testimony in court cases as needed.

- Developed a new process that allows tracking of researched records.
- Improved process for computerizing lab notes and record keeping.
- National Society of Professional Surveyors.
- Coordinated a successful summer survey student camp.
- Prevented a major litigation case over boundary disputes.

Education

Idaho State University, Pocatello, Idaho
Bachelor of Science Degree in Surveying. 1988.

- Dean's List, two Years
- Recipient, Michael Roberts Scholarship Award

Interview Q&A Using Keywords

Why should we hire you, what are your strengths, and how do you see yourself contributing to our company?

I meet all the qualifications outlined in the job posting, including a Bachelor's degree. I have been a successful surveyor saving each company money by improving existing processes with state-of-the-art technology. I am dedicated to the project from conception to completion. My physical stamina allows me to stand for long periods of time. I enjoy the outdoors, walking, climbing, and using scientific instrumentation. Researching, analyzing, interpreting, and technology are some of my greatest strengths.

SWITCH ENGINEER

Resume

Willy Garrou
29587 Compo Parkway
Westport, Connecticut 06880
(203) 555-1122 / email@email.com

> **Switch Engineer**
> **10 years' experience in Telecommunications**
>
> **Ethernet Specialist**

Experienced switch engineer with background in installations, conversions, configurations, infrastructure design, and architecture. Ability to support all aspects of system life cycle from inception to implementation.

Core Strengths

Circuit analysis	Troubleshooting
Multivendor systems	Testing
Fiber optics	Design
Simulations	Architecture

Professional Experience

Network Engineering, Inc., New Milford, Connecticut

Switch Engineer

Provided on-site support and deployment/integration services to companies in the United States and abroad. Performed installation, configuration, troubleshooting, and maintenance of LAN/WAN hardware, server, PC system construction, and NetWare. Resolved applications problems and software interface issues. Designed wireless connections to accommodate multiple locations and remote access.

- Reconstructed switch rooms to upgrade 31,000-station network
- Designed new switching systems with gateways to new technologies
- Worked with Lucent Technologies to customize switch for project
- Developed simulation model for testing operations

Education

Fairfield University, Fairfield, Connecticut
Bachelor of Science, Computer Engineering. 1991.

- Alpha Sigma Nu
- Summa Cum Laude

References Furnished Immediately upon Request

Keywords

Telecommunications
Circuit Analysis
Troubleshooting
Signals
Ethernet
Architecture
Design
Testing
Simulation
Fiber Optics
Digital
Analog
Network
LAN
Outages
Multivendor
Life Cycle
Software Interface
WAN
TCP/IP

Interview Q&A Using Keywords

Why should we hire you, what are your strengths, and how do you see yourself contributing to our company?

I have extensive experience in circuit analysis, switch, hub, and router design in LAN/WAN hardware installation and configuration. I am skilled in network infrastructure design and troubleshooting, as well as applications troubleshooting. My background includes new product and upgrades to existing networks and integrations. I have worked in analog and digital design. Taking a project from inception to implementation supporting the system life cycle, I can set up and maintain multivendor system operations.

SYSTEMS ADMINISTRATOR

Resume

Brook Garrou
597 Rice Street
St. Paul, Minnesota 55104
(651) 555-2201 / email@email.com

> **Systems Administrator**
> **For-Profit & Nonprofit Background**
> **10 Years of Broad-Based Experience**
> **Proactive Technology Solutions**

Technology: Hardware: LAN,; Multiuser Interface; **Systems:** Windows NT/2000, DOS, Novell, UNIX, PC; **Applications:** MS Office 2000, Photoshop, PageMaker, CAD, SQL, IndDesign, C++, JavaScript, ACT!; **Other:** optics, CD-ROM, videos, phones, diverse peripherals.

Core Strengths

Hardware and software	Peripherals
Emerging technologies	Multimedia technology
Help desk	Data and disaster recovery
Staff training and support	Object-oriented development

Professional Experience

MILLENNIUM SYSTEMS INNOVATIONS, Minneapolis, Minnesota   1995 to Current

Systems Administrator

Direct engineering team responsible for configuration and field installation of customer sites. Capitalize upon high-growth market opportunities with e-commerce, videoconferencing, CD-ROM, and Internet enhancements. Staff and operate a 24/7 help desk supporting both internal and external customers. Build computer systems from "nuts" up. Oversee hardware, software, networks peripherals and related technology systems. Guide all aspects of administration to ensure optimum acquisition, development, methodology, functionality, and security.

- Redesigned development/engineering protocols *ahead* of changing user requirements.
- Introduced time-sensitive data recovery processes, and virtually eliminated all data losses.
- Authored Seagrams' in-house disaster recovery process.
- Received *Outstanding Performance Awards*, six years consecutively.

Education

St. Cloud State University, St. Cloud, Minnesota
Bachelor of Science: Business Computer Information Systems (BCIS), 1992

- Computer & Technology User Services Work Study
- BCIS Club Secretary, 1990–1992

Interview Q&A Using Keywords

Why should we hire you, what are your strengths, and how do you see yourself contributing to our company?

My expertise covers system engineering, database administration, system implementation, and security. Proactive with emerging technologies, I frequently advance object-oriented and multimedia systems into development. I am frequently the key resource for all hardware, software, network, and database training and support. I've developed a reputation as the help desk and data/disaster recovery "Dear Abby," approached 24/7 by colleagues. My leadership, training, and technical expertise allows me to contribute immediately in managing projects and resources.

TAX SPECIALIST

Resume

Ronald Lockwood
47 Plymouth Avenue
Duluth, Minnesota 55811
(218) 555-4712 / email@email.com

Senior Tax Specialist
Expert Qualifications in Strategic Planning & Financial Leadership

Corporate Tax Policy / Tax Assessment Reduction
Negotiations / Audits / Appeals / Protests / Compliance

Hands-on financial executive with 20 years of experience in all aspects of corporate taxation. Consistent record of accomplishment planning and implementing tax strategies to achieve competitive advantage.

Core Strengths

Tax Planning Opportunities	State & Federal Tax Work Papers
Financial Statement Reporting	Corporate Tax Policy
Revenue Apportionment	Tax Allocation Specialist
Forecasting & Management	Federal & International Tax Issues

Professional Experience

E. I. DUPONT DE NEMOURS & CO., Duluth, Minnesota   1995 to Current

Senior Tax Specialist

Challenged to direct continuous improvement and aggressive automation of all Tax Department systems and processes. Responsible for management of successful execution of all federal, state, and local tax compliance. Successful completion of all federal, state, and local estimated payments and extensions; all state and local income, property, and sales/use tax planning; and reacting appropriately to changes thereto.

- Finalized settlement with IRS reducing proposed deficiency by $7.9 million.
- Used IRS Advanced Issue Resolution (AIR) to reduce cost by $500 K.
- Successfully expedited a $4 million claim for federal refund.
- Developed and instituted completely computerized tax provision system.

Education

Cornell University, Ithaca, New York
Bachelor of Arts / Business Administration, 1983

- Concentration: Tax Preparation, Statistics, and Operations Mgmt.
- Magna Cum Laude distinction

References Furnished Immediately upon Request

Keywords

Reduced Deficiency

Tax Provision System

Disallowances

Penalty Assessment Reduction

Cash Management

Audit Controls

Corporate Tax Policy

Tax Analysis & Planning

Audit Assessment Reduction

Appeals & Protests

Tax Allocation Strategies

Consolidated Tax Return Filing System

Rapid Calculation

Financial Audits

Sales and Use Tax

State and Local Transactional Tax

Work Papers

Revenue Apportionment

Department of Revenue

Advanced Issue Resolution

Interview Q&A Using Keywords

Why should we hire you, what are your strengths, and how do you see yourself contributing to our company?

With more than 20 years of experience as a tax specialist at the director level, I offer a broad record of accomplishment in all aspects of corporate taxation. Specifically, I have designed corporate tax policy and handled extensive reporting of sales and use, and other specialized areas. I excel in the areas of penalty assessment reduction and advanced issue resolution. With a consistent record of savings in operations, planning, and successful completion of audits, I will quickly and positively affect your bottom line.

TELECOMMUNICATIONS/E-SOLUTIONS

Resume

Dan Schmitz
2288 Water Street
Long Beach, California 90806
(310) 555-1122 / email@email.com

> **E-Solutions Specialist—Telecommunications
> Network Engineer**

10 years' experience providing e-business solutions through Internet access and legacy systems integration and redesign.

Core Strengths / Technical Skills

- Network operating systems: Banyan VINES, Novell NetWare, Windows NT Server
- Network hardware: Ascend, Cisco, FORE, Nortel, Xylan
- Network protocols: SMTP, DNS, Telnet, FTP, TCP/IP, IIS
- Operating systems: Microsoft, Red Hat, SCO, Silicon Graphics, Sun
- Programming: C++, C, Perl, TCL/TK, Python, Fortran, and Shell Scripting
- Software applications: Adobe, Corel, Microsoft, Lotus, SAP
- Internet: HyCurve, Microsoft, Novell, Open Market
- Security: Check Point, ISC2, ISACA
- Certified Cisco Network Professional and Cisco Design Professional—CCNP and CCDP
- Microsoft Certified Systems Engineer + Internet—MCSE and Internet

Professional Experience

SENIOR NETWORK ENGINEER (E-Solutions)   **1995 to Present**
Sprint Communications Company, LP
Alameda, California

Assess medium to large business data communications needs for high-speed digital, telephony, internal/remote LAN/WAN networks, and enterprise applications. Present project proposal to clients along with cost-benefit analyses. Project management activities cover installation and testing, acquisitions, personnel, schedules, and budgets. Work closely with business and technical teams to ensure minimal disruption of services and maximum customer satisfaction.

- Transitioned a major sporting goods chain from host-based, proprietary platforms to open, client/server architectures. Expected cost savings of $200,000 by the second year of operation.
- Built enterprise architectures and application systems for on-line transaction processing, decision support, and workgroup computing. Net profits increased over 20% in the first year of ownership.

Education

California State University at Long Beach, California
Bachelor of Science in Computer Systems Engineering—1991

References Furnished Immediately upon Request

Interview Q&A Using Keywords

Why should we hire you, what are your strengths, and how do you see yourself contributing to our company?

I offer a substantial history of economical network design and installation successes in a variety of platforms, including wireline, wireless, third generation, and fiber optic. Along with my degree in Computer Systems Engineering, continual recertification in popular networking platforms assures you that I have a solid background in current technology. In fact, I have deployed two WANs of both voice and data for two enterprise operations of over 100 sites each. My practical understanding of e-commerce infrastructures allows me to develop cost-effective architectures that stay technologically viable for many years.

TELEMARKETING MANAGER

Resume

Jessica Lane
4311 Ipmire Blvd.
Columbus, Ohio 43219
(740) 555-1122 / email@email.com

> **Telemarketing Manager**
> **Driving Sales Within Advertising, Marketing, and PR Industries**
>
> **Data Analysis & Interpretation / Product & Program Marketing**
> **Revenue-to-Expense Projection / Telemarketing Operations**

Accomplished, extremely motivated telemarketing manager offering three years of continuous sales achievements and company recognition for ability to maintain optimum performance levels with minimal employee turnover.

Core Strengths

Solicitation Improvement	Revenue-to-Expense Projection
Goal Setting / Problem Solving	Compensation Reward/Recognition
B-to-B/B-to-C Telemarketing	Incentive Programs Design
Long-Term / Short-Term Forecasting	Training Coordination

Professional Experience

SOLID EDGE CONSULTING GROUP, Columbus, Ohio   1999 to Current

Telemarketing Manager

Foster extremely productive and positive call center environment for prestigious, high-volume public relations company. Accountable for all telemarketing operations including workforce management and reporting, staff recruiting/coaching and development, and problem analysis/decision making. Demonstrate expert knowledge over a variety of telemarketing applications and methodologies.

- Executed strategic telemarketing sales campaign that increased sales by 300%.
- Improved overall productivity by empowering staff with effective sales techniques.
- Recognized as Top Telemarketing Commission producer throughout employment.
- Contributing author for innovative script development/ objection handling.

Education

Franklin University, Columbus, Ohio
Bachelor of Arts: Sales and Marketing, 1995

- GPA 3.5
- Student Services Assistant

References Furnished Immediately upon Request

Keywords

Data Analysis & Interpretation
Product/Program Marketing
Workforce Management & Reporting
Recruiting/Coaching and Development
Telemarketing Applications/ Methodology
Revenue-to-Expense Projection
Problem Solving
Telemarketing Operations
Script Development/ Objection Handling
Compensation Reward/ Recognition
Business-to-Business Telemarketing
Business-to-Consumer Telemarketing
Problem Analysis and Decision Making
Ergonomics
Goal Setting
Incentive Programs Design/ Implementation
Short/Long-Term Forecasting
Training Coordination
Solicitation Improvement
Call Center

Interview Q&A Using Keywords

Why should we hire you, what are your strengths, and how do you see yourself contributing to our company?

One of the major difficulties in telemarketing is employee retention. With a strong talent in team building, I am certain that I would identify, recruit, and encourage qualified employees. I would design and implement worthwhile incentive programs and empower my sales staff with strong scripting and training in handling objections. My business-to-business/business-to-consumer telemarketing experience, my ability to motivate, and my in-depth understanding into telemarketing operations are good indicators of my long-term performance with your company.

TRANSPORTATION/LOGISTICS SPECIALIST

Resume

Robert Kavanaugh
1953 Orchard Street
San Diego, California 92108
(619) 555-1122 / email@email.com

Logistics Specialist
Transportation Solutions & Disaster Prevention through
Early Design Influence
Trade-Off Analysis / Alternative Solutions

Certified Professional Logistician (CPL) with 10 years' experience in logistics transportation and distribution management. Driven to attain "seamless transportation" and cost reductions through early participation in the system design review process and employment of holistic approaches that consider social, political, and environmental issues.

Core Strengths

Program Development & Management
Transportation Modeling/Simulation
Government & Industry Contacts

Global Information Systems
Federal Regulations
Disaster Planning

Professional Experience

BOOZ, ALLEN, HAMILTON   1996 to Current
San Diego, California

Overland Transportation Programs Manager

Develop or redesign transportation plans and emergency plans for companies experiencing losses in their transportation infrastructure. Select best and alternate plans based on simulations of transportation modes, routes, characteristics, limitations, and program constraints.

- Identified the logistics infrastructures for and negotiated a strategic partnership between a major overland freight carrier and a local telecommunications company, to provide a global information system utilizing global positioning system and Internet technology for tracking its $50 million truck fleet and scheduling deliveries.
- Recommended safe alternate routes for Coca-Cola® deliveries into volcanic activity areas, based on intimate knowledge of the trade corridors along Interstate-35 and government and industry contacts.

Education

Oxnard Community College at Oxnard, California
Certified Professional Logistician / 2000

References Furnished Immediately upon Request

Interview Q&A Using Keywords

Why should we hire you, what are your strengths, and how do you see yourself contributing to our company?

I am a Certified Profession Logistician who can reduce transportation costs and cut delivery times dramatically through early development of master transportation and distribution plans. My practical logistics experience ranges from arranging military airlifts and sealifts to the uninterrupted distribution of Coca-Cola® during a volcanic eruption. If there is a better way to deliver a product safely, I will find it through my familiarity with global information systems and domestic and international carriers and routes.

TRAVEL AGENT

Resume

Tammy Tice
1234 Paradise Road
Las Vegas, Nevada 89104
(702) 555-4523 / email@email.com

Professional Travel Agent
Certified Travel Counselor Since 1985

Corporate Travel / Family Vacations
Ecotours and Recreational Activities

Capable and confident travel industry professional. Extensive knowledge of global distribution systems. Proven success in developing new business and cultivating long-term client relationships.

Core Strengths

International Travel   Customs Regulations
Travel Crisis Information   Vacation Packages
Charter Flights   Cruises
Customer Service   SABRE

Professional Experience

TRAVEL PARTNERS, Las Vegas, Nevada   1995 to Present

Travel Consultant

Help walk-in clients with all travel needs, including flight reservations/ticketing, transfers, hotel accommodations, and car rentals. Partner with area businesses on customized corporate travel packages. Take twice-a-year familiarization trips, acquiring first-hand experience at various domestic and international destinations. Responsible for maintaining travel advisory pamphlet.

- Assisted owner with successful transition from antiquated computer reservations system to state-of-the art global distribution system.
- Memberships: American Society of Travel Agents, Institute of Certified Travel Agents, International Airlines Travel Agency Network.

Education

University of Nevada, Las Vegas, Las Vegas, Nevada
Bachelor of Science / Hotel Administration, 1983

- Member, Hotel Alumni Association
- Treasurer, Student Hotel Association

Keywords

American Society of Travel Agents (ASTA)

Institute of Certified Travel Agents (ICTA)

International Airlines Travel Agent Network (IATAN)

Certified Travel Counselor (CTC)

Computer Reservations System (CRS)

SABRE

Vacation Planning

Corporate Travel

Charter Flights

Hotel Accommodations

Rental Cars

Cruises

Family Vacations

Tour Packages

Ecotours

Recreational Activities

International Destinations

Customs Regulations

Familiarization Trips

Travel Crisis Information

Interview Q&A Using Keywords

Why should we hire you, what are your strengths, and how do you see yourself contributing to our company?

I am a true travel industry professional recognized for my ability to build relationships with customers, ensuring their repeat business. You won't have to spend much time training me since I have been a Certified Travel Counselor for 17 years, and am an expert in the SABRE computer reservations system. I pride myself on my knowledge of international destinations and can skillfully assemble a range of packages, from corporate travel to family vacations.

TV PRODUCTION MANAGER

Resume

Lori Nuss
1359 Highland Avenue
Burbank, California 91510
(818) 555-1111 / email@email.com

TELEVISION PRODUCTION MANAGER
10+ Years' Production Experience

Skilled Manager and Negotiator
Reputation for Coordinating Diverse Teams in a Fast-Paced,
High-Pressure Environment with Critical Deadlines

Industry reputation for expertise in managing business and production functions with attention to meeting timelines and budget concerns. Proven ability to negotiate contracts securing favorable terms for equipment, supplies, locations, services, and top talent. Background includes features, commercials, and television broadcasting. Works well with diverse temperaments; adept in scheduling, directing, and coordinating cross-functional crew members.

Core Strengths

Budget Development/Management	Script Breakdowns
Negotiations	Shooting Schedules
Set Design & Props	Crew & Staff Management
Time & Resource Management	Planning & Delegating

Professional Experience

ZYX NETWORK Burbank, CA   1995–Present

Production Manager

Advanced through series of progressive production positions. Key member of team responsible for ensuring success and high ratings of "The Hollywood Journal" daily entertainment news show. Previous projects included the *6:00 News* and *L.A. Morning*.

- Recognized by Television Academy for contributions to profession.
- Conceived and guided production of numerous special remote stories, showcasing up-and-coming talent in Southern California.
- Suggested and oversaw details of station participation in numerous fund raising drives including AIDS Project L.A. and campaign for Santa Monica's homeless population.

Education

UNIVERSITY OF SOUTHERN CALIFORNIA, Los Angeles, CA
B.A. in Film & Television

Excellent Industry Recommendations Available upon Request

Interview Q&A Using Keywords

Why should we hire you, what are your strengths, and how do you see yourself contributing to our company?

I have 10 years' progressive experience managing production, from inception through the end of production. I have a keen eye for breaking down scripts and developing detailed cost and crew budget requirements. I realize how important it is for you to have someone focused on meeting deadlines while staying within budget, and that has always been a priority for the projects I managed. I am skilled in negotiating contracts including talent, locations, equipment, and supplies.

Resume

Mary Jane Young
728 River Road
Trenton, New Jersey 08608
(609) 555-2345 / email@email.com

Mortgage Loan Underwriter
Technical Expertise in Mortgage Loan Process and Underwriting

Mortgage Banking / Consumer Lending
Wholesale Mortgage Operations in Production Environment

Analytical, decisive underwriter experienced in all types of consumer loan products, including home equity, second mortgages, and FNMA/FHLMC, as well as "A" paper jumbo loans sold into the secondary market.

Core Strengths

Consumer Loan Underwriting	Funding and Loan Documentation
Commercial and Investor Banking	Home Equity and Second Mortgages
Desktop Underwriting	Underwriting Team Motivation
State Fair Lending Act	FHA D/E, VA, FNMA/FHLMC

Professional Experience

FIRST NATIONAL BANK, Trenton, New Jersey   1994 to Current

Mortgage Underwriter II

Underwrite conventional first trust deed residential mortgage loan requests using bank mortgage credit policies, as well as standard secondary market guidelines. Serve as technical resource for mortgage loan criteria, with strong knowledge of state and federal lending regulations, and jumbo loan underwriting. Promoted from loan processor with signing authority.

- Overachieve line production/sales standards for mortgage underwriting, while carefully analyzing credit and collateral packages for compliance with Fannie Mae, Freddie Mac, and FHA investor guidelines.
- Efficiently and accurately produce heavy underwriting services caseload with ease, making credit decisions within acceptable service levels.
- Consistently surpass annual goals for volume and customer service.

Education

Mercer County Community College, West Windsor, New Jersey
Associate of Science, Business Administration—1994

- New Jersey Underwriters Certification (HUD / MVA)—1994
- New Jersey Mortgage Banker's License—1994

References Furnished Immediately upon Request

Keywords

Mortgage Loan Underwriting

Mortgage Banking

Consumer Lending

Wholesale Mortgage Operations

Production Environment

Consumer Loan Products

Home Equity

Second Mortgages

FNMA/FHLMC/ FHA/VA

"A" Paper Jumbo Loans

Secondary Market

Consumer Loan Underwriting

Funding and Loan Documentation

Commercial and Investor Banking

Desktop Underwriting

Underwriting Team

State Fair Lending

Conventional First Trust Feed

Residential Mortgage Loans

Jumbo Loan Underwriting

Line Production/Sales

Interview Q&A Using Keywords

Why should we hire you, what are your strengths, and how do you see yourself contributing to our company?

Overachieving line production goals, while maintaining sound consumer loan underwriting decisions, has been the hallmark of my underwriting career. I bring extensive knowledge of conventional, conforming/jumbo, FHA, Fannie Mae, Freddie Mac, and VA loans, as well as state and federal lending regulations. Accustomed to decisive customer interaction and collaborative team relationships, I can model high-level underwriting services while producing results for you.

UNIX MANAGER

Resume

Glenna Hazen
103 Dylan Street
Patchogue, NY 11772
(631) 555-1122 / email@email.com

UNIX Manager
Install, Configure, and Maintain UNIX Workstations and Servers

Support Business Processing Requirements
Skilled in Wide Array of Technical Principles, Theories, and Concepts

---

Seven-year background in UNIX systems administration. Strong skills in system installation, configuration, troubleshooting, tuning, planning, backup, and disaster recovery. ERP and Sun Solaris experience.

Core Strengths

UNIX Server Architecture	Failure Recovery
UNIX-Based System Security	Budget Management
Installation/Maintenance	Problem Resolution
System Interoperability	Team Technical Support

Professional Experience

Computer Associates, Hauppague, NY   2000 to Current

Senior UNIX Manager

Administer all changes and upgrades. Install, configure, and maintain all company UNIX systems using various Sun performance commands. Monitor, repair, document, and report on systems' operation and performance. Oversee server administration, server revision control, and maintenance, including software, firmware, and updates. Communicate clearly with technical and nontechnical staff. Provide team leadership.

- Designed innovative UNIX-related team-wide technical support model.
- Delivered new server performance analysis adopted companywide.
- Trained staff in new application development environments/utilities.
- Developed leading-edge end-user support methodology.

Education

St. Joseph's College, Patchogue, NY
Bachelor of Science: Computer Science, 1995

- GPA 3.75
- Vice President, Future Business Leaders

References Furnished Immediately upon Request

Interview Q&A Using Keywords

Why should we hire you, what are your strengths, and how do you see yourself contributing to our company?

I believe in operating IT as a contributing value addition rather than a fixed cost. As a broadly experienced IT professional, I bring a wide array of hands-on skills to this position including operation and support of UNIX-based systems and system-level applications. I have a unique ability to bridge the communications gap that often exists between the tech side and the business side, translating both areas' needs and solutions so that operational goals are met, budgets are kept, and internal and external customers are supported.

VETERINARY ASSISTANT

Resume

Theresa Pizano
207 Dorothy Place
Kenmore, New York 14226
(716) 555-8390 / email@email.com

> **Veterinary Technician**
> **Specialized in General Practice, Dental Care, and Surgery**
>
> **Caring and Compassionate Small-Animal Health Professional**

Licensed Veterinary Technician with over 10 years' clinical experience in pre- and post-operative care, as well as general pet examination and treatment.

Core Strengths

Intensive Care   Emergency Treatment
Preventive Dental Care   Surgical Preparation and Assistance
Wound Care   Medication Dispensing

Professional Experience

TRANSIT ANIMAL HOSPITAL, Eden, New York   1992 to Present

Veterinary Technician

Assist veterinarians and surgeons during examinations, treatments, and surgery. Perform fluid therapy, oxygen therapy, catheterization, and venipuncture. Monitor vital signs and administer injections and anesthesia. Educate owners on patient care and provide comfort and sympathy. Oversee and schedule laboratory tests. Purchase medical supplies and control drug inventory.

- Provide clinical supervision to team of 12 veterinary technicians, animal caretakers, and animal handlers in busy, urban veterinary clinic.
- Specialize in care of domestic and exotic birds, as well as all dog and cat breeds.
- Write *Tips and Tails* monthly community outreach newsletter that educates owners on appropriate and timely pet care.

Education

Medaille College, Buffalo, New York
Associate in Science: Veterinary Technology, 1992
New York State Department of Education
Licensed Veterinary Technician, 1992

References Furnished Immediately upon Request

Keywords

Pre- and Post-Operative Care

Clinical Supervision

Veterinary Medicine

Patient Examination and Treatment

Fluid Therapy

Surgical Assistance

Owner Education

Wound Care

Injections and Inoculations

Preventive Dental Care

Medication Dispensing

Anesthesia

Oxygen Therapy

Emergency Treatment

Venipuncture

Laboratory Tests

Inventory Control and Purchasing

Patient Preparation

Community Outreach

Small Animal Specialty

Interview Q&A Using Keywords

Why should we hire you, what are your strengths, and how do you see yourself contributing to our company?

I currently provide clinical supervision to a team of 12 veterinary technicians, animal caretakers, and handlers in a busy, urban veterinary practice, as well as assist veterinarians and surgeons during examinations, treatments, and surgery. Our practice specializes in care of domestic and exotic birds, as well as all dog and cat breeds. I also write *Tips and Tails* monthly community outreach newsletter that educates owners on appropriate and timely pet care.

VOLUNTEER COORDINATOR

Keywords

Multilevel Recruitment

Task Assignment/
Scheduling for Peak
Coverage

Community
Outreach/Public
Awareness

Public Relations

Staff Mediation and
Management

Turnover Reduction/
Participant Retention

Interviewing and
Screening

Multiple Event/ Project
Coordination

Nonprofit

Community Liaison

Confidential Records

Leadership/
Motivation/Team
Building

Telefundraising and
Events Planning

Volunteer Participation

Community Resource
Development

Program Enhancement

Training and
Supervision

Cost Savings

Advertising, Promotion,
and Media Relations

Volunteer Network

Resume

Patricia J. Houston
127 Elmwood Street
Cheektowaga, New York 14227
(716) 555-3711 / email@email.com

Volunteer Coordinator

**Leadership/Motivation / Team Building
Multiple Event/Project Coordination**

Solid track record of developing and implementing creative programs that substantially increased levels of volunteer participation. Provide training and supervision to an enthusiastic and hard-working corps of volunteers.

Core Strengths

Interviewing and Screening	Community Resource Development
Advertising and Promotion	Staff Mediation and Management
Events Planning	Multilevel Recruitment
Turnover Reduction	Confidential Records

Professional Experience

UNITED SERVICES, Buffalo, New York   1994 to Current

Coordinator of Volunteer Services

Recruit, train, and motivate volunteer network of 120+ participants. Create promotional materials to expand community outreach and heighten public awareness. Coordinate task assignment/scheduling to guarantee peak coverage. Identify opportunities for program enhancement. Design materials to improve public and media relations.

- Developed 40-hour training program and monthly in-service seminars, improving quality of service and increasing participant retention.
- Created and promoted "Share-an-Idea Program" for volunteers, resulting in cost-saving suggestions that reduced operating expenses.
- As community liaison, built a visible presence and increased recruitment by 37%.

Education

Villa Maria College, Buffalo, New York
Bachelor of Science—Human Development, 1994

- Graduated Cum Laude with 3.72 GPA
- Youth Leadership Award and "Doing More" Award

References Furnished Immediately upon Request

Interview Q&A Using Keywords

Why should we hire you, what are your strengths, and how do you see yourself contributing to our company?

I led the effort to develop a 40-hour training program and monthly in-service seminars, improving quality of service and increasing volunteer retention. We created and promoted "Share-an-Idea Program" for volunteers, resulting in cost-saving suggestions that reduced operating expenses. As community liaison, I built a visible presence and increased recruitment by 37%.

WAREHOUSE MANAGER

Resume

Nicholas Carrington
573 Emerald Plaza, Apt. 2D
Somerset, New Jersey 08873
(732) 555-1234 / email@email.com

> **Warehouse Manager**
> **Warehousing and Distribution Operations**
>
> **Materials/Inventory Control Management**
> **Inbound and Outbound Shipments**

Warehouse Manager experienced in directing teams to meet tight deadlines in a results-oriented environment. Ensure product quality and customer satisfaction through responsive, accurate, on-time scheduling.

Core Strengths

Materials/Inventory Control	Cost Containment/Budget Controls
Human Resource Management	Safety Training/Management
Distribution Accountability	ISO 9000 Certification Standards
Troubleshooting	Written and Verbal Communications

Professional Experience

MOHAWK CARPETS, Montclair, New Jersey   1989 to Current

Warehouse/Distribution Manager

Senior warehouse manager for multimillion-dollar wholesale distributor of high-end imported wool rugs, supplying 350 mass merchandisers such as Macy's, Sears, and QVC. Full supervisory responsibility for 25 warehouse personnel, safety management and training, cost controls, equipment reliability, and shipment verification. Maintain an orderly stock and staging area for finished goods inventory in a fast-paced department.

- Doubled warehouse and shipping operations efficiency and productivity by transitioning to computerized inventory system for 200,000 SKUs.
- Effectively maintained tight inventory controls through internal auditor reviews and immediate troubleshooting. Achieved cost management goals and percentage of loss 25% lower than industry standards.
- Ensured expeditious materials transactions while meeting budget goals.

Education

Burlington County Community College, Pemberton, New Jersey
Associate of Arts, Business Administration—1988

- Computer Skills: Windows NT/2000, Microsoft Office 2000 (Word, Excel, Access) and automated inventory tracking applications.

Keywords

Warehousing
Distribution
Inventory Control Management
Inbound and Outbound Shipments
Customer Satisfaction
Scheduling
Human Resource Management
Distribution Accountability
Troubleshooting
Cost Containment
Budget Controls
Safety Training
Safety Management
ISO 9000 Certification Standards
Warehouse Personnel
Shipment Verification
Stock and Staging Area
Finished Goods Inventory
Warehouse and Shipping Operations
Automated Inventory Tracking

Interview Q&A Using Keywords

Why should we hire you, what are your strengths, and how do you see yourself contributing to our company?

With 13 years' experience leading and managing warehouse and shipping operations for a major finished goods inventory distributor, I have a proven track record of maximizing customer satisfaction while achieving cost control goals well below industry standards. Efficiently scheduling warehouse personnel and closely monitoring warehouse and distribution procedures has yielded high levels of productivity. I believe I can produce similar outstanding results for you!

WEB DESIGNER

Keywords

Artistic Talent

P&L Mindset

35 mm & Digital Photography

Life Cycle Development.

Web Design & Development

Search Engine Optimization

HTML & Cutting-Edge Software

E-Mail Campaigns

E-Commerce Initiatives

Message Development

Project Management

Brand Development

Static and Animated Images

Typography/Text & Font Management

Image Management

Client-Server Concepts

Cross-Browser Issues

Revenue-Enhancing Sites

Troubleshooting

Color Theory & Manipulation

Resume

Marit Johannsen
1812 Waterford Court
St. Paul, Minnesota 55102
(651) 555-0090 / email@email.com

Web Designer & Developer
Successfully Transform Concepts Into Interactive Reality

Artistic Talent, P&L Mindset, and Technical Savvy

Draw on artistic vision, business acumen, and passion for the field to create aesthetic sites meeting client-driven goals. Proficient with HTML, DHTML, Cold Fusion, MS Office, JavaScript, C++, WebLogic, Oracle, Photoshop, Fireworks, QuarkXpress, SQL7.

Core Strengths

Client-server & object-oriented concepts	Cross-browser issues
Image, brand, & message development	Search engine strategies
E-commerce initiatives/e-mail campaigns	Total Web lifecycle development
Static/animated images	Photography/color/topography

Professional Experience

VISIONLINK, LTD., St. Paul, Minnesota   1995 to Current

Web Designer and Developer

Contribute as integral member of development/design team. Perform object-oriented and client-server-focused Web applications and development. Create original art and graphic layout of content, banners, logos, and merchandise. Code new programs. Incorporate interactive elements and e-commerce initiatives; perform technical coding, review, and testing; and work closely with senior executives to conceptualize, design, and launch Internet/Intranet sites furthering company goals. Serve as primary "troubleshooter."

- Enhanced Internet site for bank garnered a 42% increase in unique user sessions.
- New Internet site for distributor generated a 57% increase in qualified sales leads.
- Initiated interactive "Me & You" bulletin board, growing communication flow.
- Handpicked by management to revamp home page, praised in *Web Design Monthly*.

Education

University of St. Thomas, St. Paul, Minnesota
Bachelor of Arts: Computer Information Systems, 1990

- Graduate of first program emphasis in Interactive Web Design & Development
- GPA 3.85

References Furnished Immediately upon Request

Interview Q&A Using Keywords

Why should we hire you, what are your strengths, and how do you see yourself contributing to our company?

I am able to transform concepts into on-line, interactive reality, managing all aspects of Web life cycle development. My combined artistic talent and P&L mindset have resulted in the delivery of revenue-enhancing, market-oriented sites. My innovative sites, tapping into my expertise in photography and managing images, fonts, text, and color, are in demand. I optimize search engines through keyword research/selection, meta tagging, engine submission, and position tracking. My career is marked by success in incorporating interactive elements and e-commerce initiatives. I have earned a reputation as an effective troubleshooter, resolving technical issues and managing ongoing support.

WRITER/EDITOR

Resume

Cheryl Franks
425 Range Road
Harrisburg, PA 17107
(570) 555-1212 / email@email.com

Writer / Editor

Excel at identifying & developing compelling news angles

Award-winning writer/M.A. in Writing
Analytical/Excellent command of the English language

Award-winning journalist/reporter/editor with nine years of professional writing experience in traditional print media and Web publishing. Extensive experience writing and editing for newspapers, businesses, and health-care-industry organizations. Specialize in writing about business and technical topics. Maintain high-quality standards. Produce on or ahead of deadline.

Core Strengths

Identifying news angles	Technical & business writing
Creating Web copy	Interviewing
Supervising writers	Researching complex topics
Editing	Meeting deadlines

Professional Experience

WALL STREET REVIEW, New York, NY

Freelance Writer   1999-Present

Research topics, interview senior executives, and write business articles. Produce market forecasts concerning new technologies in the pharmaceutical, automotive, chemical, and medical equipment industries. Contribute to writing business news summaries for *www.wsr.com*. Edit business articles. Supervise five other freelance writers.

- Wrote a feature article for the Biotechnology section on market trends
- Won "Best Technology Article 2000" (News Publishers Association)
- Selected to provide editorial direction to six freelance writers
- Contributed to 10% growth in circulation

Education

Smith College, Northampton, MA
B.A. in English 1990
Goddard College, Plainfield, VT
M.A. Writing, Journalism Concentration 1995

References Furnished upon Request

Keywords

Journalist
Newspaper Reporter
Editing
Features
Editorials
Interviews
Supervising
Web Copy
Business Writing
Newspapers
Magazines
Reports
Newsletters
Deadlines
Analytical
Creative
Research Skills
Print Media
Copy Editing
M.A. in Writing

Interview Q&A Using Keywords

Why should we hire you, what are your strengths, and how do you see yourself contributing to our company?

My professional specialization is writing and editing for technical and business publications. My research and interviewing skills are excellent. I have a particular gift for making complex material both understandable and interesting to the general public. My ability to write compelling articles has had an impact on the ability of a publication to grow and gain market share in a competitive market.

Index

About the Authors

Jay A. Block, CPRW (Certified Professional Resume Writer), internationally certified career coach and resume strategist, is the contributing cofounder of the Professional Association of Resume Writers and Career Coaches (PARW/CC). He helped develop the PARW/CC national certification process and is a widely respected national speaker, author, and career coach. Contact him at www.jayblock.com.

Michael Betrus, CPRW, has been a hiring manager in the telecommunications industry for several years, and frequently engages in academic seminars for students on campus. Michael is the author of *The Guide to Executive Recruiters* and co-author, with Jay Block, of *101 Best Resumes, 101 More Best Resumes, 101 Best Cover Letters,* and *101 Best Tech Resumes.* Contact him at betrus@earthlink.net.